As If Kids Mattered

As If Kids Mattered

WHAT'S WRONG IN THE WORLD OF CHILD PROTECTION AND ADOPTION

Marlene Webber

KEY PORTER BOOKS

Canadian Cataloguing in Publication Data

Webber, Marlene, 1947-

As if kids mattered

ISBN 1-55013-931-2

1. Adoption. I. Title.

HV875.W38 1998   362.73'4   C97-932455-6

THE CANADA COUNCIL   LE CONSEIL DES ARTS
FOR THE ARTS   DU CANADA
SINCE 1957   DEPUIS 1957

The publisher gratefully acknowledges the support of the Canada Council for the Arts and
the Ontario Arts Council for its publishing program.

Key Porter Books Limited
70 The Esplanade
Toronto, Ontario
Canada   M5E 1R2

www.keyporter.com

Design: Jean Lightfoot Peters
Electronic formatting: Heidi Palfrey

98 99 00 01 6 5 4 3 2 1

*To my son, Clay Carter-Webber, who every day draws
me deeper into the most precious love of all*

*To my parents, Ethel and Harvey Webber, for their
unconditional love, even when it wasn't easy*

Contents

Foreword

I received Marlene Webber's book with interest but, I confess, also with trepidation. As an adoptive mother, the book's subject is of inherent interest to me, but I was nervous that Webber's judgment of what I'd done to become a mother would somehow find me wanting. My husband and I adopted two children, one in Canada, through a private social worker, and another through international adoption—an area of pretty dubious moral ground. So it was with great appreciation, and a small measure of relief, that I read what she had to say. Webber's coverage, not only of international adoption, but all aspects and kinds of adoption, is remarkably thorough and balanced.

Ten years ago, when we began exploring adoption as a means to have a family, we were venturing into unknown territory. Our information was gleaned through friends and rumors and not much else. Ten years later, there is still such a remarkable lack of information on the subject. Like Marlene Webber, we were greeted with how difficult, how long, how few infants, etc.—almost all negatives. And surrounding those negatives was a void.

Had it existed ten years ago, *As If Kids Mattered* would have filled that void, relieving me of a lot of stumbling and, more importantly, removing some of the barriers in my own thinking. Like many, we wanted a healthy newborn—or as close to one as possible. As time went on, my boundaries started to widen, but only gradually. After reading this book, I wonder how much further and how much more quickly those boundaries might have been extended. Would we have considered a 'hard to place' child? Maybe. But if anyone was advocating adoption for such children, we weren't aware of it. One would think, or at least like to believe, that the child protection bodies hold the best interests of children—all children—in highest regard. But, as Webber so clearly illustrates, kids who could be adopted are constantly lost in the shuffle.

Lost, too, are birth families, whom society has treated with such terrible negligence. As a woman, knowing that your child—the most precious thing in your life—was borne by another woman who may have had no other choice than to make an adoption plan can be difficult to handle. Although we have what I considered to be an open adoption arrangement, Webber's examination of open adoption has made me reconsider it. Her recommendations on this subject are humane and sensible.

Adoption forces us all to redefine family. As an adoptive parent, I've encountered suspicion and even downright hostility. I have come to realize that making that choice to love and commit to a child you didn't bear comprises a threat to some people; perhaps because if one can love another's child as one's own, the next step is loving one's neighbor as oneself. Yet, I have also been fortunate that in my immediate circle of family and friends there are a number of adopted children, all of them crossing racial or cultural barriers. This is my norm.

As If Kids Mattered replaces the false notion of the "normal" or "perfect family" with a much more encompassing one—an adult or adults who provide a child, not born to them, with a loving, stable, permanent family, a real family. It should be required reading, not just for those thinking about adoption or for those working in the field, but for all people interested in forming a family.

—SONJA SMITS

Introduction

In 1988 I was forty years old and unintentionally pregnant. For the preceding decade, I'd waffled about parenthood. It wasn't that I didn't like kids. As far back as I can remember, I was crazy about them. Indeed, growing up I was so mad for infants—and horses—my mother figured I'd be down on the farm making babies and mucking out stables before I was twenty.

Though my fondness for children never fizzled, I wasn't hooked on the idea of having any. Besides, the time never seemed right. Either I was unattached and uninclined toward single-parenting, or I was coupled, including a brief marriage, but unconvinced that state would last. Or I was busy building one career, then another. Eventually I settled on writing and on earning the typical income that brought—more reason to delay a decision. But bad timing, being single, and earning *bubkes* weren't the only things stopping me. I loved belonging to the first generation of women to see motherhood as a choice, not an inevitability or an obligation. Except, though I was normally decisive, I chronically postponed exercising my prerogative.

Come the big Four-O, I was still undecided. The difference: I was now pregnant. The timing—you guessed it—was the pits. My relationship with the father wasn't yet a year old and I couldn't predict how he'd react. Free-lancing might have been covering the bills, but royalties weren't exactly pouring in. Yet, suddenly none of that mattered. All my fancy excuses evaporated in a flash. I felt euphoric, brilliantly clear. I was having this baby, come hell or high water. Though I enjoyed free-lance writing, I could get a regular job. Though I wanted him to stay, David could split. Luck was with me, because, as it turned out, David, too, was thrilled.

We started nesting. Five months later, our daughter was born dead, reasons unknown.

It would take me two years to get through the emotional slaughter and to contemplate motherhood again. When that time came, I wanted to know why I had lost my baby and what the chances were of a repeat performance. For the next few months, I trundled off to a hospital fertility clinic for a lot of bloodletting, urine-sampling, and uterus-snipping. The specialists ordered ever-more tests. I asked ever-more questions. The doctors shrugged in response. The invasive, time-consuming, emotionally draining process to which I'd surrendered was clearly a dead end. No one in a lab coat, however, was about to admit it. As long as I'd keep coming, they'd keep probing. Finally, I stopped the madness.

Either I could chance another pregnancy, which might or might not be trouble-free, or I could adopt. The number of readers who can relate to what I'm about to say could probably fit in a phone booth: I longed to become a mother but couldn't care less how a baby might come to me. In fact, from my first twinges of interest in having kids, the question had always been "Yes or no?" Assuming an agreeable partner, if I ever got to "yes," I always figured I'd toss a coin. Heads: adopt. Tails: give birth.

Why don't I give a hoot whether my child comes from my womb? I don't know exactly, but I do know that it's not for any of the usual reasons. For example, it's not because I want to wave a placard against adding to our overpopulated planet while so many kids, already here, need families. Though I applaud people who think it better to parent existing children, to my way of thinking every new life is one more fighter for a better world. So, I can't say my politics tell me not to multiply. Nor can I blame my family. I come from a loving, normally dysfunctional household. Maybe, as I'm beginning to believe, the aberration is not in me but in society, in the way it drenches the very idea of family in blood and, hence, blinds us to options every bit as good as, though different from, genetic kinship.

The bottom line for me was: I could love anyone's child, so why become a guinea pig when what I really wanted to become was a mother? Once I got over the big hurdle of deciding whether or not to have a family, deciding to adopt was a breeze. Though David wasn't as blithely comfortable with adopting, he wanted to be a dad, and he took the view that it was my body, and hence my call.

All of this may make both of us seem pretty strange. Yet, from my point of view, what I see out there is less intelligible, kind of a never-ending episode of *The X-Files*. I see the constant parade of women, including many from my own circle, who are desperate to have a baby. That mission overtakes their lives. They agonize through repeated miscarriages, but never give up. Or, seemingly infertile or having a sterile partner, they go to the extremes of genetic engineering. Some bankrupt themselves financially (then borrow from relatives) and emotionally. More and more venture into the ethical fringes of surrogacy, even into global reproductive tourism. Under the strain, their relationship with their partner—who may be the one hell-bent on biology—frays. But once on the baby treadmill, they can't bring themselves to get off, not when going the extra distance with one more bit of hocus-pocus might make their dream come true. If it doesn't—as, statistically speaking, it likely won't—few go on to adopt. Instead, most abandon their consuming desire for children.

Though over the years I've felt for friends in this predicament, if the truth be known, their choices have been incomprehensible to me. Intellectually, I have tried to understand. But, emotionally, I've never been able to grasp why anyone so intent on having children would sacrifice the dream rather than adopt.

Obviously, in my six-of-one, half-dozen-of-another attitude toward the how of becoming a parent, I was out of kilter with the community around me. I took comfort, however, in assuming that traditional notions about family-building wouldn't infect the world from which we hoped our baby would come. Little did I suspect that the adoption system, too, would have jitters about lineaments of kinship that don't begin in blood. Less did I imagine it might be caught in a time warp, hardwired to a view of family that I thought went out with the fifties.

I wasn't what you'd call adoption literate. I had a few clues but nothing the guy in the street can't tell you. On trashy and even on less-sensational TV, we've all seen clips of tearful reunions between adult adoptees and their graying birthparents. So I knew, vaguely, about search and reunion. From feature-article headlines, I'd gathered that supply and demand were out of whack, and that faraway adoptions were making up the shortfall. I was also aware that some newer types of families were cracking the system, that mature single women, possibly even lesbians, could sometimes adopt. It was common knowledge that parental age and matching by religion were no longer imperatives. That pretty much covers the insights I brought to the table. And on the basis of these info tidbits, I reckoned we wouldn't look so bad. If older solo applicants were in the running and religion wasn't, then presumably an aging, theologically mismatched, unmarried couple would pass muster, especially if we were flexible about the child we'd welcome.

David and I were already past forty. We both worked long hours. Beyond an extended adoptive leave for me, neither of us pictured staying home or cutting our careers in half. Given these factors, plus every child's need for quality time, we figured we'd be a one-tyke-only family. But we didn't want to miss out on any stage, not even the diaper days. Hence, the child had to be youngish, though not necessarily newborn. We were squeamish about babies who'd been badly bruised *in utero* or battered in early life. We ruled out AIDS, fetal alcohol or narcotics exposure, plus a known history of hard abuse. While profound or multiple handicaps scared us, we felt we could cope with some wonkiness, say, imperfect sight or a deformed limb. Call us cowards, but we wanted a relatively healthy, quite young child with not-too-intimidating special needs.

Race mattered. By now, most people know something of the tragic history of Native adoptions. On government say-so, tens of thousands of kids across the continent were forcibly removed from their families, then relocated to church-run residential schools, where they were culturally exiled. The children born of this demoralized generation were then scooped up in frightening numbers for transplant into "good Christian homes." Little wonder that North American Indians now reclaiming their nations have clamped down on adoption. In the United States, the Indian Child Welfare Act curbs such adoptions, whereas, in Canada, provincial laws and policies affect them but don't effectively stop them.

What's more, even if First Peoples weren't beseeching outsiders not to adopt their children, David and I didn't have the cultural savvy or connections to make us fit parents for a Native youngster. Otherwise, a child of color was fine. Given our city, Toronto, our rainbow neighborhood and circle, and David's biracial nephew, an adoptee who is now our young-adult friend, we imagined any child could feel, if not perfectly at home, at least snug enough in our family and milieu.

When we set out, we planned to adopt domestically. Surely, we speculated, there must be familyless little ones not far from our doorstep who fit our bill. To the superficial extent that we analyzed the issue, we weren't unalterably opposed to international adoption, which usually means children from poor countries joining families in rich ones. But we did feel ethically uneasy, not to mention nervous, about the unknowables.

A famous Argentinian movie, *The Official Story*, which had made a deep impression on me, hovered over our brief discussion about looking abroad. I couldn't imagine finding myself in the lead character's position: mothering a stolen child. And the thought of that child, who could be with his or her original family, stuck with us, oceans away, horrified me. At that time, I knew little, save the odd headline-grabbing scandal, of the shenanigans that sometimes go on in making global families. I didn't know, for instance, if there were any "safe" countries from which to adopt, places where middlemen can't get away with pulling a fast one on gullible, baby-hungry foreigners with fat wallets. Maybe ending up, unknowingly, with a bought baby or a missing child was a long shot, but the risk made me shudder.

Having sorted out these preliminaries ourselves, excited, I checked the Yellow Pages listing for "Adoption Services" and called the Children's Aid Society of Metropolitan Toronto. Talk about a rude awakening. In my ignorance, I assumed we'd be welcomed as a resource for a baby who might not be a cinch to place. Instead, a coolly officious intake worker couldn't get me off the phone fast enough. (She wasn't just having a bad day. Later I would hear many stories like mine.) She told me that: (a) there are "no babies"; and (b) given our age and marital status, we had virtually "no chance" of adopting a preschooler, let alone a newborn, since they go to "typical" parents.

Next, she pulled the "homestudy" from her bag of discouragements. What's that? I asked. The government-required screening process for all adoptive hopefuls. It includes office interviews and home visits by a social worker, forms to fill out, documents—a medical report, for example—and character references to submit. Okay. How long would it take to get our study done? Longer than anyone past forty could afford. A private agency might get around to us faster, she advised. And then we could come back to Children's Aid for a child? I asked. No, they don't set any store by outside homestudies, she explained. But you just told me they're done by licensed social workers, so you must be joking about not accepting them, I said. No, she wasn't kidding. Even if they did permit external homestudies, there was still the problem of our being less-than-choice candidates, she reminded me. Shell-shocked by her attitude and everything she was saying, I requested an information packet, then hung up, without, I regret, getting rude.

Back to the Yellow Pages, where I found a list of private agencies. I phoned the closest one, and a week later we were in a cluttered, home-spun office with a sympathetic social worker for the first of our home-study meetings. Over the next couple of months, on a schedule of visits to his workplace and our home, we'd answer personal questions about our upbringing, values, relationship, and our parenting style. (Who knew what that was? We just winged it, tried to second-guess the "right" answers. No, we wouldn't hit. Yes, we'd encourage any child to find his or her own path. The child wouldn't have to become an x, y, or z to satisfy us.) We wouldn't, I should mention, have much beyond a one-minute exchange about our competence, or lack thereof, to raise a child who might be racially and culturally different from us.

We'd discuss our work, income, assets—you name it, and the government wanted it in the homestudier's report, which would recommend us, or not, as adoptive applicants. We'd also grimace our way through the usual bureaucratic paperwork, and bother some friends who have impressive letterhead to write glowing references.

Though we both liked the guy grilling us, I was a nervous wreck. Trembling at his power to award or withhold our parenting badge, I went into performance-art mode. I measured my words, worked to convey my best impression of a correct parent, shot loaded glances at my laid-back partner when he said anything I imagined might weigh against us. I remember a tellingly ridiculous incident after one of these sessions. In answer to a lifestyle question, David had volunteered that he spent some university years living in a commune. "How could you?" I shrilled as we waited for the elevator. "He's going to think we're a couple of overgrown hippies. We'll never get a kid."

Whew! Although we'd both veered from beaten paths, we did get stars on our report card and could get in line for a child. Before the homestudy, I hadn't realized that in private adoptions, original families, not facilitators, choose their baby's adopters from those on file. Usually, they want to meet the parents they're considering, perhaps negotiate terms of an ongoing relationship between the two families. Though it came as a bit of a shock, open adoption seemed to make sense. At least, it gives adoptees access to background data the rest of us take for granted. At most, it gives them contact with the people who gave them life. I'd be incensed if anyone tried to deprive me of these rudiments, so why would I want to deprive anyone else, least of all a child of mine? That is not to say David or I automatically warmed to the idea of a wide-open arrangement—later, we'd want it—where we'd know each other's last name and phone number. But meeting the birthfamily and staying in touch appealed. It sounded healthier than the traditional silence separating birth- and adoptive families.

Once the homestudy was completed, our social worker prepared us for the competition. There weren't many birthfamilies out there, he warned, but there were plenty of parent wannabes who'd look more attractive than us to the typical young mother or father. It might help, he nudged, if we brought our relationship "up to community stan-dards"—in other words, get married. He also coached us on how to write a winning "Dear Birthparent(s)" letter, which is usually known as a "Dear Birthmother" letter because so many pregnant young women go it alone. In addition, he equipped us with a starter kit of ideas for tracking down a baby ourselves.

I cranked out a form letter to be sent to doctors in small Ontario towns, all within a manageable radius, drafted a letter of introduction to go to birthfamilies, and hired a student to label and stuff envelopes. We shipped a few hundred. Over the next six months or so, about a dozen replies dribbled in, all from retired physicians with time to answer their mail. They sent their regrets and wished us well. Everything else we tried, such as ads in college newspapers, was equally effective: zero productive leads. Meanwhile, I bugged our social worker. He put us onto one birthmother, but she decided before our scheduled meeting to keep her baby. There were a few other teasers along the way, but none got as far as a face-to-face.

It seemed as if I was constantly busy with the search, and with pay-ing the miscellaneous bills that were piling up, on top of the $3,000 or so we'd already put down on the homestudy. Yet, somehow, two years had gone by and we were no farther ahead. We were married though—to please ourselves, not to placate birthfamilies who surely wouldn't be any more impressed with mid-life newlyweds than with old cohabitors. I cut back my free-lance writing and got on the phone. That was in November. Six months later, we hit the jackpot.

I'll never forget that eye-opening half-year. I canvassed just about everyone in private adoptions across an in-reach swath of the province. We restricted ourselves to Ontario, by the way, because adopting across provinces can be a bureaucratic nightmare. We registered with roughly ten agencies within car-shot of Toronto, as far away as Ottawa. We met with a variety of adoption arrangers. Some gave us valuable advice. A lawyer, for instance, who scrutinized our "Dear Birthparent(s)" missive, suggested we further minimize my Jewish background. Why? Since even nominal Christians tend to celebrate Christmas, some birthparents might nix us for fear their child would forfeit a special family day. So, for its next of many incarnations, an artist friend sketched into our pitch—by then an illustrated pamphlet on aqua onionskin!—a cartoon of us with child next to a Xmas tree.

Most professionals were friendly, empathic—and pessimistic. As they took our fees, they warned us that pregnant teens rarely choose adopters who grew up with the Beatles. While they blamed the place-ment pattern—newborns going to married couples under thirty-five—on birthparents, I wondered how much supposedly neutral intermediaries influenced the outcome.

Take note: no one telling us we'd likely never get a baby tried sidelining us toward toddlers in the public system. No one edged us over with "You guys are of an age to have kids in school and it just hap-pens that lots of such children need people like you. Maybe you could think about adopting one of them?" "Waiting children" simply weren't in the vocabulary. Yet, the adoption world is so small that operators trip over one another. Everyone knows who's who and what's what, including what we would later learn: Children's Aid is indeed Fort Knox, but even the oddest of couples can break kids loose. It's a matter of knowing the right workers and the right doors. No one urged us to knock. Instead, in conversations with adoption arrangers, they regur-gitated our uninformed bias for an almost-new baby adopted privately.

Conversations were strange in another way too: race was often the foremost concern. It came up before HIV, crack cocaine, cerebral palsy. One way or another, facilitators said, "Presumably you want a white baby." When we'd come back with "Not necessarily," they'd raise an eyebrow, as if something were inherently wrong with mixed families. (In the United States, where race relations are impossibly strained, you'd expect workers to be jumpy about transracial adoption. In Canada, where tensions are more muted, knee-jerk assumptions about racial sameness in families seemed more at play.) A Windsor social worker told me the biracial babies she places are born of young white mothers from "good families" who get mixed up with black criminals from Detroit. She confided in me in a "one of us" way she'd dare not use with blacks. I couldn't believe my ears. It was from her, though, that I got my first inklings of the race-in-adoption potboiler in the United States.

By then, we'd decided to cast our net south, where there'd be far more babies but no more red tape than that tangling adoption between provinces. Besides, the U.S. was culturally familiar (how's that for Canadian understatement?) and accessible for open adoption. At that time, we were under the impression that if any parents in the States chose us, they'd likely be white, or black and white. Our letter to birth-parents gets revised again: we feel an ivory, or ebony and ivory, child would fit nicely in our family.

Very determined now to find a little bundle and frustrated to tears as our birthdays stack up (I'm forty-five, David forty-three, at this point), we turn to a California baby broker. Our signatures are barely dry on the contract before we get antsy about what this gambit might cost before we're rocking a cradle. Around this time, two things happen. On our own initiative, we attend a public meeting on waiting children at which a couple of kindergarten-age kids presented in pictures and stories hit a soft spot in our hearts. Shortly thereafter, our social worker tips us to a nonprofit Missouri agency, founded by a religious order, that recently placed an African-American baby with a Toronto couple somewhat like us: older and secular. Next day I'm on the phone to the family and to Independence, and our package is *en route* by courier. Before David and I even have time to discuss the Children's Aid kids, we get a call from Kansas City: they have a baby for us! He's one week old, apparently healthy, and in foster care. His mother is African American and Hispanic, his father black. Together, they've selected us. Can we come straight away?

The rest, as they say, is history. We went. We met our son's birth-mother and her mother. We wept and hugged and made our plans. Each family gave the baby a name. David and I fell in love with little

Clayton Marcus. About four weeks from the phone call, we brought Clay home.

So, what do I have to *kvetch* about? The system worked for me. Even though I was practically menopausal when I entered, I managed to walk away with the prize. Believe me: I am eternally indebted to a cockamamie setup. Were it otherwise, I might have found a child, but I would not have found Clay. And it is not the idea of having a child, but this one, my son, who makes my heart soar.

What's askew then? Plenty—which accounts for my feeling fidgety from the day I stepped into the adoption arena. My first contact with the icy intake worker made me wonder what that was all about. My consternation, however, didn't go away when I detoured from the public into the private domain. Throughout our journey, a funny feeling that some things were terribly wrong continued to gnaw at me. If you'd asked me at the time what was getting under my skin, I think I'd have put my finger on three issues. First, I sensed there was more cultural subtext than spoken truths floating around in this unfamiliar world. Second, I was increasingly aware that the type of family we were trying to create meant we'd be joining a marginal club. Since I'd always thought of adoptive families as normal, this hunch that we were doing something abnormal threw me off. Third, and related, a glint of suspicion shadowed the whole process.

In the throes, however, the momentum carried me along. Too caught up getting through the gate so we could get to a child, I had no mental time to examine the philosophy or *modus operandi*. But, later, on reflection, my vexation took more definite shape and propelled me to write this book.

It's the resource I wish I'd had before we bumbled, naive, into the weird world of adoption. Better I'd been an informed consumer than a wide-eyed tyro stumbling across ethical land mines. How-to books are a dime a dozen, but I needed briefing on the hot buttons, such as the prejudices against unconventional families. We should have gone in knowing about the controversies of race and place. We did consider these issues, as I mentioned, but not in the deeply informed way that behooves people making socially sensitive decisions that rebound on the child, on both his families, and on his root community. Our education was also sorely lacking on open adoption, though this was one area where social workers brought us up to steam as we went along.

But the biggest lapse in our repertoire was knowing so very little about waiting children in this country, about the viability of adopting one past infancy. Before I first rang up Children's Aid, these kids should have been in my mind's eye.

Our story has a happy ending. Yet, it is needlessly sad for the one system child—perhaps even two siblings—who'd have a family today if the child-welfare/adoption complex sided with waiting children, with all kids who should be readied for adoption, and with all sorts of potential adopters. Though we couldn't be more satisfied with the outcome, the fact remains that, in many ways, our sojourn should not have happened the way it did. I offer this book in hopes that other searchers will go in with their eyes open wider, steeled against the barriers, prejudices, and stupidities that may greet them. Above all, I hope the lives you will enter in later pages soften your hearts to the possibility of parenting a child different from the baby of your dreams.

ABOUT THE FAMILIES, NAME USE, SOURCES, AND SOCIAL WORKERS

My journey through adoption so jolted me I became almost obsessed with understanding what was going on in the low-visibility world I'd stumbled into. Even though it was after the fact—I'd already adopted an African-American child—I wanted to sift through the surrounding controversy. If I knew more, how would I really feel about what we'd done? Other nagging questions: what should I have known about third-world adoptions before halfheartedly rejecting them as we did? What about open adoption? At first explanation it felt right, but how do experienced birth- and adoptive families assess it?

I wondered if others who don't fit the nuclear-family mold got flak when trying to adopt. Were they barred from babies? Were our son's teenage parents exceptional in choosing mid-lifers? Were birthfamilies usually as turned off by everyone but the young, the married, and the privileged as we'd been led to believe? Were less-conventional families almost invariably thrown together with kids the system describes as hardest to handle? And how much of a role did money play in matching? Was I right in guessing that income was *the* critical variable in determining who got in the door, which children they'd get, and how quickly? Was it the case, as I was starting to suspect, that the system, or crucial parts of it, dedicated to creating adoptive families itself nurses deep ambivalence about parent–child kinship among strangers?

I figured the best place to take soundings would be with North American adoptive families. By the way, there's almost nothing uniquely Canadian about adoptions today; the hot issues are more or less the same, though not equally inflamed, in all super-industrial countries. But I knew it was important to include the United States. As in so many fields, in adoption Americans have a knack for extremes, exhibiting the worst and the best on offer. Canada has much to learn from their voluntary-sector innovations in finding families for so-called hard-to-place kids and in appreciating so-called hard-to-match adopters.

This wasn't to be a scientific study, just informal get-togethers with a convenient sample of less-familiar adoptive families and with more controversial ones as well, and, for open adoption, with birthfamilies. I put together my tour of thirty-seven families in ten cities through personal networking, flukes, and cold calls to organizations in the child-advocacy, private or specialty adoption sector. It's safe to assume intermediaries paved my way to reasonably functional families, not to botchups. Otherwise, there's not much bias built into the loop.

In looking for families—except for adoptions involving distance and racial difference, which happen in "traditional" as well as newfangled families—I specified characteristics of adopters, not of adoptees. That is, I asked contacts to help me meet the kind of adults who normally wouldn't have had a prayer of adopting even a decade ago: poor people, older folks, those with differing abilities, gays and lesbians, unmarried hetero men. I sought single women too, though there's little scandal left in allowing them to parent. I didn't narrow the field to households that had incorporated infants, or adolescents for that matter, only to those who had come lately to adoption.

Yet, as it turned out, in a standout number of cases, irrespective of income, people adopted system kids, whether local or from afar. The pattern reflects a built-in bias against A-Okay newborns going to anyone but youngish mom-and-pop families. (The silver lining: older kids get homes.) This observation, plus other noteworthy coincidences and the existing research, lead me to believe my chance family assortment is remarkably representative.

Another intriguing feature: most families contain more than one oddity, whether, for example, they are single *and* international adopters, or homosexual *and* transracial adopters. Given the teensy domestic supply of adoptable healthy babies, even married white yuppies, seen as most desirable for Caucasian newborns, have to consider kids viewed—though often wrongly—as hardest to place. Hence, in general, the more "wrong" you are as an adopter, the less likely it is you'll gain access to those adoptees who are most in demand.

Not everyone I approached agreed to an interview. Some felt, as I might in their shoes, that their story belongs to their children, too young to give informed consent. Others wanted to guard their privacy completely; pseudonyms wouldn't be enough. One guy, who, interestingly, has differing abilities, refused because he objects to grouping unusual families in a book. He felt I was doing more of the same old thing: ghettoizing and marginalizing those who diverge from the hallowed norm. A few others balked too, though some for baffling reasons. Unfortunately, they did it at the last minute, after I'd flown to their cities. Several families who appear could be called "adoption missionaries." To their credit, they want to use their own success to help spread the word.

Most contributors chose to be fully identified. As a rule, gays and lesbians were most worried about disclosure. Some opted for first names only, as did a couple of straight adopters. A few participants requested total anonymity. In two cases, I use fictional names and locations for real cases I just happen to know about, though one family wasn't interviewed at all. An asterisk with the first use of a name or place indicates it has been changed.

Bear in mind as you read that I blundered into the lives of gracious strangers for anything from scant hours to a full day, with or without their kids, at home or elsewhere. I took what they shared at face value. Yet, our lives and our family ties are hopelessly complex, even mysterious. When it comes to intimate human relationships, transparency is always an illusion.

Another caution: for easier reading, I've kept my citation of sources to the minimum.

The most important caveat: this book is not meant as an attack on professionals who arrange adoptions. Whether they believe birthfamilies are always best, or that adoptive ones are the best thing since *Wednesday's Child*, or that having both families brings children the greatest advantage, whether they think that only well-off, legal couples should get babies, or that choice adopters for any child defy categorization, is beyond the target. My bull's eye is the system they work in.

It is riddled with policies and practices allowing individuals' prejudices full play to harm children, birthfamilies, and would-be adopters. I've made no attempt to bracket my bias: this book goes after a system out of tune with the times and with the urgent needs of children in care.

Far from having any beef with this adoption facilitator or that one, I'm a fan of anyone with the gumption to unglue kids from dangerous parents and a deadly child-welfare system, and seal them into competent homes of any configuration. Such homes include those of birthfamilies brought back, with professional help, from the brink of wreckage. And I'm on my feet for any fixer trying to build access ramps to adoption for a broad cross-section of the population. This point is not lost on me: while shakers and movers are in the trenches, sticking out their necks, all I'm doing is mouthing off.

Of Blood Voodoo and "Real" Families

*... Contracted parenthood cannot compete: there is no equivalent
aspect of parenthood the social parent can absorb that will have the strength
of the "blood" tie.... [Adoption] is just paper ... not as binding as birth.*

—Judith S. Modell, Kinship with Strangers

"I'm infertile. So what?" read T-shirts worn by a Japanese contingent at the 1995 international women's conference in Beijing. Since females are raised to repeat the cycle of giving birth, it's safe to assume relatively few could strut around comfortably with such a slogan emblazoned on their chests. Though baby-boomers have made mind-boggling leaps since their mothers' generation, women are still seen as unnatural if they choose not to produce offspring, or inadequate if they want to but cannot.

Biological motherhood as the greatest accomplishment of a life, both in a woman's eyes and in the eyes of the world, has more staying power than almost any other cultural symbol. So exalted is producing "your own" children that couples and single women flock to fertility clinics. Even a decade ago, Americans were already shelling out about $1 billion to battle infertility.[1] Late last year, when an Iowa couple produced septuplets after infertility treatment, the press reported that the industry had grown to $4 billion U.S. a year. "Of course," says Harvard law professor Elizabeth Bartholet, herself unsuccessful in the quest for a medical miracle, "the infertile are begging for treatment, and of course those who manage to produce a child will say it has all been worth it."[2]

But is it? The vast majority of women who devote themselves to getting pregnant at the hands of the wizards *do not* walk away with a baby. Their chances of slumping away bankrupt, emotionally drained, physically exhausted, and suffering side effects from their stay in Clomid City far outweigh their chances of leaving with a baby carriage. Janice Raymond, a University of Massachusetts professor of medical ethics and women's studies, and author of *Women as Wombs*, claims that 90–95 percent of women who try *in vitro* fertilization (IVF) don't become pregnant. Yet, ever-increasing numbers of women risk their health, suspend any misgivings they may have about genetic engineering, and surrender their lives to trial and error, even with the odds so heavily stacked against pregnancy.

This phenomenon reflects a cultural fiction of gargantuan proportions: replicating your own flesh and blood is the only way to have *bona fide* family. Hence, it's a cultural norm to mourn infertility. Indeed, many women are so pained at being barren that they need counseling for years. Some never get over their grief.

Blood voodoo is so potent it puts a hex on adoption. Among women who go through purgatory in their failed bid to produce progeny, only a fraction go on to adopt. You could argue most are too broke or too pooped, or have too-resistant partners, to take on the long, arduous adopting process. But there's a more likely explanation for why adults who will do almost anything to make a baby, but can't, forgo their chance to parent. Though polite company wouldn't express it in these words, adopting a child is not as good as having "your own."

Patricia Irwin Johnston, an adoptive mother and writer, explains it this way:

> Historically people have been considered to be members of the same family when one or more of several conditions are met: they are linked by blood (e.g. father and son), they are linked by law (e.g. husband and wife), they are linked by social convention (e.g. woman and her husband's sister), they are linked by love. We don't blink at the concept of two non-genetically-related people being members of the same family if one or more of the other criteria are met ... except in adoption. Though in adoption parent and child are linked by love and by law, the fact that they are not connected by blood has often meant that some people are unwilling to acknowledge their relationship as genuine and permanent.[3]

When was the last time you saw a probably adoptive family—one that makes you wonder how the child "belongs"—on TV, not in an adoption story but on a commercial for any product, say, cereal or soap?

Although not all adoptive families are obvious, lots are, including all-white households like that of my olive-skinned Italian friends and their blonde, blue-eyed daughter. Looking at them, few could "make it work" by imagining that the girl came from the parents' loins, or from one of the parents with a different partner. Television tolerates blended families, especially as sitcom subjects, where two adults bring their cookie-cutter kids together into a unit that, on closer inspection, might not otherwise look to be a fit. But programming almost never gets any closer than that to adoptive families.

Figuring out how society, and popular culture, above all, sidelines adoptive families is a no-brainer; they are simply excluded from the image marketplace. We're not talking about underrepresentation here, a complaint that many atypical individuals—such as the blind or quadriplegic—as well as newer types of families could legitimately spindle. We're talking about almost full-scale blackout. True, every now and then a feature film touches the topic through a controversial lens. For instance, Hollywood discovered transracial adoption in *Losing Isaiah*. More to the point, made-for-TV tearjerkers have been mining search-and-reunion. A quirky British movie, *Secrets and Lies*, that explored this theme with a dash of race issues thrown in even walked away with the 1996 Palme d'Or prize for best picture (sort of a European Oscar). But, take note, with all the potentially exploitable adoption-related subjects—the tragedy of children denied a central adult link for life, for example, or openness between birth- and adoptive families—none excites the media more than the reconnection of the "real" mother with her long-lost child.

Recall the buzz when recording artist Joni Mitchell recently came face to face with the daughter she gave up for adoption over thirty years ago. The headlines and language used by the papers made it seem as if the only rightful parent–child bond is the one birthmother and daughter share. Don't get me wrong. Reunion, as I see it, is a wonderful trend, the next best thing to openness from the start. Mitchell's story was heartwarming. But her birthdaughter has a family, the one who raised her, and the one both she and Mitchell acknowledged in their statements to journalists. My point? The press played up the "real" family bonds while almost ignoring the presumably synthetic, that is, adoptive ones. Because such families are seen as a shell game, not in the running with the real McCoy, the hype centers on the only supposed good in the situation: reunion.

In situations like Mitchell's, aside from the odd groan coming from the adoption community, it seems hardly anyone bats an eye when the media spouts its usual claptrap. Unthinking prejudice against adoptive families has held its course despite the growth industry in equality. While the modern culture of inclusion has shattered many orthodoxies about individuals, human relationships and families, adoption has been shut out from the club of enlightment. The press can get away with its ignorance only because it's still socially benign to talk about adoptive families as knockoffs.

Adoption isn't a four-letter word, but it's often treated as if it were. Prevailing cultural discourse reinforces the adoptive-family image as a fake. This overheard conversation should make the point. Two mothers, let's call them A and B, were discussing the Paul Bernardo case, speculating on his parents. What must it be like for them to stand by their son, a convicted serial sex-murderer? The women agreed that, despite the horrific crimes, any good parents would feel, as B put it, "he's our child and we love him, no matter what."

Then A says, "Okay, but what about the Chrétiens [referring to Canada's prime minister and his wife, whose son served time for sexually assaulting a young woman]? I wonder how they feel?"

"That's different," says B, without skipping a beat. "He's adopted; he's not their flesh and blood.... They're probably there for him, I don't know, but you can't blame them if they're not."

After the twosome meander around in this territory, with no dissenting opinion, the conversation switches back to the Bernardos, who, they say, must have had a hand in shaping their son's deformed psyche. The women agree that both genes and upbringing count: they see it in how their own children have turned out. Yet, B goes on to make an exception for the younger Chrétien, who probably has "bad blood" and "came perverted." She also observes that he's Native Indian, as if that explains everything.

Their conversation never strays from the fiction that adoptive family bonds are tenuous, nowhere near the same in kind or in strength as "normal" family ties, and that the kids have a strike against them from the start. The lingo that rolls so comfortably off these women's tongues is laced with lamentable social conventions about supposedly regular versus pseudofamilies. No wonder Elizabeth Bartholet, in *Family Bonds*, has this to say about adoption language:

[It] conveys the additional message that adoptive parenting
relationships are less powerful, less meaningful, less loving than
blood relationships.... The clear implication is that people
would not adopt for the same reasons that they would produce
a child....Therefore, some aberrational and perhaps altruistic
motive must be involved.[4]

Adoptive-family members also complain that nonadopters view the
parent–child tie as weaker. *The Stranger Who Bore Me*, by Canadian
researcher Karen March, cites, for example, a contemporary study in
which seventy-two adoptive mothers said their community regarded
the birthmother, not them, as their child's authentic parent. Onlookers
assumed number-two mom couldn't love the youngster as deeply as
number one could. In addition, respondents noted how people seemed
to think less of their children because they were adopted. March herself quizzed a large sample of adult adoptees about social stigma. She
found they, too, grew up intensely aware of doubts cast on their attachment to their adoptive parents and with misgivings about the legitimacy of their family structure.[5]

Perhaps you assume only those not personally acquainted with
adoption see such families as phonies. On the contrary, the belief that
blood is thicker than bonding ripples through the adoption world
itself, where, presumably, you'd least expect to find it. You'd hope, for
example, that those responsible for state children would put themselves
on the cutting edge of family reinvention. They've been in enough hor-
rible homes to witness how bad blood can be. They've seen the psychic
laundry kids collect as they lurch from one temporary foster address to
another. They know there's no prayer of washing it clean unless the
little ones find loving stability. And they've seen adoption provide that
ballast. Yet, ironically, some of the most virulent anti-adoption senti-
ment originates in the house of child protection and placement.

Authorities carry on as if families that share DNA were a sacred
hinge of society with which we tamper at our peril. So lacking is their
faith in adoptive families that they would sooner, and do, shunt kids
back and forth between foster settings and dysfunctional birthfamilies
throughout childhood than see them settle in one place with loving
adults who have no blood ties with them. It's no accident that only a
fraction of kids trapped in the game of bureaucratic hopscotch are ever

freed for adoption, and that only a trifling number of those given the green light actually end up in adoptive homes. It's no accident that adults hoping to parent often have to beat down an agency's door rather than stave off persistent appeals from them. The motto seems to be "Family preservation, even if it kills"; witness the litany of parent-inflicted deaths of tots while under government supervision.

The systemic attitude among child-welfare authorities that grants biological families the copyright on worthiness and deems adoption to be the desperate last option will become more evident in the next chapter. But it's introduced here because it serves as a philosophical clothesline. On it hangs all the other telltale evidence of discrimination and distrust that has always dogged adoption. That discrimination, it should be said, is not purely attitudinal; in some respects it's also legal. For example, the Employment Insurance Act provides up to twenty-five weeks of parental leave benefits to families whose babies arrive by birth, but only ten weeks to parents whose children come through adoption. (Though one court ruled this provision unconstitutional, the appeal court overturned the decision. Two Ontario adoptive mothers, who've been fighting this battle for years, plan to go to the Supreme Court of Canada.)

The problem—viewing the adoptive as something less than the authentic family—starts high up and fans out throughout the system and the surrounding community. Take the homestudy. This obligatory assessment can be so invasive as to border on voyeurism. Why must would-be adopters lay bare the minutiae of their lives and prove beyond reasonable doubt they deserve a seal of approval as fit parents when every rogue can produce as many kids as s/he chooses without any kind of official imprimatur? The subliminal message? Biological parenting is sacrosanct, your business, not the state's, unless you mash your kids and Big Brother happens to find out. Adoptive parenting, on the other hand, needs heavy-duty oversight.

That is not to say I oppose screening. Obviously, those charged with protecting children must use standard criteria to measure good character. It almost goes without saying that everyone wants authorities to ensure, as best they can, that kids don't go to incompetents and molesters. But relying on a mushy, subjective test open to interrogator bias and manipulation by the respondents mocks faith in would-be parents. Were adopters assumed to be no more or less defective than average folks, and their families no more doubtful than the standard brand, there'd be no reason to put them under a microscope.

There's another major way in which the child-welfare establishment enforces its profound distrust: closed adoption. Historically, sealing biological and legal families off from each other has been a hallmark of adoption practice. While the trend now favors unlocking files and normalizing open adoption for newly made families (more on this in chapter 3), the legacy of the old school lives on. As Karen March, who researched adoption reunion, puts it: "By denying adoptees access to both the genetic and genealogical information possessed by the majority of their society, secrecy distinguishes them as a *separate category of people with suspect family membership and questionable social identity*" (my emphasis).[6]

Institutions by nature cozy up to conservatism, so maybe we shouldn't be too surprised, after all, that officialdom takes a dim view of adoptive families. But, how can we explain those adoptive parents who themselves have an iffy attitude? I was in a Toronto audience a couple of years back when one mother, who's also a respected authority in the field and who normally offers sage advice, made me want to holler. She claimed, in approximately these words, that "we can only know the joy of adopting because we remember the loss of infertility." Though her talk was supposedly about raising adopted children, she droned on and on about infertility.

She said nothing to defuse the conventional wisdom that people always prefer to "have their own children." Nor did she promote adoption as a family-building option, different from but equal to the birthbound method. Listening to her, the uninitiated would come away with the tired old impression that the adoption process begins only after the better way has failed. In this same adoption-as-second-best vein, author Jana Wolff, in *Secret Thoughts of an Adoptive Mother*, writes: "Adopting interracially is like donning a permanent sandwich board that advertises your adoption (and your infertility, too.)"[7]

Other insiders also give it a bad name. Some birthmothers of the last generation are rightly bitter that the stultifying mores of the time forced them to relinquish babies they might have kept, given a choice and minimal support. These mature women, now involved in search and reunion, hear an echo from some younger birthmothers who are also smarting because their parents, adoption intermediaries, and aggressive couples pressured them into a decision they soon regretted.

Together, these reluctant birthmothers, along with the odd professional who has sworn off adoption for one reason or another, paint it as a borderline crime that puts a curse on all who are complicit in it. Accordingly, everyone leads a life perverted by painful losses: the birthmothers because they've lost their baby, the child because s/he's lost "real" parents (as one writer wisecracked: watch out, kiddo, here comes "genealogical bewilderment"), and the adopters because they've lost out on having "their own" child. While these profound losses and inevitable grief should not be trivialized, adoption also brings gains—gains glossed over by those who've been wronged through adoption.

Also doing damage to social acceptance of this type of family are adoptive parents who give children back to the agencies whence they came. Since almost no biological parents ever voluntarily give away a birthchild they have decided to raise, what are people supposed to think when adopters choose to hand back a child they're bringing up? These tragedies hardly inspire the belief that adoptive families, like their non-adoptive counterparts, are forever. Reversible adoptions don't deliver the message that some adopted kids, just like some bio kids, screw up big time, and some parents do go berserk, *but* the family holds—even if the youngster has to find a room of his or her own or spend time in a therapeutic facility or, for that matter, in juvenile detention.

Normally, parents don't wash their hands of a demon child who comes to them by birth. More often, they do if s/he comes through adoption. Estimates of how often this happens vary wildly, but there's no dispute that some families who adopt older, especially needy kids do break down. While returning a human being as if s/he were a commodity must be its own kind of hell for everyone, it delivers a clear message about adoption: it's a "maybe" kind of arrangement. (The other more important message doesn't get out: system incompetence often creates conditions for adoption reversals. But more about that later.)

The net result? The confluence of insider and outsider prejudice keeps ignorance alive. That ignorance manifests itself in comments that wound adoptive families. Parents hear pearls like these, often in the presence of their kids:

"I guess you can't have children."

"Do you have any children of your own?"

"Don't worry. You could still have a child."

(If there are bio kids in the family) "Do they behave like brothers and sisters?" Or "Do you feel the same about her as you do about your own children?"

"Why would you want to adopt? I couldn't do that." (It's unnatural to love a child born to someone else.)

"You're a saint." (Only a humanitarian, not a regular mortal, would adopt.)

"How can you do it? God knows what you're getting." (The Bad Seed theory.)

"Aren't you afraid her parents will try to get her back?" (Birthparents are shady types.)

"If he meets his natural parents, aren't you scared he'll want to go live with them?" (Adoptive families are shaky, not permanent like birthfamilies.)

Adoptees sometimes face hurtful remarks like these:

"Your parents are great. They treat you as if you were their very own."

"I bet you're grateful that you were taken in by such loving people."

"You're the adopted one?"

(To a third party) "I'd like you to meet Sally's adopted son, Mark."

"Have you met your real parents?"

You can't blame people for thinking or saying such insensitive things. In the old days, I might have made some of these *faux pas* myself. We aren't born crass and thoughtless. The culture, blood coursing through its veins whenever it thinks of family, makes us that way.

Adopters must be bucking for sainthood—unless they're psychos, that is. Their families are *faux*. There's shame in being adopted. All in all, adoption is a last-ditch option. These dopey ideas persist despite the fact that custom adoption, whereby kin or nonrelatives raise children not born to them, is as old as Methuselah. For the past century, alongside informal arrangements, adoption has also been practiced in the way we now tend to think of it: as adults legally incorporating child "strangers" into the family.

Yet, authoritative adoption data are hard to come by. No federal agency in North America systematically or regularly collects it. This lapse is probably related to casual indifference toward the kids, who, not incidentally, tend to come from families with zilch social status or clout. Every time one of these children dies while under some form of government care, the media lament the paucity of databases that would allow the system to track the children it supposedly monitors. The sorry state of adoption information is part and parcel of broader institutional neglect, so pandemic it's almost impossible to find out how many kids are knocking around in the system, where they are, who they are, or how ready they are for adoption. How many families are actively looking to adopt is another near-mystery. Available figures on any aspect of the subject come principally from voluntary child-welfare organizations. Not surprisingly, information often conflicts and estimates vary. As incomplete as the picture is, American data are abundant compared with Canadian. With this situation in mind, here are some basic numbers on which all sources agree.

Every year, Americans adopt more than 100,000 children (estimates range from 115,000 to 140,000); Canadians, about 6,000. More than 60,000 adoptions in the United States involve nonrelatives; the rest, kin or stepparents. Another half-million or so people, from the nuclear and extended families adoptees join, are affected by the event. In Canada, adoption touches an estimated one in five people. At this point, 5 to 6 million Americans count as adopted, about 1 million of them still children. "Count" because many others, dating back to the era of shame and secrecy, remain statistically invisible. Guesstimating from known numbers, about 30 million Americans have a direct, personal stake in this kind of family, as adoptee or birth- or adoptive parent.

As you see, adoption hits home for incredible numbers of people. Yet, for the most part, society still views it as the great compromise: adults who can't have the children they want settling for the children they can have. Though they've been arranging adoptive families for the best part of a century, child-welfare authorities, hoist on the petard of their own halfheartedness, have done little to help the world get over its love affair with ties of blood, or to elevate adoption into the same ether.

The Pecking Order

In the world of adoption, demand and supply are dramatically out of alignment, and for well-known reasons. On the supply side: birth control, abortions, single-parenting. On the demand side: later parenting interest, soaring infertility, and the emergence of new family types that have discovered adoption. In Canada, for every infant that public agencies place, eight other applicants wait, according to the Royal Commission on New Reproductive Technologies. Bear in mind that private agencies arrange most newborn adoptions, so competition is much stiffer than the public record suggests. In the United States, at least twenty couples jockey for each adoptable child. Every year, more than a million prospects queue up for a scant 25,000 babies.[8]

The lineup can get so long that some agencies worry more about managing the waiting list than they do about matching families. Some turn newcomers away. What they don't usually do is everything they can to encourage those in line to consider a child long out of a crib. Instead, a consumer-service mentality reigns. You want a healthy white baby? (Most comers are Caucasians in search of infants who resemble them.) That's your choice. But, sorry, we're fresh out. Take a number.

This situation is very odd, considering that adoption came into being as a service to children, or so the theory goes. Ideally, society would find suitable homes for youngsters who didn't, for whatever reason, have one. In practice, adoption has wandered far from its original intent, coming full circle, from child-centered to adult-focused. Now, it's a marketplace that encourages customers to shop around.

Comparison shoppers are more likely find what they're after— untarnished babies and fast service—in the nongovernmental sphere. Because over time public-sector adoptions proved so slow, so user-hostile, so wary of families that break the mold, the system paved the way for takeover by the private sector. While fee-based services aren't new to the adoption world, the private domain's dominant market share of healthy infants is. Now, for almost anyone who can afford it, the alternative route is the only way to go. In the United States, even those with little money but with access to a subsidized adoption through a specialty agency will likely choose it over the bureaucratic route. To put it plainly, people hoping to adopt a baby turn to the public system only if: (a) they don't know any better (as many rookies, like I was, don't); or (b) they can't afford to adopt any other way.

For adopters, avoiding government agencies brings a major benefit: it shaves years off the process. For birthparents, it brings a measure of control. Traditionally treated as incidental to adoption, original families found that they, as possessors of precious commodities, had new powers in the money-based adoption economy. The leverage allowed them to count, to get some of what they wanted in the exchange. It turned out they wanted to choose who'd raise their children. More than that, they wanted to figure into the family equation, not to be erased once their babies found new parents. Open adoption, where the bearing and rearing families relate for the sake of "their" child, has been gaining acceptance in part because birthparents bring something—babies—the cash quarter needs. Indeed, it's no coincidence that paid-for adoptions started to boom just as the baby supply started to go bust.

The perks from a parallel system, however, come at a price. The private sector attracts the parents of newborns, leaving the public domain with dwindling numbers of infants, except those apprehended at birth or soon after. As a result, the child-welfare system has become primarily a repository for older children. Today, virtually anyone intent on adopting a baby, and on bringing the child home while s/he can still be considered one, has to go private, which can cost a bundle. That means such adoptions are usually off-limits to families of modest means unless they sneak in as foster parents and later manage to keep the child. The upshot? A richer/poorer division in which the former get the babies and the latter get the big kids.

There are lots of ways in which the private system offers privilege to the more pampered. For starters, though there's no getting away from the homestudy, a healthy cash flow allows you to jump the queue. Instead of watching your hair go gray, and hence your chances of adopting diminish, while you wait your turn at a public agency, you can purchase a private homestudy for $2,000 to $5,000 in Canada.

Costs for adopting are all over the map. In Canada, if you bring your business to one agency, get a flat-fee homestudy, then wait for the phone to ring with news of a match that works out hitch-free, you could spend under $5,000. But good luck to you. More likely, you'll tire of waiting for that call and pursue other avenues: register with a raft of agencies, investigate international pathways, maybe hire an independent "baby broker," who is usually a lawyer. Fees, fees, fees. The irony is that most places you turn to for help qualify as nonprofit.

Beyond requiring a homestudy, government regulation of private adoptions is, in most respects, a joke. For instance, though chargeable services are limited, what licensed operators can charge isn't; the market sets the price. It's hard to predict what you'll pay in the end, because so many factors influence the bill: incidental costs, such as homestudy updates, plus optional extras, such as pre- and post-adoption counseling for birth-parents. Also, it's a pay-as-you-go plan. You wake up one day and realize you've spent maybe $10,000 and don't yet have a baby. You can easily fork over $20,000 to make your dream come true. And it's not unusual to cough up considerably more, especially if you roam far from home.

In this context, averages become meaningless. Among families you'll meet in this book who adopted outside the public system, but not from a specialty source, no one in Canada or the United States spent less than $10,000, in either currency. Most estimated $15,000 to $20,000 per adoption, and a few admitted, with embarrassment, kicking in an unspecified king's ransom. Spending $50,000 isn't unheard of.

In the United States, costs can really skyrocket if you're matched with a birthfamily that has no health insurance. While you can't, technically speaking, buy a baby, you can cover an expectant woman's reasonable living expenses, such as legal and health-care costs. As a would-be adopter, you pay on spec, knowing that once baby arrives, mom may change her mind. Flush families may very well sponsor several birthmothers before they themselves have anyone to coo over.

I said you can't buy a baby, but in fact some people do. In the 1980s, scam artists operating baby-selling rings were busted in Arizona and Texas. With its lenient private-adoption laws, Texas attracts entrepreneurs who rake it in compliments of gray market conditions and adopter desperation. Though the hot one, Texas isn't the only spot for schemers. Stories from the American baby underground make headlines from time to time. They typically follow one of two patterns. In the first, a go-between, usually a lawyer, purchases infants for clients directly or indirectly from birthmothers, often, but not always, from outside the country. Mexico is popular. In the other, legitimate-looking agencies defraud unsuspecting couples. But, while crooked practices litter some stretches along the international adoption highway, as you'll read in chapter 6, domestic adoptions cannot as easily skirt the law.

Even observing the rules, you can take a toll road to a baby, fierce competition notwithstanding. You have to do your homework, which is a bother. But once you locate the agencies and brokers who do the most business, and you spread the greenbacks around, *boom*, baby makes three (or two, if you're single). Doubtless, had we stuck with a California adoption lawyer we hired in a moment of total frustration, we'd have had a newborn pronto—within a year, which is instantly in the adoption world—and been maybe $30,000 in hock. In our case, we worked a lot of angles simultaneously. Luckily an affordable one paid off just as we were getting cold feet about the broker's bills, and we were able to weasel out of our contract for a small penalty.

The point is: if money and time pose no obstacle, you probably can find a made-to-order child. The baby supply is so slim that it's never simple, but often it's doable. The way things work, chances are in the United States you'll pay more to adopt a white baby than a brown one, and more for a brown one than a black one. In *The Case for Transracial Adoption*, the authors mention, for example, one U.S. agency that in 1990 published this fee chart for infants: white, $7,500; biracial, $3,800; black, $2,200.90. They conclude: "It appears that an agency can demand and receive greater fees for white or biracial infants than it can for black infants, because the former are scarcer."[9]

The money rule still applies, though not with the same rigor, if, as a prospective parent, you're not such a hot commodity yourself. Suppose you're past forty, a single heterosexual man, deaf or differently abled, a lesbian, or even a gay male (lowest on the adopter totem pole). Even with these supposed liabilities, which in the public system normally mean "Buzz off," you might still be able to find a newborn or near-newborn, if that's your desire.

The system favors the rich and the "normal," and the richer and more normal you are, the more it favors you. Examine adoption from the receiving end, and the verdict, however unattractive, is inescapable: highest-demand babies (read: healthy and white) usually go to families who own the most cultural capital. Meanwhile, the riffraff, defined foremost by income, but also so labeled by other factors—race, age, gender, marital status, able-bodiedness, and sexual orientation—get the rest, *if* they get a child at all. As Elizabeth Bartholet puts it: "They [meaning children] are categorized in terms of their marketability, with the 'undesirables' handed off to those deemed marginally fit to parent."[10] Or, as a child-placer, quoting someone else in her agency, said to me off the record, "Weird kids go to weird families."

No primer on the adoption arena's pecking order is complete without mention of race, tackled in chapter 6. Here, suffice it to say that, except for specialty agencies, in general, minorities get the short end of the stick. They are underrepresented in the halls of child-welfare power, and in standard agencies, from top management to frontlines. At the same time, for all the obvious reasons—take your pick: racism, disproportionate poverty, or the knapsack of troubles slung onto these two—in the United States their children are overrepresented among waiting kids. In Canada, except for Indians, who, among those snared in system limbo, far exceed their population share, it's impossible to know background descriptors. Nonetheless, you can say that the system has a long and inglorious history of fawning over well-off white adopters for nonwhite children while erecting barriers to families of color.

These days, given two families, one white, one not, both interested in a black child, the system will choose the lookalikes. But, usually, that's only if the applicants show up on the agency's stoop. Otherwise, almost no one, unless employed by a trend-setting organization or by a specialty unit for Native children, will go very far afield to find adopters culturally akin to the children in care.

To the extent that things have changed, they've done so because affected communities and their supporters have been hammering the status quo for at least twenty-five years. They've forced changes in laws, policies, and practices that have opened the door to some minority adopters who don't have bags of money. Nonetheless, when it comes to class and race, the playing field is still far from level.

In adoption, two things, you can be sure, still count: the old wrappers of privilege, and the old supply-and-demand rules of capitalism. Robert L. Woodson, founder of the National Center for Neighborhood Enterprise, in Washington, DC, fumed in the *Wall Street Journal* about this state of affairs:

> It will never be acceptable or moral for children to be reduced to the level of a commodity; adoption should not be included in the list of entitlements of the wealthy and powerful.... We must demand an end to atrocious double-standards that cater to the familial whims of society's elite but rebuke the earnest attempts of ordinary people to adopt.[11]

BOLDER THINKING
The adoption world, its governmental wing worst of all, has been warped by a bunch of antiquated canards. The most pernicious of these: adoption doesn't work. Its corollary: biology does work. Accordingly,

birthfamilies, no matter how derelict, deserve life-saving heroics (which is not to say that the jaws of life always free families from the wreckage, but that's another story). If all else fails, the thinking goes, give the go-ahead to adoption, but don't get carried away. It's bad enough kids can't have their "real" mom and dad; don't further sully their normalcy by saddling them with unorthodox parents. The last thing those poor kids need is, for example, some lesbian as their mother. Old chestnuts like these, still rattling around in society, infiltrate the workplace culture of mainstreet adoption.

Instead of redesigning assumptions about parent–child unions, by and large the institution of adoption continues to make a fetish of yes-teryear's sentimentalized family. On the one hand, by bringing together adults and children not connected by genes, it invents a new cultural meaning for "family." On the other, it too often operates to make that icon resemble the old one: youngish mom and dad, duly married, with newborn babe, though if you don't fit the formula, money might buy you a way around it.

Off on the sidelines, it allows, though it's skittish about doing so, for the supposed aberrations to come together: nonbabies and noncon-forming adults. And then, only if proven beyond a shadow of a doubt that a child cannot go back to his or her birthparents, or visit them occasionally while wasting his or her entire childhood in foster-care drift. The theory seems to be: bad birthparents are hardly ever bad enough, whereas garden-variety families of today, who might adopt and who rarely fit the old formula, are hardly ever good enough. Kids caught in the ideological snafu are cheated out of, or very delayed in getting into, a stable, secure home, while many could-be parents never get to provide one.

Is the picture all bleak? No. In the protection/adoption edifice, which is chock-full of contradictions, the most forward-looking and the most retro practices coexist. On one side of the street, you find offices plagued with the mentality that greeted me, where workers ward off those they consider weirdos, that is, would-be adopters who don't satisfy the antiquated criteria for normalcy. Behind sanctimo-nious concern about children going only to the right kind of family, whatever that is, you'll probably find an agency that sits back while kids in its care, far from going to any home at all, birth or adoptive, get lost in the bureaucratic shuffle.

Across the street, you find agencies, occasionally even of public-sector persuasion, that believe, as evidenced by their actions, children deserve an early life that's better than a dress rehearsal for lifelong despair. From a tender age, they need a family to forever call their own. Here, an adoptive one will do every bit as well as a birthfamily.

On this stretch of the road, you mostly find specialty agencies, which are sorely lacking in Canada. They're dedicated to finding homes for so-called hard-to-place youngsters, the ones who've been around the system too long or who have acquired complicated stories. The motive: place them fast before their stories accrue new complexities through exposure to the discredited system of care. Kin count—as well they should—on both sides of adoption row. But, on the modern side, attaching a child to at least one nurturing adult for life counts more.

Other beliefs distinguish the new from the old breed of gatekeepers. They shun the concept of adoption as the last stop for adults at the end of their rope. Instead, they trumpet it as just another means of family-making: no better, no worse—different mechanics, that's all. They assume every child needs and deserves a family, and that there's a taker out there for each and every one, no matter what challenges the little ones face. Through this lens, there's no such thing as an unplaceable child.

What's more, the upstarts don't subscribe to passé beliefs about who stacks up as a choice parent and what makes a desirable home. They're open to any self-defined family—one-headers or two, rich or poor or in between—capable of providing a loving anchor. They stopped thinking babies belong only with adults who, by virtue of their age, appear to have given birth to them. They gave up on the notion that older kids belong only with parents, no matter how terrible, who did, in fact, give birth to them. (I'm not arguing against family preservation here, only against reliance on fixup to a fault.)

These talismen of broader thinking, however, aren't exactly ubiquitous. It will take a firestorm of change to catapult the rescue and resettlement of children from where they are today to where they should have been a quarter-century ago: a humane deal for emotional starvelings across the continent. That deal has a better chance if the established monitors of parent–child kinship forgo dated creeds and come to hold dear a conviction already precious to some child-placers, many adopters, and child advocates: the adoptive family is not an aberration, but is every bit as prosaic as its idealized competitor. Adoption doesn't warrant the brouhaha its doubters have surrounded it with.

Unless those positioned to bypass genetics in family-building shake their hangup on biology and stop making a secret of adoption, who will? Overrating ties of blood and underrating ties of love are costly habits. For, more than any other obstacles, fixating on birthfamilies and being finicky about adoptive ones jeopardize efforts to guarantee that children will have families. Given the crush of kids hungry for homes, and the exacting criteria often used to screen potential adopters, these cultural reflexes needlessly condemn children and competent adults to life without each other.

In the current *zeitgeist*, the notion that we'll have social justice any time soon may be a pipe dream. Attempting to achieve this book's piece of that dream, however, is not a lost cause. All we're talking about here, after all, is making room on the biological family's pedestal for another family form. Conferring legitimacy on adoption, bringing it up to social standard and giving it recognition, and thereby opening doors to kids otherwise shut out from having a family of their own—these rate with realizable social changes even in these cruelly conservative times. The old guard on the adoptive family front, first cousins to the grumpy throwbacks making such a hullabaloo about "family values," can be defeated. All that's required is that we do it.

System Kids and Family New-Sorts

There are no rules, or at least none with any teeth, that give children a right to a nurturing home or that limit how long they can be held in limbo.

—Elizabeth Bartholet, Family Bonds

By the time I reach Sandra Craighead's bungalow in downtown east-side Detroit an hour late, I feel like going to a bar, not an interview. I arrive sweaty and swearing. Sorry, I was lost in freeway hell, sucking back truck belch, trying to read the map perched on my steering wheel. While my consciousness whispers, "This burnt-out, segregated city gives me the creeps. Why am I writing this bloody book anyway?" Sandra, without effort, melts my misery.

Step through her doorway and enter the orbit of mother earth: welcoming, warm, relaxed. A young-looking forty-five, Sandra has one of those faces fixed in a permanent smile, dimples so deep they never disappear. She's wearing a jaunty cap and a jumper, like you see on high-school kids; it suits her to a T. In the halo of her sunny calm, I feel the knot in my right shoulder dissolve as we settle in for a chat.

It's so quiet, where are the kids? Latasha, six, Lashawnda, fifteen, and Michael, twenty-one, are at special schools. Richard Thomas, two, the foster child she's now adopting, is napping. That poor waif got cocaine before birth, then a series of foster homes after, where he was likely abandoned in his crib. He still eats his feces, destroys pillows, and has "picked through" three playpens. His behavior tells Sandra he was caged in, unstimulated, and starved.

How would she know what his habits mean, or what to do about them? Insights come from ongoing training, and from commiserating with other fost/adopters (parents who foster first, then adopt) raising injured, delayed children. The education, and resources that include all-important respite, come from the Judson Center's LIFE (Living in

Family Environment) program and Sandra's worker, Brenee Moore. "She's there for me twenty-four/seven," Sandra emphasizes.

LIFE is a leading-edge idea from an award-winning nonprofit organization, funded by public and private money. It recruits families who love children and hate being on welfare. Judson doesn't buy the fashionable political line: welfare mom as urban menace culpable for all evils, ranging from the deficit to demoralized kids. Instead, it harnesses skills the poor accumulate from a lifetime of going up against the system. Many learn how to overcome adversity despite crushing obstacles. These survivors, Judson has found, given a chance, some courses, and oodles of support, can make first-rate parents for supposedly unadoptable kids. It trains and licenses them as foster parents.

By 1996, sixty kids, most of them African American, were living in thirty-three such families, eleven headed by couples, the rest by singles, primarily women. By then, twelve families had adopted their charges. The families earn $21,000 for their first child, plus medical expenses, then $12–27 per diem for each additional one. The youngsters get healing homes in place of a crazy-making system, the parents escape soul-destroying dependence, and the public purse saves an estimated $30,000 a year per child.

Sandra is the survivor-type LIFE looks for. With a buffer of services around her, she's crafting a new life for the kind of kids who, left in the system's hands, typically founder. And creating a new world of satisfaction for herself. For instance, to prepare for adopting Lashawnda, who is deaf, Sandra and her birthdaughter, an only child, learned sign language—no simple task—and now Sandra aims to become an interpreter.

She regards the chance to parent her three adoptees and one permanent foster son, Michael—who, by the way, is white and needs "total care," as he has muscular dystrophy and limited mental abilities—as a gift. When this book is out of print, I'll still take inspiration from her attitude.

It echoed at Silvan Burden's house in westside suburbia. She's also a LIFEr, and, like Sandra, an African American in her forties. Silvan raised her two kids alone, on and off aid, after single-handedly bringing up her two siblings. Their mother died young, and their dad was no help; he was too drunk. Making it through the hardship imbued Silvan with sympathy for the dissolute birthparents of the children she now raises as a fost/adopter.

Take her son William, for example. Of his mother, an alcoholic Silvan has known for years, she says, "I know it's a sickness. I know how sweet they can be.... I want William to know that there's some great things about his mom." And the boy, what's he dealing with? For starters, fetal alcohol syndrome (FAS). He was born, on the street, with syphilis, caught TB at six months, spent a year in hospital on a feeding tube, went blind in one eye and deaf in one ear. When Silvan first saw him at Judson, where she was a volunteer respite caregiver, William was a two-and-a-half-year-old basket case.

"I feel I could do something for him," she told his worker. "I bet you could" was the response. William went home with her, supposedly to give his foster family a break, but he never left. How did he endear himself to her? She laughs, her straight-laced, no-nonsense demeanor softening for a moment. By being "hyper and mean.... If he wasn't hurting himself, he was hurting someone else ... pulling his hair or digging in his face ... blood everywhere." She and her adult son had to watch William round the clock, napping only when he did. Silvan learned from a FAS clinic how to handle the boy. And now? "I wish you could see him. Oh man, he's a totally different person."

Her other two have also come the distance. At first, her severely mentally challenged son, who never had contact with typical kids, ripped down curtains, overturned tables, shredded clothes, and drank from the toilet. Now he plays with his peers, attends special classes at a regular school, tinkers with his beloved motors, and helps with the chores. "You got to give him story. Routine. Routine. He doesn't like change," Silvan explains.

Her daughter, age nine, who has cerebral palsy and whose birth-parents abused her every which way, was wild and terrified in the beginning. "The first thing she did when I brought her here was to go to the sofa and root around for trash to eat under the cushions." She'd fight for food, stuff herself, vomit, smear the walls with excrement. She'd moan to keep herself awake at night, protection from the sexual attacks she expected. At age eight, she was in diapers, couldn't walk, and wouldn't talk. And today, one year later? She shares food, doesn't throw up or dirty the walls. She's out of diapers and dresses herself. She walks, speaks some, and signs beautifully. "She's very smart. Her problems mostly came from abuse," Silvan believes.

What does Silvan get from parenting these kids? "It's wonderful to see a child like William ... do something new.... The doctors said he wouldn't make it to five ... [and] he'd be in wheelchair. Man, I have to chase him to the corner like nobody's business. That's the best feeling you could ever have.... To know Nannette can sleep all night—the way she used to stand behind the door.... It helps me forget how tired I am.

"I get a good living and a good feeling about myself. Whereas before I never had much self-esteem, [Judson] made me believe in myself." Silvan adds that the experience is "very rewarding" for her whole family, helping her two older children understand "what real problems are" and what they can accomplish. "My daughter [age fifteen] is on the dean's list."

As I gather my gear to leave, strange squeals come from a bedroom. They sound like an animal in pain. What's that? A twenty-three-year-old foster child, just waking, who's like an infant. Silvan wants to keep the girl so she won't get dumped in the same back ward in which she has vegetated most of her life. Silvan thinks maybe she should pull back from Judson because she wants to keep all the kids she encounters. "That's one of my problems."

FAMILY PRESERVATION, EVEN IF IT KILLS

At any given time these years, 500,000 to 600,000 American and 40,000 to 60,000 Canadian children have Big Daddy as their mom and dad.[1] About two-thirds of all kids who enter care go home and, presumably, more or less stick. For the remaining third, child protection is not, ultimately, a round-trip ticket, though it does come with a stack of invalid return stubs. They get used up as kids come and go from home into fostering and home again on a dizzying journey through childhood. In the United States, on average youngsters rebound seven times in four years. In Ontario, not exceptional for Canada, they zip around three times in five years, while going through three workers.

Why all the switching? Because faulty laws and practices governing child protection usually give even the worst parents the benefit of the doubt. Are appalling parents born rotters who hate their kids? Of course they aren't. While every neglected and abused child has her or his own particular family tragedy, story lines rarely change. Some parents suffer from mental illness and don't comprehend the harm they do. Some, lost in the haze of one addition or another, couldn't take care of a cat let alone a kid. Some, lost to a single emotion—rage—are too busy beating up themselves or their spouse to do much else. Scads of bad parents come from bad homes themselves, where they learned incompetence and cruelty. To their way of thinking, they love their kids, and show it in ways their parents showed them. Many have had more than their share of grubbing in the socio-economic margins, with all the self-hate, demoralization, and escapist longings that breeds. However much so many damaged parents are products of mental instability, social injustice or substance abuse and however much they need help, not contempt, the fact remains: their kids cannot be left to start life with a kick in the head.

Yet too many unstable adults have more clout with child-protection services, and with the courts, than do children in need of stability and safety. The evidence? Even if mom and dad continue to neglect and endanger their kids, they may get them back time and again. How do they manage to pull it off? By, in social work argot, "presenting well." In other words, some borderline parents, who've usually been around the block when it comes to dealing with helping professionals, can snow anyone who comes snooping around. Besides, the typical investigator labors under an impossible workload and lacks both the time and the skill to accurately assess risk. These factors favor otherwise unimpressive cases for reclaiming kids.

Estimated numbers of minors living like boomerangs vary from one source to the next. But all the data-collectors present a uniform portrait of what government custodians will do for children in the United States. It's not a pretty picture. Though Canadian figures are either uncollected or inaccessible, kids are no better off here.

If the system labels a child "hard to place"—too old, too sick, too slow, too troubled, too many siblings, or too different from a healthy white newborn—and if that child is among the 33 percent or so who won't be reunited with his or her family, here's the plan: though the child effectively has no parents, in most cases s/he will never be freed for adoption. Between 10 and 16 percent of children who need families get clearance. Even the low end of that estimate can be wildly optimistic. In Ontario in 1994, for example, adoption was the system's goal for only 2.7 percent of its children, according to a review of crown wards by the Ministry of Community and Social Services.

It's hard to distill reliable data from those available, but based on reports from the Canadian and Ontario adoption councils, here are some safe estimates. Countrywide, 40,000 to 45,000 children now find themselves in foster care. Excluding Quebec, roughly 18,000 permanent wards are legally free for adoption, perhaps 7,000 of them under age twelve. About half are Native and unlikely, given prevailing sensitivities, to be placed with nonaboriginal adopters. Yet—and here's the rub—*fewer than 1,250 per year find homes.* The American ratio is also grim. According to the Child Welfare League, from the approximately 100,000 available children, only 20,000 were adopted in 1995, while an additional 7,000 went into legal-guardianship, a variation on adoption.

Why this situation? In part because preserving families, even after they've failed miserably and their children have been taken from them, is the Holy Grail of protection work today. In part because legions of people with power over the lives of the state's small fry suffer from bureaucratic inertia: they don't do a heck of a lot to move kids into lifelong homes. Maybe they secretly don't believe in adoption, or they subscribe to the myth of unadoptability. At the 1996 national adoption conference in Toronto, I asked an Ontario child-welfare honcho how many kids were awaiting placement. He was vague on stats, but clear that numbers are misleading because some very challenged kids would "obviously" never be adopted. (Can we lock this guy up for a spell at Silvan Burden's or in any other household gladly raising "unadoptable" children?)

As a result of my official's kind of thinking, says Charlotte Vick, assistant director of the North American Council on Adoptable Children, those who should often don't take steps to terminate parents' rights. "The rationale becomes: no one will ever adopt this child, so why sever parental ties—even abusive ones."[2]

Another clue to why only a fraction get freed for adoption: bizarre though it sounds, many professionals themselves regard nonbiological parents as inferior. At the same conference, an adoption supervisor explaining why a plan at her Quebec agency to boost adoption rates flopped, cited, among other factors, colleagues' attitude; they won't give up on the bio family, she said, no matter what.

Finally, relatively few come up for adoption because system incentives usually aren't there. Most of the money is earmarked for fostering and, lately, though far fewer dollars, to shoring up rickety birthfamilies. Hence, careers and pensions come from maintaining the tired old system, with trendy new twists now and then. But the spine of government care for kids needing protection—supposedly temporary, but in reality long-term foster care—has never been noticeably flexible from day one. Only the servicing budget has changed.

So, chances of getting onto the adoption rolls are slim. If, after the standard long delay, a child does make it, s/he will likely wait four to six years before being matched with an adoptive family. In the meantime, the child will probably have too many addresses, ersatz parents, and passing siblings to keep track. Keeping count of the helping professionals will also be a challenge, though rest assured there'll be enough to make anyone zany. As a street kid once philosophized to me, "When they sic that many shrinks on ya, ya know ya must be nuts." Most system kids will tell you that a phalanx of strangers, each with a wall of credentials, has poked around in their heads. They probe, analyze, make notes, then turn the case over to the next expert—or, more likely, don't pass along the file, leaving the new interrogator to start from scratch. To quote the young prophet: "They try to fix your head, but they don't do nothin' 'bout fixin' your life."

Among the painful details kids share over and over, and often to no apparent good, is the story of where their life in free-fall began. Since they typically love/hate their neglectful or abusive parents, the story begins where somebody with a highfalutin title arrives out of the blue, announcing what they already know: Your parents have problems too big for them to handle. So you have to bunk in with some nice strangers for a while. Forever? We'll see. Just try to understand; it's for your own good. Get your stuff together, and let's go. No, you don't have a say. Yes, we're leaving right now. Then, after all the pain and confusion of finding their place in a new household, and making whatever peace they can with stop number one, another authority arrives. S/he directs them through the same routine—for their own good—just as others to come will sweet-talk them through a sad progression of places.

Little wonder kids risk developing something called "attachment disorder." It may start in the womb, but it certainly comes from an early childhood spent like a rubber ball. Being kicked around can, understandably, turn a kid off love. They start to view caregivers as disposable, interchangeable parts, and themselves as all they've got. Once that dial's been set, there are no easy fixes for a child's faulty emotional and psychological equipment.

Since under 8 percent of children cleared for adoption are actually placed, however, they needn't much worry—though part of them may desperately want to be adopted—about having to do the near-impossible: get close to anyone. There probably won't be an enduring adult in their life. These kids are more likely to "age out" of the system at eighteen than find a place to call home. In this country, a child who comes into care at age seven will most likely get stuck there for the next eleven years. In the United States, 15,000 to 16,000 foster kids leave every year, twisting in the wind. About 25 percent wind up on the streets; 34–40 percent, on welfare. That's not surprising, considering how many zombies the system turns out, or the fact that 60 percent who do graduate from state care do not graduate from high school.

You have to ask: is this prognosis worse than it might have been had these kids stayed in the contaminated environment from which they were ostensibly rescued? This is not to trivialize the fact that pulling some kids away from the home fire may literally save their lives. Neither is it to overlook the fraction of evacuees who land in one wonderful foster family and who, along with some others, feel lifelong gratitude for the salvage effort. Nor is it to argue for leaving children with toxic parents. The point is: the system should provide a safe haven with staying power, the antithesis of the original home. Coming into care should uplift children, not leave them, when all is said and done, as stranded as they would have been had they stayed with their folks. Instead, the demolition derby between families that clobber kids and the system supposed to soften their blows is more often an equal contest. On the face of it, the two do different kinds of damage, but for the kids, crying inside all the while, it doesn't always feel different.

Every day, authorities remove more than 2,000 children across the continent. Protection workers who do the deed don't have an enviable job; they're damned if they do and damned if they don't. Weighing the factors, checking the facts, assessing the degree of danger, predicting how never-straightforward and ever-shifting family kismet will uncoil, then deciding to take or leave a child, is not an exact science. It's more guessing game, in which gut instinct, gutless laws, heavy caseloads, stingy budgets, empty foster beds, and recent child-abuse deaths load the dice. Besides, even in clear-cut cases, decision-makers have only two choices: a menacing home or an often-hazardous system.

Given this scene, you wouldn't want to be in the average protection worker's shoes. They do a high-stakes, sometimes rewarding, but often heartbreaking and thankless job. When things go wrong and a child dies, caseworkers can get hung out to dry. Some end up taking the fall for higher-ups and for what many child advocates describe as a philosophically and functionally bankrupt system. Hence, the deep undercurrent of frustration and the high staff turnover in the front ranks of child protection make eminent sense.

In the bad old days, parents in poor districts quaked at the system's power to snatch their kids for any transgression, especially the crime of poverty. In these bad days, the snatchers do penance for the sins of their forebears. The pendulum has swung. Today, the same authorities—new faces, old powers—now swear as an article of faith that children belong in families. Not in *any* able family, mind you, but in their birth one. Family preservation is the new gospel.

It's a worthy catechism. Even if it romanticizes prospects for 180-degree reversals in parenting behavior, it sure beats the wisdom that said poverty and bad parenting go hand in hand. And were the art of gluing together crumbling households practiced the way it's preached, many families at risk would survive. Early-intervention models with impressive track records are out there. From intensive home-visiting to screening expectant mothers, preventive programs find households threatened by a cluster of high-risk factors. Then they wrap a tailor-made rescue net around those units until they're out of harm's way. Plus, the helpers come back if the dangers do.

Such preemptive action, unfortunately, has little in common with resurrecting families long and deep in trouble. Not to be too pessimistic, late intervention in children's lives, given intensive, appropriate services over time, can and does mend, even in some cases that appear to be sunk. But, judging by the chronic reentries of kids in many families supposedly under repair, you have to wonder: is the system hooked on offering too little, too late? And is help too often pegged to points of no return rather than to the ongoing counsel fragile families need?

Every time parents kill, it's uncanny how you know the story before you read the gory details. It will turn out everyone suspected the parents were lethal weapons. Helpers will have swarmed the house during explosive episodes. As one columnist wryly observed: "Indeed, some mothers scarcely have enough time in the day to see all the helpers who are involved in their cases."[3]

When parents or caregivers murder a child hooked into some form of government care, if the case gets any notice—which usually means the media is onto it despite officials' attempts to sweep it under the rug—what normally happens? We investigate. Government appoints a very sturdy citizen to head up a probe that begins with a specific case but broadens into the question "What's wrong with child-protection services?" Pick any major Canadian or American report from the 1990s. Read, for example, former Alberta child advocate Bernd Walter's assessment that came after foster parents beat eighteen-month-old Jason Carpenter into a vegetative state. Better yet, try British Columbia Provincial Court judge Thomas Grove's words, written in the wake of little Matthew Vaudreuil's demise. This five-year-old was finally finished off by his developmentally delayed mother, who had a well-known habit of torturing and starving him. Or flip through the findings of Governor Pataki's Commission on Child Abuse and Neglect. It grew out of a spate of highly publicized child-abuse deaths in New York City, especially the harrowing life and death of Elisa Izquierdo, age six, whose head was pummeled in by her crack-addicted, deranged mother.

These documents and others, including the 1997 joint report from the Ontario coroner's office and provincial children's aid societies examining suspicious child deaths, invariably reach similar conclusions. In this ugly business, the old saw applies: there's nothing new under the sun. Flaws are standard, long-standing, and well documented.

Here's a quick primer. In preface, bear in mind that a faulty conscience is not the exclusive preserve of the child-welfare component. Rather, there's blood on the hands of all interventive systems: criminal justice, health care, and social welfare. The primer: Police, social workers, doctors, and nurses often have a blind spot for hints, and even for hard evidence, of child abuse. In Matthew's case, for instance, Grove found sixty clues they'd overlooked. *Toronto Star* reporters, analyzing eighty-three child deaths from 1991 to 1996, found many cases where professionals saw not enough evil, such as multiple fractures, and hence did nothing. Even where danger signals were crystal clear, it took the system forty-four months on average to rescue young victims. "The child was let down by a domino effect of one screw-up after another."[4]

How many helpers does it take to fail a child? Grove counted twenty-one different social workers and twenty-four doctors spread over seventy-five visits, resulting in sixty filed reports. The shocking thing is that this tally is noteworthy only for its averageness.

Why such colossal incompetence? An array of factors: wishy-washy definitions of abuse; laws that give abusive parents more rights than their victims, thereby tying the hands of those meant to come to the rescue; too little in the way of child-abuse prevention programs and education for professionals and the public; cruel cutbacks that make an always-difficult job impossible to do; far too few frontliners, most of them carrying caseloads from hell; inadequate training, especially in risk assessment, for the vanguard of all helping trades; child-welfare management and personnel recruitment that aren't up to scratch; spotty data-keeping; no coordination of services and service-providers (hence, those in the same profession working the same case may never speak with one another, or with any of the multiple professionals in touch with the family).

The helping circuit, it appears, doesn't groom team players often enough. As a result, conditions rarely exist, as they always should, for policeperson A to learn automatically that colleague B has already seen a parent's nasty handiwork. The same systemic oversight leaves caseworker C in the dark about D's visits, while Doctor E doesn't get to consult with F, and no one from these three sets of players realizes that everyone else is concerned that parents or stand-ins may be deadly. To make matters worse, some who suspect a child is being deliberately hurt are nonetheless lackadaisical in pursuing more evidence or reporting their worries. And should an outsider—say a neighbor of a victimized child, or a journalist who has somehow got a whiff of the story—ask pointed questions, some authority may invoke "confidentiality" to cover up what is probably a snail-paced, if any, investigation. Meanwhile, in the normal course of events, an obscene number of intervenors operate almost or even totally solo, without the benefit of interactive databases to track kids at risk and to team up all would-be rescuers.

The buck stops nowhere, and the child gets trapped in a dangerous home.

All the deficits above, and then some, routinely get singled out in a system, which, overall, *slavishly adheres to process without due regard for a child's physical safety and emotional security*. Worse, the whole mess is buttressed by a hodgepodge of laws that lack strict time frames and adequate protections for children. Although tinkering won't do, and the child-protection behemoth almost needs gutting and rebuilding, as Grove and some other investigators have insisted, these probes have a long history of *not* being a wakeup call. At best, the response is superficial repair, not reconstruction to save innocents from hellish lives, or even death sentences.

However, observers hope British Columbia will prove an exception to the rule. After Grove delivered his indictment, the province undertook major housecleaning. Yet, after the shakeup and reorganization, a familiar kind of system-neglect fiasco depressed the optimistic: a toddler was found in filth, clinging to the body of his addicted mother who'd OD'd about six days earlier.

Whatever the outcome in British Columbia, all is not gloom. It may be getting safer to hold your breath in anticipation of sweeping changes. The dark corners of child welfare have come under such heavy scrutiny this decade that real progress is becoming harder to avoid. Remember, though, that the child-welfare system doesn't operate alone when it under-protects children. Yet, its partners, particularly justice and health care, usually get off much lighter. It seems that fewer brooms sweep out the dark corners of those systems.

The most recent probes, such as Governor Pataki's, include what's supposed to be a revelation: family-reunification efforts are often not in a child's best interests. Tell us something we don't know. The problem is: reconstructing families that have been blown to bits, even with the right tools, often takes an eternity, and may not work in the end. Worse, the system too often proves incapable of ongoing quality control. Meanwhile, their childhoods stolen, kids drift, growing detached, restless, and enraged. Yet, child welfare and the courts still crawl along, their gaze fixed on this mystical thing called "family of birth."

Don't misunderstand. If families can be shored up to *safely* keep their kids, that's the best outcome. But only if patching can be achieved in a reasonable time, usually defined as one year. What's more, if a child can't go home within twelve months—ideally after a stint with *one* foster family and *one* case team—with solid prospects for staying put and without the revolving-door syndrome, then another door to permanency should be ready for fast entry. Called "concurrent planning," this approach is gaining in popularity, but not nearly as widely or quickly as the kids need.

By contrast, what usually happens? Children get sandwiched between parents desperately trying to hang onto them, though they can't handle the responsibility, and a system that lacks the imagination to keep the adults in the picture while ensuring their kids get steady succor elsewhere. If parents weren't forced to lose all contact, some might come around sooner to the realization their children would be better off with another family. Instead of doing what must be done, authorities stall for years while childhoods slip farther and farther from stability's reach.

This is one for the books. Ontario invented a compromise between severing parental rights and liberating a child for adoption. The province assumes legal guardianship but allows key relatives to visit, a scenario covering about 80 percent of wards. So long as kids have court-mandated "access orders," they can't be adopted. That might make sense if their loved ones dropped by regularly. But do those with access use it? In most cases, not at all or only sporadically.

In its wisdom, the law ensures that, instead of finding adoptive families who'd agree to access by those allowed—called "cooperative adoption"—these kids will sit and wait in case the adults who supposedly love them pop in for a visit. Lots of experts must have stayed up late writing this statute! (Astoundingly long overdue, proposed changes to the Child and Family Services Act, including getting kids out of the access order/no adoption bind, have recently been circulated by the Ontario Association of Children's Aid Societies.)

The Adoption Assistance Act in the United States intends that kids should be fast-forwarded through child welfare and the courts, and into families. The legislation, however, isn't worth the paper it's written on. Birthfamilies typically get two years to clean up their act before Uncle Sam moves to cut off parental rights, a process that can snake through the courts for two more years. Canada is no speed demon either. Here, too, everybody's rights get coddled except the child's. As for getting their act together—kicking drugs, attending counseling for abuse, getting up in the morning, whatever—parents can't count on accessing the services and breaks they need to move their lives from the Lost to the Found department. Some do get useful help, but many get useless warnings: change, or else!

While their parents may be going nowhere but deeper into grief, anything could befall the kids. The luckiest enter "kinship families." Although usually a relative, "kin" means anyone who feels like family to the child: a neighbor, a teacher, a coach. The trick lies in backing these stand-ins with whatever they need to become effective parents: subsidies, parenting courses, therapy, community resources. And respite, respite, respite. Big surprise: the system hardly ever delivers enough goods.

Kincare can be excellent, nonetheless, but is rarely a cure-all. Mostly, it saddles low-income grandmothers—in the United States, especially African American, poorest of the poor—with yet another generation to raise in scrimping conditions. There's a risk that dumping kids on people who care about them without supplying the essential supports will script another disaster for the child. A case in point: I recently met an Ottawa senior raising two grandchildren, now state wards, who suffered ghastly abuse: cigarette burns, heads held under water, the lot. Problem is, granny can't afford help, doesn't have a support network or a car, and has been housebound with two emotionally churned-up gradeschoolers and a resentful husband for a year.

Children's Aid, bungling at every turn, has provided no respite. Grandmother now regards it as the Evil Empire. Instead of insisting on backup that might make her home viable enough, she keeps her distance. Children's Aid, meanwhile, isn't exactly breaking down her door to offer a hand. As a result, it's only a matter of time before the fragile container cracks and the kids tumble into the system like human flotsam.

Sorry ... We were talking about the lucky ones. They find homes with kin or kinlike folks buoyed by publicly funded supports. There's one approach that comes in different shapes and sizes, with renditions variously called "subsidized" or designated "guardianship" or "custodianship." Here, a court-appointed adult assumes custody and care of a minor, though parents still have legal rights and may have visits. A cross between fostering and adopting, it aims to give children the best of both worlds: ties with their root family, whose name they keep, but with the security of another, more stable household.

The big attraction of such schemes: they don't force an older child to spurn the incapacitated first family s/he may love (or love/hate) in order to have a healthy second one. The idea that having both is best may alarm old-fashioned caseworkers. Yet, in today's world, having several families simultaneously—and feuding ones, at that—is far from exotic. It's more like the great equalizer.

Other winners in the placement lottery go to unrelated families recruited to foster with a view to adopting if parents don't rehabilitate. This is fost/adopting by design. In the more common default scenario, foster child and parents bond. Then, when the youngster comes up for adoption, the fosterers try to legalize their *de facto* relationship to the child. Until recently, it was unlikely they'd be approved. Now, they have a decent chance as foster parents have finally made a dent in the system's ambivalence toward them—good enough to do the dirty work, but not good enough to be real parents.

However, since foster families tend not to be the most solvent, many who'd gladly adopt don't step forward. The way the system works, fostering pays a per diem, but adopting not a farthing. Unless the child has extraordinary needs, the family loses its make-it-or-break-it subsidy when switching modes from temporary to permanent parenthood. (Making it financially impossible for adults to offer a child a family for keeps is another sure sign of the system's phony affection for adoption.)

Finally, some kids struggling with the most awesome demons and delays find their way into treatment foster homes in the United States. They get a permanent, familylike setting with wraparound specialized medical and therapeutic services.

If the cafeteria of options impresses you, don't be fooled. Although the menu is improving all the time, especially south of the border, only relatively few kids get to taste the best items. By and large, if a youngster can't go home, care is still an either/or proposition: either scatter-shot foster care—by far the most likely fate—or an adoption by strangers, which usually breaks the cord to the child's birthfamily.

Most often, the system goes for the human-debris option. Care is often as cruel as life was at home. Kids enter it emotionally raw. What do they need? An island of stability with at least one reliable adult who comes to adore them and win their trust. A parent substitute who'll be there whether or not the youngster goes home again. What do they get? Too often, moved to avoid precisely what they most need—attachment.

Though this happens less frequently now than it did in the old days, maybe they get shunted elsewhere because they or a caregiver "cares too much" (what a concept!). Or they may be forced to move for the system's convenience or because of worker turnover. Or they get bounced because the best foster homes are overburdened with too many hard-to-parent kids and receive too little support to do the job. As kids wing in and out of care, they may go to a different foster family each time. Maybe an earlier placement is no longer in the program, or full at the moment. Maybe the child wouldn't mix well with other kids currently in the house. Maybe the family's not keen to have that one back.

Whatever the rationale, kids move and move and move. Entrants will likely wander through a series of placements, not infrequently carrying their worldly possessions in garbage bags. Healing, indifferent, or harsh—they could find themselves in the hands of any type of caretakers. If ever there was a quality crapshoot, foster care is it.

The yank-around comes from the wait-and-see school of casework. No matter what the permanency plan, those responsible may do a lot—or nothing much—to make the plan feasible. Meanwhile, children's lives are put on hold as they're stored here and there, according to space considerations.

Louise Armstrong's words, penned a decade ago in *Solomon Says: A Speakout on Foster Care*, still ring true today. "It is nothing if not impressive, as I was to learn, how little 'happy endings' had to do with a 'plan,' and how much to do with sheer luck: the child fortuitously endowed with charm, intelligence, spunk; the coincidental appearance of a compatible adult...."[5]

MANUFACTURING "PROBLEM KIDS"

When Elmy Martinez, a single adoptive father of five, had to wait four months to bring home brothers Juan and Luis, he couldn't believe it. The boys, then thirteen and twelve, had been orphaned and in the state's jurisdiction since the older one, Juan, was a year old—latterly in separate places, but that's another story—yet their paperwork wasn't ready. Though the pair was supposedly on the adoption track, it was clear to Elmy the plan was a sham. As far as he could discern, no one had done anything other than capture the money that keeps the foster system thriving and adoption in the fringes. And the twosome would, Elmy's sure, have "aged out" unless he or someone else rescued them. After eleven lazy years, surely the boys' agency wasn't about to get the urge to find them a family.

Luckily, Elmy found them. His son, Luis Martinez, talks about his life in two compartments: "in New York" and "in Virginia." New York means the East Bronx, where he grew up. That's where his Puerto Rico–born birthparents, both of them, died in drug-related murders. Luis, not yet two, was toddling home with his mother, her arms full of groceries, when she was taken down. He doesn't remember the incident, only the legend of it.

His life, age two to thirteen, was a smidgen better than the typical government childhood. Better because, through sheer luck, he spent four formative years in one loving home with a single foster mom, originally from Cuba. He still feels connected to her and to his foster sisters, later adopted by the woman.

Why didn't she adopt him and his kid brother, Juan, also part of the family? Luis answers with what I quickly learn is his way of dealing with old hurts: don't dwell on them, stay positive, move on. He mutters something about a blood relation who stepped in to stop his foster mom from adopting the duo. Except the relative's motive for taking the boys in was the per diem. When she mistreated them, they were apprehended again.

Since their original foster mother was no longer on the roster, the boys were introduced to the standard bounce-around. First, a trial period with a suburban Anglo couple broke down. Afterwards, a residential school back in the Bronx. Next, a year with a family that treated the boys as free labor and punished them if they spoke their only language, Spanish. "She'd make me do reverse push-ups." (Elmy later tells me that, thanks to the system's cultural insensitivity, the boys went from fluent Spanish to swear words only.) Though orphans, not delinquents, their last stop was a group home for young toughs. Not one group home, but two, one for each child—separation, the ultimate in the system's ability to hurt in the name of help. Luis took it in stride. "That's the way it was."

Fortunately, a counselor latched onto him, "taught me right from wrong." On weekends, he'd make sure Juan and Luis got together. That man is still a friend. So, too, a teacher from his "LD" (learning disabled) classes, the only teacher who ever believed Luis had a mind and a future. These two formed his lifeline in a treacherous neighborhood, a stone's throw from the projects. Luis didn't get into trouble; he tried to avoid it, which was trouble enough.

By age ten, he gave up hope of being adopted. Let it go. Look at the bright side. Move ahead.

Enter Elmy Martinez, journalist on the government payroll, and single father to a Cambodian orphan adopted shortly after Elmy emigrated to the United States from his native Puerto Rico. Although Elmy is gay, being out "wasn't an option" where he grew up and he didn't dare mention it while adopting. Perhaps due to Latin-male stereotypes, no one ever asked. In fact, Elmy only recently came out to his sons and in the adoption community, where he has so long been an advocate for straight and gay single adopters.

When Luis meets Elmy, he is thirteen, and doesn't know why he and Juan have been driven to an office to shake hands with a stranger speaking a language he no longer understands. Soon the boys find themselves visiting Virginia. "We kept watching our backs ... but there were hardly any people in the street, and they weren't arguing over stupid things. Nothing threatening. No garbage, even. Later, at the schools, no armed security guards; they had supplies and equipment."

This was heaven, but it surely wouldn't last.

It would take a year with Elmy for Luis to start believing in the impossible. That first year, he entered grade 7, special classes, having been assessed as performing at a grade 4 level. "Here the teachers wanted me to succeed. In New York, even the psychiatrist said I wouldn't amount to anything."

By grade 10, he'd caught up. By graduation, and through two years of college, he pulled down As and Bs. So much for learning disabilities. He credits excellent teachers, his own hard work, and his father. Elmy also gets praise for keeping "the family tight," and, most of all, for giving Luis cause to dream. "In New York, I lived day-to-day, never thought about the future."

When I interviewed Luis by phone at his family's home, he was twenty-one, on furlough from the armed forces, where he's working toward his dream of becoming a police officer. We said good-bye after he boasted, but only a little, about his pride in being a role model for his four brothers.

Elmy Martinez, angry enough that Juan and Luis weren't always kept together in care, is livid that Luis, never a punk, was placed in a setting for young hoods. Elmy has other gripes, the same ones you hear over and over from parents whose kids come up through the ranks. One of the biggest complaints: kids see specialists *ad infinitum*, get overlabeled, misdiagnosed, and excessively medicated. The good news is that these youngsters often turn out to be in much better shape than their files suggest. Parents like Linda Miles, for example, whom you'll meet in another chapter, think they're adopting a developmentally delayed youngster and then find out the kid's a whiz.

When a child with a mixed bag of problems accumulates a whack of diagnostic labels, some agencies or individual workers deliberately underplay the severity of the child's condition in hopes of more easily placing him or her. Or the agency, not having done its homework, may simply not know. Ill-prepared parents find out the hard way that their adoptee has, for instance, a life-threatening disease. In the United States, such cases have led to so-called wrongful adoption suits. From 1983 to 1987, sixty-nine adoptions in California alone were annulled after county agencies fraudulently misrepresented a child's profile.[6]

These tragedies don't necessarily come before a judge because adopters want to give the child back. Perhaps they can't afford the medical costs and hope the suit will ante up. Believe it or not, though, some misled parents do return their child after a legal adoption, as if s/he were a faulty product going back to the manufacturer. (When this happens, rather than judging the agonized family, you have to question the quality of agency work in matching, preparing, and supporting families.)

While some adopters are bitter because their children were treated like lab rats, others are bitter because their kids' problems weren't assessed. Why might obvious needs for medical or psychological intervention get ignored? The thinking goes: this kid's a writeoff anyway, so why bother? Hence, some throwaways never get the help they need, and their problems worsen. One of Elmy's sons, for instance, who entered at age seven and spent four years in foster care, bombed at school. But only after he was adopted were his learning deficits diagnosed and dealt with. Elmy blames agency apathy for many struggles still crippling the young man today. What's more, the backgrounder didn't hint at how severe the boy's learning lags were.

Tom Cusick on Staten Island knows all about holes in histories that come with the kids. This beefy, gruff, one-of-a-kind guy, playwright and songwriter, has had his tunes recorded by the likes of the Carpenters and Olivia Newton-John. Despite career success, Tom is far more famed as a father. Starting when he was eighteen—he's now forty-four—he has raised twenty-two kids, including fourteen adoptees, often as a lone parent. Among his complaints: sloppy reporting. For example, "I have a boy here who is a fetal-alcohol child with severe hearing loss and speech loss, and *not one thing* in his record indicated that he had a hearing problem." Hello. Is anybody home?

I heard many anecdotes like this, where kids had easy-to-diagnose difficulties, not medical mysteries, that went undetected. Misinformation can be so bad—with critical details totally missing, wildly inaccurate, or overly bleak—Elmy says you have to take with a grain of salt the written blurb on the child's background, which the placing agency usually pieces together.

To be fair, accurate, up-to-date information is hard to come by for kids who've had bales of handlers and been all over the map for years. But some do come with detailed records. Those agencies that have exacting standards expect their workers to verify as much data as reasonably possible, and to share findings with adopters. And to help parents decipher the coded messages behind cold, hard facts. For instance, Johnny survived crack cocaine in the womb, and hunger and fists in his first year—how might these affect his health and behavior? Also, to be fair, let's remember some adopters may be told the whole truth but refuse to hear the half of it. They nod in seeming acknowledgment as the counselor fills them in, while clinging to their errant belief that love cures all.

Nonetheless, shabby tabs-keeping follows predictably from the overriding problem of institutional neglect. If the system does not play Russian roulette with their lives, if it does not worsen existing, or produce new pathologies in them, kids can count themselves lucky.

THE WALL: NEEDY KIDS ON ONE SIDE, EAGER FAMILIES ON THE OTHER

Though the house of care is straining at the seams with kids who need families, you'd never know it. The scattering of newspaper columns, such as "Today's Child" in the *Toronto Star*, and TV spots, such as *Wednesday's Child* throughout the United States, do make all the difference for children featured one by one. So do innovative approaches launched by the handful of individuals and organizations that realize kids can't wait for families, and who've taken it upon themselves to make families happen. Witness, for example, the work of the Dave Thomas Foundation for Adoption (as in the famous founder of Wendy's, himself an adoptee). Despite the headway exemplars make here and there, the scope of the crisis remains invisible to the general public. Even after kudos are handed out to the dedicated few, waiting kids still have less profile than endangered animals.

Meanwhile, adults who badly want to parent usually pick up two messages about adopting: (a) There are no babies—False. There are, though few relative to older children. The message breeds from the assumption that searchers will accept only the flawless newborns they initially imagine; (b) To complete your homestudy and get matched with an adoptee could take years—True. Yet, instead of solving the problem of delays, more often than not the system merely laments them, as if correction were impossible. The odd agency and American state make it a mission to cut red tape and time. But these are exceptions. Normally, the system sends the very people who might welcome the kids scurrying to private homestudies and foreign adoptions, which can be much faster. This nonsense has reached such a pitch in Canada that we now adopt more children from outside than from inside the country.

The national adoption conference ran a brainstorming workshop on the need for, and the potential how-tos, of public- and private-sector cooperation, for which, to no one's surprise, there's a crying need. A Children's Aid panelist kicked off the session by wondering aloud if attendees could figure out why so many adopters cross borders. (I wasn't the only one in the room who had to stifle a snicker.) That was an interesting meeting, actually: a room full of adoptees, adopters, wannabes, adoption supervisors, and line workers, not to mention a sprinkle of apologists for the Ontario government, hacking to ribbons the social safety net for vulnerable families and kids. My jaw dropped at the amount of rage in the room. Rage from people on both sides of the wall separating families that want to reach a child and from workers committed to placing them but thwarted by system idiocies. For example, intake, a newcomer's initial point of contact with the system by phone or in person, got a resoundingly bad review. Outsiders related how summarily they'd been dismissed—no infants, long queue, the usual jive—from their first "hello."

Indeed, consensus on what's holding kids hostage runs throughout the stakeholder community. The problems are old hat. They include the sacred status ascribed to bloodlines and the low priority given to adoption both by the community at large and by the very system responsible for family-making. The fragmented and user-unfriendly services that baffle potential adopters. The sluggish bureaucracy, which takes forever to bring families and kids together—if it doesn't drive candidates to drop out along the way. The paralyzed judicial system, which can waste a whole childhood pushing a ward through the courts. In court reviews, the judges who rubberstamp the "go home" plan even when the same child, going nowhere, shows up in court year after year.

Atop these routine barriers, dinosaur attitudes toward certain adopters lock families out and children in. Bring any major factor differentiating you from the family doused in nostalgia—youngish father/mother (married, of course), able-bodied, overachieving, more-than-middle income—and you can expect a lukewarm reception from many standard agencies. As they remain leery about people who could provide children with consistent love, the kids are left at the mercy of serial foster homes and random acts of kindness.

DINOSAUR ATTITUDES

Differently abled people (or "diff-abled," my word) typically get stonewalled—though in dulcet tones. When Patricia Andrade of Washington, DC, tried repeatedly to get so much as an information packet from a series of public agencies, she got the same polite promise: they'd promptly send one out. Did anyone she contacted, using the relay service which identifies her as a deaf caller, ever say "Forget adopting, you're deaf"? No. But they were "very embarrassed on the phone.... They would talk to me as if they were talking to everyone.... What [kind of child] are you interested in? That kind of thing.... [When the kits didn't arrive] I'd call back and they would tell me that they don't have anything available at that time.... 'I just want information, that's all,'" she'd respond, but the info never came. Pat and her husband, Carlos, also deaf, eventually gave up trying to adopt at home. They went to Russia, where they adopted two little girls, both deaf.

Nadine Jacobson, a Minneapolis social worker who in her varied career has licensed foster homes, and who, like her programmer/analyst husband is blind, first tried to adopt in the late 1980s. The couple faced one roadblock after another, all clearly related to their blindness. An adoption lawyer who almost placed a baby with them backed out at the last minute, admitting he flipped because of their sight. Other facilitators, who seemed more amenable, were adamant that the only right baby for this couple was a blind one. In the end, they adopted a girl from South Korea who has partial sight.[7]

Barbara White, a deaf adoptive mother and social work professor at Gallaudet University, has a special interest in adoptions by diff-abled parents. Her research confirms the Andrades and Jacobsons faced standard, not exceptional, discrimination. Everyone's polite. No one blatantly admits to having no intention of helping the family adopt. They obstruct through omission, like not mailing out materials, and deliver "subtle messages" by, for example, refusing to pay for an interpreter, as they did in Barbara's case. They pretend to ignore the difference in ability, while focusing on other factors supposedly making the family hard to match. When it comes to deafness, agencies tend to lump it in with other differing abilities, insensitive to the deaf community as a cultural minority.

Particularly irritating, White says, is the assumption that comers should have access, if at all, only to children like them. This stubborn prejudice persists, she adds, despite the fact most deaf kids have hearing parents and will themselves produce and rear hearing kids as competently as the next guy. Besides, White emphasizes, while research singles out diff-abled parents as superior caregivers for similar children, no evidence suggests they make inferior parents for typical kids.

Yet, many agencies would sooner place a deaf child with hearing parents than a hearing child with deaf parents. What's more, by unofficially restricting candidates to like children, the system quietly prevents such applicants from adopting. They're able to bar them because deafness and physical diff-abilities are low-incidence. In other words, domestically at least, few deaf or blind children—to carry through with the example, though we could use others—are waiting for adoption. It's no accident that disproportionate numbers of diff-abled adopters turn to foreign countries, just as it's no fluke that other nontraditional types follow the same path. At home on agency row, the welcome mat has been removed.

MATCHMAKING

Ask your average custodians of state children why so few wind up in families and they'll demur that finding good homes for "problem kids" is next to impossible. Ask your average child advocates the same question and they'll claim there are families galore out there, provided you aren't hung up on finding Ozzie and Harriet. In response, the bureaucrats will balk, pointing to what's evident from the adoption exchanges, or central databases set up by some jurisdictions to list waiting kids and searching families—namely, that the two sides don't jibe. Searchers want younger children; older ones are available. Parents prefer girls; more boys need homes. Across North America most adults looking are white; about half the kids on hold in the United States are not. In Canada, disproportionate numbers of Native kids wait.

Are these obstacles between searchers and waiters surmountable? Child advocates think so. For openers, adoption exchanges list adults who, on their own initiative, are on the trail. They don't tap into the many who might be wooed were government guardians in the mood to sell new recruits on the idea of adopting. More telling, specialty agencies that believe all children are placeable and deserve families manage to find them, even for those, such as AIDS infants, whom others might call impossible to place. And private agencies, too, with their stacks of people waiting for a baby, could stop watching the till long enough to lure a few folks away from the nursery. What's to prevent a passel of them from being won over to, let's say, a preschooler? I use myself as an example. Had anyone been on the case for waiting kids, I'd guess we'd now be raising a child of the system.

But, are families like mine, headed by professionals, who themselves tend to come from privileged backgrounds, right for kids who've been through the wringer? While no foolproof predictors exist, specialty agencies do notice trends. When I ask Debbie Kelly at Project Star, in Pittsburgh, which places troubled preteens, who makes the grade, she mentions social class first. Working-poor families shine. Is that because she sees more of them, since they can't afford fat-fee agencies? No. It's because of hardship. The key to assessing prospects, she says, is in discovering how creatively they've endured tough times—because the kids are bound to press all their buttons. "It's hard to trust a family whose worst experience was not making cheerleader!"

Pat O'Brien, an adoptive father and feisty Brooklyn social worker, voluntarily heads up You Gotta Believe! The Older Child Adoption and Permanency Movement. He also claims that "working-class parents are best. If they've raised kids already and didn't have an easy time of it, they're ideal.... They hang onto their kids better than anyone else.... These kids need ... families who'll ... visit them in jail if necessary."

Throughout O'Brien's career in placing children, he's seen markedly more instances where white collars, as opposed to blues, who began the process of adopting a system kid didn't close the deal. He shares a heartbreaker about a boy brought back by his adoptive father, a doctor, because the child's IQ was too low for the family's liking.

Elmy Martinez, whose sons were booted around for years, and who helps other single people like himself adopt, would agree with Kelly and O'Brien about one thing: adopters of older children must have a passion for them. But he doesn't endorse the equation: roughed-up kid plus hard-pressed family equals better chance of success. Indeed, in coming pages, you'll meet others like Elmy: well-educated, well-off parents of varied ethnoracial persuasions, happily raising kids with brutal beginnings. Nonetheless, if the link between class and adoptive-family outcomes with older children went under the microscope, I suspect we'd find that O'Brien is mostly right.

He's probably right on this one too: he says careful screening, training, and matching matter, yet you can't predict which families will endure the rigors "until they're in it." It's a bit like fixing up single friends you figure are made for each other. Some don't make it through a first date, some become pals, and some end up life partners.

Could You Parent a Child from the System?

Nobody's saying that welcoming a half-grown girl or boy with extraordinary hurts and needs is for everyone. Who's made for it? Who's not? These are tough calls. In some families, things go smoothly. In others, attachment and healing come in small doses over the long haul. Yet other parents say that what you see is what you get; the child basically stays as s/he was on homecoming day.

Remember, "system kids" is a broad category, covering those with atypical hurts but otherwise typical needs, *and* those with profound and multiple conditions, medical and psychological. They can be very young, bearing minimal baggage, or late teens, lugging heavy loads. They might also be newborns with burdens, or mid-teens with surprisingly few scars. And lest you think that those with developmental shortfalls must be the toughest to parent, some adoptive parents say "no way." If they're experienced with different types of kids, they'll probably tell you that a child with Down's syndrome, for example, can be a breeze compared with a "normal" one whose emotions have been whizzing in a blender for years. Perhaps you imagine teenagers must be the most impossible. Yet, parents like Elmy say "not always." They admit to the migraines, yes, but also lay claim to the joys.

Not to glamorize—it's well known behind the scenes that far more multineed adolescents stream back into the system than other adoptees. Adoption breakdown, for good or for an extended time out, apparently happens in 10 to 25 percent of cases. Bear in mind, though, that "breakdown" is a problematic concept, not always implying complete or irreparable rupture. Some families that have supposedly disintegrated may still have members who actively care for each other.

Whether a full-scale or half-tilt disruption, adoption may dissolve before it's completed or after the legal fact. Children have been known to ricochet through countless foster homes, and three or four adoptive ones, before they land—if they ever do. A wrecked adoption has to be excruciating for everyone it touches. Besides delivering a body blow to the kicked-out kid, what does it say to other children, especially adopted ones, in the family? You might be next? Let's be clear about this problem, though. It's far more about failure to carefully match, prepare, and support kids and families than it is about the complex personality factors inevitably at work.

Take the Summerses*, for example, a Caucasian, mid-income couple in their forties, living in a white-bread small town, who adopted three troubled children from Los Angeles*, two sisters born in Puerto Rico and an African-American boy. This combination promises trouble. Trouble number one: The threesome have stories that hurt to hear, which means mega-business to sort out. Number two: They are used to big-city excitement, not the boring sticks. Number three: They have moved in with not only an Anglo family, but also one that cannot easily open doors to their heritage.

Indeed, Mrs. Summers wasn't initially all that concerned about roots anyway—quite surprisingly, since this family adopted through a specialty agency, where cultural sensitivity-training tops the preadoption prep list. "We anticipated that the child would be racially different [from us], but we figured the child was American, we're Americans. . . . I don't see that [they] are any different from us." As it dawned on her through parenting that race and culture do matter, she tried to interest her girls in an Hispanic church in a nearby community, to no avail. Her son will start to meet other black and minority children in his next school.

Even with the assorted factors weighing against a happy home, the boy and one of the girls have settled in and settled down remarkably well. Their affection for their parents and each other is palpable. The Summerses boast about the amazing progress the two, despite their share of problems, have made. The third girl, however, now sixteen, who lived five years in her adoptive home, is another story. Mrs. Summers is obviously in pain as she speaks of it. It involves a "terrible crowd," a "vicious gang," threats against the family—"we were afraid for ourselves"—stolen credit cards, arrests—you get the picture. The girl is now in a residential treatment facility, has virtually no contact with her family, and no one thinks she'll ever live at home again. The best the parents hope for? A truce in the distant future. (This case, by the way, is a kind that shows up in the adoption-breakdown data. Yet, family members, though separated, remain committed to each other, and will probably reach a peaceable denouement down the road.)

For any potential adopter of an older child, there's much to learn from the Summerses' saga. Most telling, two of the adoptions are bringing stability and healing to the kids, and deep satisfactions to the parents. This, even with the odds patently against it. Were you to add well-thought-out matching, preparation, and followup—on which adopters themselves must insist, given the slapdash system—anything's possible.

You can sense that at the Jackson home in Brooklyn. Things aren't all sorted out, but they're cooking. Chester and Karin—he's black, she's white—adopted an African-American brother and sister, then aged fifteen and thirteen. Chester, an adoption worker himself, met his son, Robert, on the *Sally Jesse Raphael* show when Chester appeared as a panelist. As Chester and Robert got to know each other through preadoption visits, each felt drawn to the other. "I see a lot in him that I see in myself," twenty-year-old Robert says. It was just one of those "magical things," Chester adds. Despite an in-system life that could have—should have—made him sick with anger, Robert never succumbed, making his adjustment to family life relatively easy.

His sister, Ebony, on the other hand, who chose to join the Jacksons, is more typical. Awash in rage, she's self-absorbed and wary of attachment. When not busy sabotaging herself, she showers her saved-up fury on her new family. To survive the system, she learned her lessons well: I'm unlovable, no good, not worth keeping, and you're gonna kick me out. "Parents are supposed to be bastards," Chester says flatly. Her behavior, subtle as a grenade, includes everything she can invent to keep the household in a tizzy around her, and to test her parents' limits. She had a baby at age fifteen. Instead of evicting them, Karin and Chester clenched their jaws and now pinch their pennies to raise mother and daughter. The hardest part, Karin finds, is teaching Ebony right from wrong.

"The kid [from multiple placements] does not know or care what you consider wrong. . . . [But] kids *want* us to have values, even if they fight against them," claims Barbara Tremitiere. She should know. Most of her brood of fifteen are adopted. Tremitiere, who's a bit of a legend in the adoption world, runs the Tressler-Lutheran Agency in York, Pennsylvania, known for its preadoption course pitched at people planning to take on kids like the Jacksons'. Among the things they teach, the "Gotcha!" game. System kids, denied control over their lives, play it in a bid to gain the upper hand.[8]

The Jacksons try not to be got. That's not easy, especially considering the other demands on their patience and their purse. They're also bringing up two preschoolers who came by birth after the adoptions. "We're getting 'No!' at both ends," Karin quips. They take a measured attitude. It's rough now, Karin elaborates, sometimes unbearably so, but Ebony's got the basic intelligence to smarten up, and Karin and Chester have got the support system to survive if and until. Besides, she emphasizes, there are no other options; *adopting children, like giving birth to them, is for life.* Whatever may happen to Ebony, the Jacksons will be consistent people who care about her. Ebony will always have parents to call her own, and someplace to call home.

The Jacksons didn't go into adoption expecting to bring home choirboys. They didn't anticipate magic makeovers. They figured they'd hear more f-yous than thank-yous. They knew that bad families and their partner in crime, a bad system, often turn out child con artists so emotionally shallow they seem sociopathic. Though they'd have had no hand in raising the rage quotient of whomever they'd adopt, they knew revenge might be directed at them. Kids come with twisted beginnings; you can only hope they unwind as smoothly as Robert's. When they don't, there's no formula for instant parenting, no 800 number to dial for all the answers. You must, Chester says, "accept that [you] may not be perfect parents ... [but] you're doing the best that you can ... and sometimes you're not going to be adequate."

Lynn G. Gabbard, who finds homes for special-needs children and whose family includes seven, writes about "loving without 'fixing'":

> Adoptive families need to be encouraged to take risks, to love and to nurture children without assuming the responsibility of "fixing" them. If indeed we believe that children grow better in families, we need to nurture and respect those families, understanding that they are not perfect and do not need to be, that they cannot repair the injuries and damages that their children have sustained.... We need to help adoptive families to continue to emotionally and legally parent children who can no longer live within the family system....[9]

TINKERING WON'T DO

As things stand, you have to be pushy *and* have the patience of a saint to get your hands on a system child. At worst, child welfare is impotent. At best, it's lethargic at preventing family breakup, reuniting rollercoaster families and keeping them running, ending parents' rights in a timely fashion in unfixable families, and promptly engineering loving permanence for kids. Instead, excuses are found for passing children around like stray cats and keeping them unclaimed for years while the bureaucracy dallies. This time-dishonored process limps along, waiting, one can only suppose, for a miracle.

Miracles aren't needed. A paradigm shift in philosophy, practices, and spending habits are. "We have to put an end to foster care as we know it," says Elmy Martinez. "It connotes something almost evil," echoes Pat O'Brien. Lest anyone misunderstand, the evil is not in the shelter-giving families (except for the few mercenaries who are in it for the pittance fostering pays but who don't give a damn about the kids). Far from it. Foster parents now adopt more "unadoptable" children than anyone. And well they should. They've likely been through enough torment with the players—the child, the system, the birthfamily—to know what they're getting into. Some have a working relationship with the child's relatives, which maybe they're willing to maintain. What could be better? The adoptee legally joins a family of which s/he's already a part without sacrificing links to the family of birth.

But, back to the evil. It rests in the system's stubborn resistance to moving kids out once they're in, and in its tendency to trot them from one setting to the next. It rests in the refusal to let them love or be loved by people who could become their psychological parents for life, whether or not they go home. Why, pray tell, aren't wards allowed extended family who mean more to them than their own folks? Lots of regular kids with wobbly parents count on aunts and uncles or neighbors for nurture more than they do mom and dad. So what? What's all the fuss been about these past hundred years?

If the system put half the manpower, money, and mental resources it now sinks in foster and congregate care, such as group homes, into guaranteeing permanency, what could happen? Far fewer children might have to lie down in the darkness of insecurity night after night, year after year. If the system focused on supplying training and services to prospective permanent homes, including families of birth, foster care, in its familiar incarnation, could get what it deserves: the junkyard. It could finally fulfill its original mandate: a temporary haven in an emergency. If child-placers would lighten up on their vision of family, and concentrate on publicity and recruitment, good adoptive homes would spring up like crocuses.

Government's stunning failure to put children into permanent families has given rise to private adoptions, catering to the privileged few who can afford the baby chase. But it has also given rise to specialty agencies that sneer at the lame "hard-to-place" mantra the system chants to cover its sins. The new kids on the block (some have grown up by now) have shown beyond a doubt that connecting up the dots between waiting kids and families who already want them, or who could be persuaded, is possible. Think back, for example, to the beginning of this chapter, reenter the homes of Sandra Craighead and Silvan Burden. The Judson Center, a specialty agency, turned a nontraditional adoptive family–type—in this case, welfare moms—into a positive force for kids with over-the-top needs.

Here's the rub: such ground-breaking efforts belong to the "brave little tryout" syndrome: ever the pilot project or outsider, never the system norm. They tend to remain embers flickering in the dark.

Does child welfare malfunction because it's underfunded? Yes, even at the best of economic times, say the bureaucrats. They rightly point out that today's cutback craze crushes the most forward-looking services, such as experiments in prevention. Fewer resources forces them, they say, to go back to basics: crisis intervention, child removal, and foster care. Because they're obliged to do more with less, and at a time when youngsters are pouring into the system as never before, more kids fall through the cracks.

There's little doubt they're right about increasing numbers coming into care. Every government bragging about its deep welfare cuts tears families apart to do the dirty deed. In the United States, an estimated 100,000 more children will descend into foster care if the ax falls as expected.[10] There's already been a scatter of reports from social workers in Canada and advocacy groups across North America of previously managing parents handing over their kids because they can no longer feed them.

Meanwhile, the system continues to concentrate money in the same wrong place. The lion's share goes to foster care, the cub's to family cohesion, and the leftovers to adoption. In 1992, for example, the American foster-care budget was $2.3 billion, of which less than 10 percent went for adoption.[11] The pie may not be big enough for the size of the problem, but there's little evidence that more money spent in the same old way would put permanency on the agenda. And there's no evidence the system radically changes its spending habits whether working with slim pickings or with a full purse.

Besides, child welfare has never primarily been about money. Nor, for that matter, has it been based on a child-first philosophy. It's been about crisis management and maintaining a bureaucracy, which, true to form, resists change. Were it about doing smart things for kids and families while getting a bang for its buck, the system would have undergone fundamental transformation ages ago. There's little doubt that serious attention to humanity *and* financial efficiency, which needn't be mutually exclusive, would have produced something better than cosmetic touchups.

Just compare the costs of reunifying families, adoption, and other permanency alternatives with the tally for foster and congregate care, and there's no contest. No matter how you slice it, families always come up bargain basement. If a childhood spent in Canadian foster care costs about $400,000, imagine what savings even a subsidized family would mean for the public purse. In the United States, the Edna McConnell Clark Foundation claims annual costs run like this: $40,000 per child for institutional care, $10,000 for foster care, and $3,000 per family for preservation work. Subsidized adoptions, which start around $3,000 a year in the United States, are a steal.[12]

Any number-cruncher will tell you the rule of thumb: community solutions are cheaper than institutions. But they are not as neat. Politicians prefer tidy. Hence, the search for simplistic bromides to sedate and contain teens who have tons of problems but no parents now finds some in the United States calling for "modern orphanages." Canada tends to catch up eventually with our neighbor's worst impulses, so if they refurbish the disgraced practice of warehousing, we may limp toward smaller, nicer-looking lockups too. Yet, as orphanage-era atrocities that have come to light prove, these institutions, no matter how pristine in appearance, tend to be hell holes for kids and havens for power freaks and pedophiles.[13]

It doesn't take a genius to figure out that families are better—families of all descriptions, absorbing kids in a creative array of lifelong arrangements, cosseted by the best community supports. The questions are: as governments aggressively embrace dereliction of duty to the most vulnerable, will we allow them to continue the slide? Will we accept the trends: either settling for system drift as regrettable but unavoidable, or shifting the burden of problem-solving onto the voluntary sector? Or will we force the system to assume its rightful place of prominence—and to get it right by following specialty-agency methods and values: all children deserve a family and are placeable, and all family types are welcome to adopt? The answers will either stop or swell the tally of broken lives.

All in the Family: Open Adoption

The memory of the long-gone mother collects more gilt than dust.
That is how much we need our mothers.

—Jan Waldron, reunited birthmother

I just feel that the more people who love this child and the more
relatives you have ... it can't be a bad thing.

—Lynda, an Edmonton adoptive mother

When our homestudier first gentled us toward something called "open adoption," which, he said, would improve our chances of getting an infant, my throat tightened from fear. I'd never heard those two words together before. They sounded a far cry from "confidential adoption," two words that, as far as I knew, always went together. Immediately, I visualized a temperamental teenager camped on our doorstep, demanding her baby back. It was news to me that most birthparents placing newborns through private agencies now pick adoptive families themselves. (Babies public agencies place have usually been apprehended, so their parents are normally out of the picture.) Many birthparents also want continuing contact with their child, ranging from occasional mail to regular meetings.

As the social worker recited his introductory patter on openness, I started to breathe easier. I warmed to the idea of less concealment and more honesty, which, as general principles of family life, have obvious merit. While my head led me to sound cool—"Open adoption, sure, no problem"—my gut was yelling "Yikes!"

I rushed out of that session and did what any writer would do: I went to the nearest library. By the time I finished my homework, I was a convert. I'd learned that openness started in the deep discontent that secrecy bred in adoptees and in the parents who surrendered them. Both typically go through life yearning for knowledge of the other. I'd learned that these relationships between families number one and two tend to make it easier on everyone in the troika, and especially on the adoptee. I was relieved to learn from the research that children usually appreciate their adoptive parents more, not less, if they have access to their original mom and dad. Nonetheless, the literature didn't sugarcoat the complexities openness layers onto the adoption drama.

By comparison, adopting used to be a relatively simple matter, compliments of Victorian morality. "Nice girls" didn't "do it," but when they "got caught" the state handed over their package of guilt to a "proper" family. Case, and files, closed. Society so little understood the emotional process or price tags pinned to loss and grief, or to family lies, that few people fretted over frivolous loose ends such as feelings. Hardly anyone guessed that ghosts of the past would haunt the fantasy lives and harm the psyches of adopted children. The notion that human beings need to exhume the skeletons from their closets in order to construct a firm emotional framework for living was beyond the times.

That birthmothers might be in pain did occur to onlookers. But, since "those girls" were sinners, it wasn't uncommon for parents or professionals to believe a little suffering served them right. Indeed, the stories, only now being told by aging birthmothers, frequently do not begin with their family's or boyfriend's (if he was told) reaction to the news of their pregnancy. Instead, they go to memories of the remarkable cruelty of strangers who shepherded them through their hidden pregnancies, shameful births, and heartbreaking surrenders.[1]

Shame tainted everyone, except birthfathers. They were so absent from cultural discourse, you'd think society had experienced a protracted outbreak of virgin births. The community regarded unmarried women and girls "in the family way" as "wayward." Indeed, in my home town, the residence where teens spent their "confinement" was known as "the home for wayward girls." Their offspring were considered stained, the families who "took in" the babies a cross between angels and oddballs—which is not to say many people openly discussed the subject. Both unmarried pregnancy and adoption got the hush-hush treatment. That the young moms were often treated punitively was of no concern; though mostly just kids, they were, nonetheless, "fallen women." The notion that they themselves rejected their newborns—remember the phrase "unwanted babies"?—was a convenience, without foundation.

A kinder philosophy also evolved. Accordingly, a "clean break" was best so the young women could "close that chapter" and "get on with their lives" as if they were not mothers. Time would help them forget—out of sight, out of mind—and it would heal all wounds. Hiding their fall from grace would also make them more marriageable, since nice boys climbed in the back seat of the Chevy with "easy" girls, but marched down the aisle with virgins.

It was assumed that babies born in disgrace needed lifelong protection from the details of their unsavory beginnings. Surely the children would grow up grateful to have escaped the stigma of their origins. Why would they possibly want to know much about, let alone know in person, the "loose" woman who'd made them "illegitimate"? Where "dark secrets" were concerned, dishonesty was the best policy. If you told the truth, you'd open a Pandora's box.

It was also presumed that adoptees would be torn apart by loyalty conflicts if they weren't amputated from their family of birth. How could kids grappling with a double identity feel secure in who they were or where they belonged? Secrecy would spare them the confusion.

Though the history of closed adoptions produced a thicket of rationalizations—albeit based in good intentions—to cover all the players, adoptive families, the most "respectable" party, got first consideration. To normalize adoptive parents' link with their child, adoption reformers pulled off a conjuring trick that would make adoptive families seem no different from birthfamilies. Between the 1930s and 1950s, depending on jurisdiction, babies were legally reborn into their second families. With the stroke of a pen, a fake birth certificate vanished birthparents and replaced them with stand-ins. This judicially sanctioned lie is still with us; typically, my son's 1993 birth certificate pretends he's our birthchild. Such pretense plays into one of adoption's rustier ideas: that one family must have exclusive ownership of a child.

The biggest impetus for keeping adoption sub rosa and sealing records was fear of birthmothers. They were young, hence unpredictable, and also viewed as ethically fringey types. What if she had a change of heart? What if she went looking for her lost child? What if she, or some shady relative of hers, were to try to blackmail the adoptive family? Better safe than sorry. Lori Clemmons, an adoptee and adoptive mother who lives near San Jose, California, vividly recalls the mistrust. At one point, fearful that Lori's birthmother might reappear, her parents "were ready to pack up and move to Canada, but at the same time they said 'she was a wonderful person.'" Lori couldn't reconcile the two messages: her birthmother as both a paragon of virtue and a potential menace. Many adoptees share Lori's dilemma: coming to terms with the mystical mother afflicted with a split personality—a saint "who loved her baby so much she gave him up" and a flighty child-dumper who might snatch him back.

When did openness start? In the 1960s, when many groups were on the march. The civil rights movement in the United States and the ensuing freedom-of-information laws in North America conferred permission for privately felt stabs of injustice to surge collectively into the public domain. Like birthparents, adoptive parents, too, had gripes: they'd had it up to here with being "judged by experts and held to standards of parenthood no one else has to meet." The mood and times were ripe to "alter the existing modes of child exchange."[2]

Women in particular were up to some very bold antics for the times, such as keeping their babies even though they were single mothers. So it was in that militant atmosphere that adoptees and birthparents built self-help organizations and raised their banners to fly with all the others demanding individual rights. Adoptees sought access to their birth certificates and to agency files. Birthparents protested what had happened to them and demanded to know what had happened to their babies. When powers-that-be demonstrated no hurry to budge, the adoption reform movement went underground, finding its own routes to reunion.

The onslaught to correct injuries of the past thrust onto the agenda a future for open adoption. The leap from prying open sealed records to promoting openness from the outset happened organically as breaking the silence exposed the terrible hurts imposed by the locked-down system. Nonetheless, reunion and openness are not always seen as logical neighbors on the same continuum. American anthropologist Judith S. Modell explains: "Reunions are perceived as *re*-activating existing, natural bonds, whereas open adoptions are seen as permitting people to construct 'unnatural' bonds, on purpose and from the very beginning."[3]

No matter. Adoption professionals started to get the message: pretending babies were born to people other than their biological parents just encouraged adopters to fool themselves and fib to their kids. Family life was at risk of becoming a fabric of lies, in which bewildered children, even if told they'd been adopted, got only scanty information. Or, never hearing the a-word but sensing themselves different, they couldn't decipher their feelings of not fitting in until the big announcement came. None of this made for healthy communication or self-esteem.

Meanwhile, birthparents, totally ejected from the picture, and usually clueless about what had befallen their babies, commonly lapsed into a state of gloom, for which they got no help. For many, even reassuring snippets about their child's progress could have been the anodyne they needed. Adoptive parents, supposedly the biggest beneficiaries because of non-competition for parental supremacy, were also badly served. Fictions in their family life often created fragile rather than secure attachments. Besides, their lack of access to medical- and mental-health history of the child's birthfamily hobbled them as caregivers.

Open-adoption advocates Marilyn Shinyei and Linda Edney explain the "faulty premise" on which the closed model hinged. "It assumed that birth and adoptive parents were adversaries instead of allies all looking to the best interests of the same child. It assumed that people were not capable of making good decisions; that they needed social workers to be in control of the process." (When professionals today oppose openness, you have to wonder if they trust parents any more than their precursors did.) "And sadly," Shinyei and Edney continue, "it assumed that people were not trustworthy. Treating people with respect and dignity is a cornerstone of social work practice but it was left out of adoption practice."[4]

PSEUDOCHOICES

Suppose you're a pregnant teen in a panic. One minute your heart tells you to keep the baby; the next, your head tells you, "Don't be crazy. Do you want to live on a shoestring in a grungy room, looking after a squalling infant?" How could you do that to yourself or to your child? On the other hand, you already love your baby and s/he's not yet born. What kind of mother would even think about giving away her own flesh and blood? You can't work it out. You consider getting help. Maybe you turn to your school guidance counselor or to your clergyperson, or to an adoption counselor from the Yellow Pages. Unlike your parents, your boyfriend, and everyone else hectoring you, at least s/he won't badger you into making a preordained choice. S/he'll help you see the big picture so you can make your own decision—or so you assume.

Maybe that's how the sessions will go, maybe not. Unfortunately, throughout the history of adoptions, even in recent times, counseling hasn't always been as neutral as you'd expect. *Within Me, Without Me,* written by a birthmother about women in Britain and New Zealand who surrendered newborns in the 1960s and 1970s, tells the tale. Eighty-six percent of 262 birthmothers reported that parents and social workers pressured them to relinquish. "If you love your baby, you'll give her up" usually did the trick.

Everyone would like to think that professionals no longer pull this old guilt-trip. For sure, chances are better today that scare tactics won't be employed to bully birthparents into giving up their baby. A pregnant young woman nowadays may well have a supportive partner or sympathetic parents. The luckiest also have access to programs that help them stay in school and get parenting lessons. None has to worry that society wants to brand her with a scarlet letter, or that no man will ever marry her, if she wants marriage. Clearly, some contemporary birthparents have real choices and opt to make an adoption plan. Many others, however, are still under the gun to pick adoption.

> While it is hard to begrudge an infertile couple the opportunity to adopt a child from a presumably willing unwed mother— such as I was at 18—I have spent the past six years cursing a society that condemns young women for becoming pregnant and then offers them redemption through handing over their children to yuppie strangers.... *Until we get over our disdain for single motherhood, and begin to provide young women with education and alternatives, adoption will never be a free, informed choice.* (my emphasis)[5]

Anecdotal evidence suggests that some helping professionals are still pointing the gun. Yesteryear's morals continue to guide their counsel, which is designed to persuade a young mom it's unrealistic to keep her baby. (Don't misunderstand. I'm not advocating for teenage parenthood, but for responsible professional conduct.) But today, financial considerations also affect advice. Conflicting interests can collide if an undecided mother-to-be happens to consult a private adoption agency. Neutrality is a lot to expect from people whose earnings depend in part on how many babies they place. Bear in mind as well that the counselors involved deal every day with deep-pocketed, desperate would-be parents, many of them young married couples, who would, unlike high-school students, enjoy society's blessings as parents. It also bears mention here that some advisers, whether lay or professional, take the opposite tack. Far from pushing young women to relinquish, they almost coerce them into rejecting all options *except* raising the baby themselves.

Apparently, there's a strong correlation between the bias of intermediaries and the decisions birthparents make. Where counselors promote adoption, a lot of clients choose it. In more value-free contexts, such as charitable residences for pregnant teens, very few select adoption.[6] While it comforts adopters to think birthparents want adoption—and, again, some definitely do—you only have to venture into birthparent publications to know that voluntary adoption is not always as freely chosen as one would hope. From the *CUB* (Concerned United Birthparents) *Communicator*:

> Today's adoption arrangers, who push ... open adoption ... would have us believe that the young moms of today ... freely choose adoption, so they will never hurt like we do. Don't believe them ... The agency that provided a place for (one 18-year-old I know) to live refused to discuss any option but adoption. She begged for information on how to keep her baby; they told her to think about the reasons adoption was best for her baby and for her.[7]

Some birthparents complain that money-making adoption agencies use openness as an inducement to push wavering parents, especially poor ones, over the edge. (Again, don't misunderstand. Birthparents usually want openness. But, understandably, they don't welcome its misuse in the counseling context.) Some facilitators seduce expectant youngsters, using the promise of a subsidized pregnancy (in the United States) followed by access without financial responsibility. They sweeten the lure by overselling the lovely family their baby will gain. Never do they hint that adoptive families are as vulnerable as every other variety to going off the rails and tossing adoptees, just as they do birthbound kids, into chaos.

FINDING FAMILY

Outside the adoption world, there's a belief that only those birthparents who were force-fed adoption, and only those adoptees who got a bum placement deal, pursue reunion. After all, why would a good woman disrupt her long-lost child's life? And why would an adoptee bother with birthfamily if s/he were happy in the adoptive home? Conventional wisdom holds that adoptees search only if they hope to find a saintly mother to replace the adoptive witch.

As it happens, there's nothing to this theory. In truth, as many studies and anecdotes testify, in most cases *no relationship* exists between how satisfied birthmothers and adoptees feel and their inclination to find each other. Elderly birthmothers who still believe they did the right thing, as well as those who all their days wear bitterness and regret like a second skin, look for the children of their womb. Adoptees who adore their adoptive parents, and others who feel little affection for their second mothers, try to locate number one. As reunited birthmother and author Jan Waldron writes in *Giving Away Simone*: "In a sense, the inner lives of those who've been rearranged by adoption have nothing to do with the families who adopt. The drive to seek and hold on to the truth of one's beginning exists only for the people essential to the moment of delivered life."[8]

People scout because of elemental longings, driven by a need to mend the holes in the tapestry of their lives. Sketchy secondhand information isn't enough; emotional closure requires pressing flesh. Many male adoptees of an age to have young families, and even some birthfathers who are now seniors, do look high and low. But, so far, females have demonstrated a much greater need to reconnect. That's not too surprising, given that emotions and child-rearing usually assume greater importance in the lives of women than of men.

While most birthmothers and daughters apparently want to search, whether or not they actually do, not all of them feel compelled to do so. Even in my own circle, I know a birthmother in her forties who, though she had remorseful days when younger, primarily feels at ease about, not deformed by, what she did. Of course, she wonders about her child and would gladly meet if the daughter made overtures. Yet, my friend, who partly fears disrupting the girl's life, mostly feels no burning need to make anything happen. (Since I first wrote these words, much has transpired. The birthfather was given medical information that affected his birthdaughter. He and my friend were able to track her down and communicate through a social worker. The young woman thanked them profusely: she has a great family and a good life.

At the moment, letters and photos are flying back and forth; the birth-family, with the adoptive mother's blessings, will probably reunite.)

But then, I know another birthmother for whom finding the son she was forced to surrender is her waking and last thought of every day. I also know an adoptee in her early thirties who feels indifferent about her birthfamily; in her words: "I wouldn't go out of my way to meet my mother, though if she crossed my path I'd be curious to see who she is."

When do people search? It used to be that adult adoptees would make furtive inquiries, even actual attempts to reconnect, while their adoptive parents were still living, but once the adoptee was getting on in years. It was easier for the lucky few whose adoptive parents were enough ahead of their times to fathom the importance of the quest, and to support it. Yet, even some of the fortunate didn't venture too far or too openly into reunion because of the prevailing attitude: if you search, you slap your adoptive parents in the face. (No matter what their parents say or really mean, which could be two different things, some still don't get moving for fear of offending adoptive parents.) Hence, many pioneers waited until their adoptive parents died, making it all the more unlikely their original set might still be around.

Baby-boomers looking for post-retirement birthparents is one of several trends in these transition years between the age of closed adoption and the coming age of open adoption. Today, adoptees usually start turning over stones earlier, often when they have a first child themselves. For Lori Clemmons, adopting galvanized her into acting on her long-standing urges. "Getting to know [my son's] birthmother . . . made me want to see . . . where I come from." (You might be interested to know that even though Lori and her husband don't have fertility problems, they elected to produce one child and to adopt one. Lori's own positive experience as an adoptee led her to repeat what her parents had done.)

What researcher Karen March found is typical: adoptees decide to search for their biological parents in concert with life-changing events, such as getting married or having children. She also found they're more likely to get the ball rolling if they have support from a significant person in their lives.

Whom do searchers initially look for? Mom, always. Doubtless they're curious about siblings and dream about dad, but he floats out there in the miasma. Mother dominates the foreground, and not only because someone somewhere recorded her name, whereas dad likely wasn't documented. Though starting with mother is the only practical approach, she, more than anyone, holds the emotional magnet of reunion. In March's sample, 37 percent of those who found their mother later went on to find their father.

Adoptees in mid-life and those in their twenties and thirties just starting families aren't the only ones looking. The third search stream, though still a drop in the bucket, involves minors reconnecting. The burgeoning appeal of adoption with contact has triggered a wave of requests to agencies by adoptive parents who can't answer their kids' questions and are hoping to find birthfamily information and hints to its whereabouts. While emerging firsthand stories of actual meetings tend to be cheery, and probably foreshadow a breaking trend, not everyone is convinced. Of coming together with her preteen birth-daughter, Rebecca, Jan Waldron writes:

> Though I had rarely doubted the value of our eventual meeting, in truth, I had often questioned the wisdom of adolescent adoptees reuniting with their birthrelations. Because Rebecca came into my life at the awkward age of eleven, she did not have the tools to balance and sort out all the information and the barrage of moods that came not only with our strange reconciliation but with her pubescent years, when identity is such a pressing confusion. She was more reckless in establishing her ground with me than a twenty-year-old might have allowed herself to be.[9]

How do people locate each other? By becoming Dick Tracy. By following a path of evidence scattered with scraps of information. By inching their way through the bureaucratic blockade: tricking guardians of the secrets into revealing a name or a place, or finding a weak link in the system who sympathizes with the searcher. Lori Clemmons, for example, who knew where she'd been adopted, spent two straight hours on the phone in transfer mode to the proper state authorities, all of whom claimed they couldn't help her. Then, *boom*, an empathic stranger came on the line. "She actually sent me staff paperwork, and—I don't know if accidentally or just because she ...

felt sorry for me—she slipped in the relinquishment form." It was signed by Lori's birthmother, and named her birthplace, a small town. Lori called a local church. Lo and behold, they had a record of her birthmother's marriage. Then she contacted the motor-vehicles branch, where another friendly voice gave up an address, which turned out to be current. (Birthmother and daughter haven't yet met face to face but are enjoying contact by phone.)

Lori's search was a piece of cake. Other people lose years and accumulate heartbreaks as they follow clues leading to dead ends. Their irrepressible need to keep going has sparked a proliferation of self-help search organizations, and sophisticated professional trackers, some of whom charge fees. These are also the boom years for government-run "adoption disclosure" registries where birthparents and adoptees sign up in hopes of getting in touch by mutual consent.

Registries, however, are riddled with problems. In most places, adoptees lack legal rights to access the information they want. As well, the registries, which normally conduct active searches only on behalf of adoptees, not for birthparents or other relatives requesting one, are swamped. In Ontario, for example, there are over 16,000 clients on the waiting list. Their wait for searching services can run up to ten years, or to two years even for nonidentifying information about birthparents. (I know one birthmother who waited five years for even these tidbits!) As you've surmised, governments don't go overboard to help birthfamilies keep abreast of kin. Indeed, in the typical jurisdiction, "token" best describes the official investment in reunion. The World Wide Web, however, is another matter. It has given a huge boost to fast family-finding, even worlds away. For instance, a Korean-born adoptee raised and living in the United States who reunited with his first family set up a computerized registry for others in his shoes.

Those trailing lost kin, and those applauding the search, agree that it's an absurd state of affairs: adults having to hunt and plead for personal information almost everyone else takes for granted. It's a case of government infantilizing grown-ups, they say. What's more, many in the adoption community feel the injury goes beyond insult into a violation of human rights.

Some locales make it easier than others for people to search. They're the same places, not surprisingly, that tend to be on the cutting edge of laws favoring open adoption from day one. In 1985, New Zealand was first in allowing adoptees and birthparents to get information, but with veto protection on request. (This is interesting: fewer than 6 percent use the veto.) Parts of Australia are as liberal. In Canada (a decade behind New Zealand), Saskatchewan, British Columbia, and Nova Scotia lead the pack. With varying provisos, these three provinces permit and assist adult adoptees and birthparents to collect data about and to reconnect with the other.

In the United States, California, New York, New Jersey, Tennessee, and Hawaii have proven most reformist around disclosure of sealed records. Globally: England, Wales, Scotland, Finland, Holland, and Israel. While easing restrictions is the trend worldwide, the law remains mulish in most of North America, a fact which has not discouraged determined searchers.

What happens when parents and children find each other? The first meeting is bound to be awkward, possibly satisfying, yet often disappointing. After all, two virtual strangers face each other against a backdrop inscribed with the motherhood myth: "some magical bond exists between a biological mother and child which no amount of time or separation can eclipse."[10] The fall from fantasy figure to mere mortal can be hard.

As a result, reconnecting often leads children to appreciate their adoptive parents more, which then parlays into closer relationships—ironic, considering adopters historically feared reunion would weaken their parent–child bond. Of her birthdaughter, Jane, and Jane's adoptive mother, a reunited birthmother writes: "Her mother once said that things were better between her and Jane since Jane and I had found each other. Now there were no unknowns clouding their relationship, no wondering about what would happen if . . . because it had already happened."[11]

But it's a long road from first attempts at contact to whatever benefits might ensue for either party. Along the way anything could happen, as March discovered tracking her sample, from "immediate rejection to deep intimacy," depending on the needs of both principals and the birthmother's situation. Did she or didn't she share her secret with the family she went on to create? If she didn't, is she ready to speak up now? Is she, or can she put herself, in a position to fold the found child into her family? Answers to these questions will have a lot to do with how reunion evolves.

Among the reconnected who develop an ongoing relationship—the majority—March found three patterns. Either they stayed in touch from a sense of duty, felt by the child for the parent, or vice versa. Or they tried to string together the mother–child mesh they'd missed. Or they came together as two adult friends. The helter-skelter in relating styles hardly surprises, given cultural inexperience with this type of kinship.

The most intriguing outcome: for the adoptee, satisfaction is almost guaranteed. Yet, it has little to do with factors you might think would make the difference: for example, the kind of person mom turns out to be. No matter who adoptees find, apparently knowing is better than not. Nor does satisfaction derive from the type of tie that develops between mother and child. Rather, pleasure primarily comes from completing the puzzle.

Vancouver journalist Rick Ouston hunted far and wide for the woman who'd left him in an orphanage more than thirty years earlier, a detective story he beautifully renders in *Finding Family*. When the author finally located his mother, whose name is Mo, in small-town USA, he didn't much like her, though "it hurts to think that thought." The woman he'd so frantically sought struck Ouston as "naive" and "small-minded" with "the world view of June Cleaver." Mo was married to a moral antique who couldn't accept his wife's lost child; hence, the mother–son relationship stopped at whispered midnight phone calls and a clandestine meeting. Did any of this matter? No, because "that which was left undone was now done.... The circle, which had been open, was now complete."

And herein, according to the research and personal stories, lies the crux of reunion. The missing piece doesn't have to be the mother of anyone's dreams; she simply has to be found. Of course some reunitees get more satisfaction than others, but, provided they make contact, few regret the ordeal, no matter where it leads. In March's group, the level of happiness correlated with how much background information adoptees gleaned through open contact with *both* birthparents.

After all, adoptees typically set out, not to find a mother who'll parent them, but to learn about circumstances of their conception, birth, and relinquishment. The more questions answered about their family tree, the better. Since mom is the stepping stone to dad, if she helps the adoptee meet him or siblings, the more gratified the searcher feels. If, on the other hand, a birthmother withholds information the adoptee craves—especially dad's name—the more dismayed the daughter feels.

Leanne Hamm, for example, who happened on her birthfamily by a fluke, lost interest in bridging the years with her newfound birthmother after the woman refused to open up. "Phyllis is very secretive.... She didn't want me to find my sisters.... She says she doesn't remember my father's name—a man she had four kids with!" (Phyllis kept one child, a boy who died from muscular dystrophy when he was sixteen.)

Leanne did find her two sisters, before she found Phyllis. It happened this way, five years ago. Leanne was working as a salesclerk, baby's clothing department, at Eaton's in Vancouver. A shopper approached. "You look just like my sister-in-law," the woman said.

"I get a lot of that," Leanne mumbled.

"No, really, your mannerisms." Turning to her kids, "Doesn't she look like Auntie Sue?"

When the kids were adamant too, Leanne became curious, especially since she knew she had two sisters somewhere. "Was she adopted? When was she born? Is she half Chinese?" The answers fit. The shopper gave Leanne Sue's phone number. Leanne, an outgoing, exuberant type, called immediately. Sue sped over to Eaton's. "I had customers standing around waiting for our reunion!" Her first reaction on seeing Sue? "I thought she looked more Chinese than I do—the same reaction Sue had. [I] dragged her into the fitting room so I could look at us both at the same time.... I'm pulling her hair up. Look at those cheeks, those teeth. Everyone was gawking at us."

To find their third sister, they turned to the media, which loved the human-interest angle and lavished ink and air time on them. A front-page picture of the reunited twosome in a Vancouver daily brought sister number three into the limelight. Phyllis was harder to find. Parent Finders, a major search organization, finally located her in Coquitlam, BC. While the sisters don't have much in common and haven't become bosom buddies, and haven't had much contact with their birthmother, reuniting, says Leanne, "really helped me feel the kind of connection I need. Just looking alike is enough."

Finding the genetic link and genealogical information, even if blood relatives don't look alike, seems to be enough for most adoptees. But what of birthparents, especially older ones who grew up with different cultural assumptions and who've guarded their past all their lives? After all, whether they wanted it or not, they were guaranteed confidentiality, which still operates as the main stumbling block to toppling the closed system. Balancing birthparent privacy and what has come to be regarded as adoptee rights to personal history is, as you'd well imagine, a juggling act. The potential conflict in interests—birthparents who don't want to be found versus adoptees who want to find them— accounts for the veto clauses of new legislation affecting parties to adoption who rejigged their families under the old, closed system.

Laws old or new aside, when a child whom birthparents never expected to see again phones them up or knocks on their door (this assumes birthparents aren't searching), how do they fare? Though individual testimonies go both ways, less is known about their feelings as a group. From Phyllis's reaction, Leanne reads mixed emotions about being found: "She's relieved I turned out so well, but she's unwilling to face her past."

The anti-adoption literature divides on the question of reunification. In *Death by Adoption*, for example, author Joss Shawyer opines that birthparents' otherwise "unresolvable grief" can heal if they meet their children again. But Marsha Riben, who wrote *Shedding Light on the Dark Side of Adoption*, disagrees. "Birthparents who complete a search are often surprised to find that, rather than an ending for their grief, their grief is renewed all the more.... They have to grieve all of the tears which were locked inside them all those years. The realization of what they have lost stands before them."[12]

OPENNESS: TAKING THE GOOD WITH THE BAD

For many generation-Xers, their cast of familial characters, the connections among them, and the roles various people play in their lives boggles the mind. So do the complicated arrangements necessary to ensure kids have quality time with their assorted parents, siblings, grandparents, and other relatives. Yet, we take it for granted that the links are precious and worth all the bother—unless the kids are adopted, in which case the waffling starts. Ironic, when you stop to consider that having two families used to put adoptees into a marginalized minority. Now, when duplicates are dandy, some people would deny adoptees the chance to be more like everyone else. Go figure.

True, no matter how bollixed the average family tree, it gets knotted in new and unusual ways when open adoption hooks up the parties. "Open" carries many meanings and misunderstandings. Here, it refers to direct contact between bearing and rearing families. Contact can begin early, during the birthmother's pregnancy, and often leads to adoptive parents attending the birth. Or, beyond the initial check-each-other-out meeting, face-to-face contact can start months, even years, later.

The continuum runs from semi-open—first-names-only, agency-mediated, minimal exposure, say, a one-time-only meeting or an ongoing exchange of letters and pictures—to wide-open involvement in each other's lives. In the latter case, the parties proceed just as if they had met outside adoption and, from mutual interest, struck up a relationship. In that instance, they, obviously, would determine its boundaries and course without external help. But open arrangements can be professionally negotiated, detailed, and contractual, just as they can be the epitome of informal, or anywhere in between. They also can and do change. Everything depends on the adoptee's needs and the comfort level of consenting adults. In this business, one size never fits all. The particular interfamily gestalt need only suit the participants.

"Open adoption is as much an attitude as a practice; to work well, it must be felt in your heart."[13] Disclosure works best, experts say, when all parties want it, when counseling prepares them well enough for it, and when everyone digs in. Recent research confirms what openness practitioners have been saying all along: it's a process, not a fixed state, that needs time and tender care so that all parties can find their bearings.[14]

Here are a few situations that hint at the range of possibilities. In an Edmonton case, from their first meeting, Bernie (for Bernadette), the birthmother, and adopters Lynda and Steve related easily. Bernie, then twenty-nine, well educated but adrift, and Lynda, then forty, a doctor and parent to an adopted preschooler, were particularly smitten with each other. From the start, they felt like friends. Formality wouldn't be right; they decided to wing it. The birthfather, Leone, wasn't in the picture at first, though the door was open. Through the pregnancy and postpartum period, Bernie and Lynda grew closer. Eight months after baby Andrea went home with Lynda, Bernie felt ready for a visit. Once there, she realized "it was too soon for me." She stepped back. She decided, and Lynda agreed, that the two women would stay in touch, and that Bernie would reenter Andrea's life much later. Bernie sees herself as Lynda's friend and Andrea's aunt. Meanwhile, Leone stepped forward, and was planning a first visit when I met the adoptive family.

Their first daughter came to Lynda and Steve in a supposedly open adoption. Except, at the last minute, the birthmother chose not to meet them. She had full identifying information and could pick up the phone at any time. Four years later, she did. By then, Steve wanted to leave well enough alone, but Lynda didn't. They compromised. Lynda met their child's birthparents, brought photos, and left open the possibility of a later meeting. Gradually the two women are building a friendship that will probably translate into family-to-family contact down the road.

Another case. In Ladner, BC, Andrea Hayward, a birthmother at seventeen, her boyfriend, Paul, and adopters Leanne and Darrel Hamm in nearby Aldergrove, in their early thirties, have lots in common. They're "casual" people, neither professional nor "pushy"; they don't live in "elaborate houses" or have "big goals." Andrea and Paul chose the Hamms because, Andrea says, "they seemed honest, they didn't make up a big story.... [They seemed to be] simple people, like me, I guess."

By the way, adopters are led to believe that birthparents prefer fresh-faced professionals who have it all, and more. In truth, says Marilyn Shinyei, who's been matching adoptive families for ages, it's not that cut and dried. "I'm picking this family because they're like my family" is the explanation she most often hears from birthparents. Usually, they want stable people, with economic security—"not wealth," she emphasizes—and one child already, preferably adopted. Two kids are a liability. In religion, fundamentalism is the big no-no. Over forty is normally out, but "there's no accounting for taste."

Andrea and Paul's choice fit the bill: people like them—modest, small-town, working-class. Andrea rated it a big plus that Leanne is adopted, and could, therefore, relate to the child's feelings. Despite the easy comfort this foursome felt all round, they decided on a written agreement. It stipulates four letters with photos the first year, then one annually until the child, Spencer, reaches nineteen, when he can meet his birthparents on request. Though it wasn't in the blueprint, eight months later Leanne invited Andrea to visit, then again on Spencer's first birthday. Later, Paul, by then separated from Andrea, came by, but it was too much for him. For now, he wants mail only. Later, he'll see. Andrea, meanwhile, has an open invitation to visit once a year. Though these families started with a laid-down deal, in practice they're taking it one step at a time until they tailor the right plan.

In none of these situations is anyone intruding on the other family's life. Yet, the very words "open adoption" can throw the uninitiated off, as if it allows principals freedom to encroach on each other. But that's not the case. As in all relationships, mutually satisfactory—or at least acceptable—borders get defined. It doesn't happen, as outsiders warn, that neither adults nor children know who the real parents are. (Leanne's friends were horrified. What if Spencer calls his birthparents "Mommy" and "Daddy"?)

In fact, unless open arrangements go haywire—which, reportedly, rarely happens—kids don't get ripped in half. Their two entwined families don't coparent. Rather, they interact like in-laws. We all know how that goes: sometimes they're people we'd choose ourselves, so it's a gift when they come by chance. With others, we could never, to say the least, enjoy a cushy relationship. In any case, there's no accounting for chemistry. But our partner's significant others love the same person we do. On that basis, we try to make allowances even for the worst of the lot.

Something else most of us experience with in-laws: feelings change with evolving needs and maturity. This truism holds particular significance in adoption, where the two sets of parents typically come together at very different life stages. Birthparents are frequently young and unsettled; adopters, older and more in a routine. The givers of the child may be surviving a nightmare while the takers fulfill a dream. Taxiing their son's birthmother back to her apartment from the hospital, empty-handed after she'd delivered a baby, drove this dichotomy home to Margery and Melanie, a lesbian couple from Sacramento. "[This was] the saddest day of her life. She's distraught, really tearful, and we feel like exploding with joy. We have our baby."

Birthparents may need time and distance to lick their wounds just when adopters hope to start forging closeness. The asymmetry may never equalize, but it will certainly change as everyone grows up. These are, after all, human beings, often as dissimilar as can be, brought and held together by extraordinary circumstances. How could there not be bumpy patches?

What do the triad parties, and especially adoptees, stand to gain in open adoption?[15] Leading experts, who invariably have children in open or reunited adoption themselves and/or work as professionals creating and supporting such arrangements, say openness mitigates the pain of separation and loss. By having birthparents inside their trusted circle, adoptees get to see that the people who gave them life value them, even if they can't raise them, and indeed value them as much as children they do keep. Adoptees learn that choosing adoption wasn't rejection or abandonment; it was circumstances.

Interacting with their biological parents gives kids a direct line to the real story surrounding their beginnings, birth, and adoption—a tale more trustworthy coming from the horse's mouth. This is no small benefit, considering that, no matter what anyone says, adopted children commonly suspect something's wrong with them and that's why they were given up. If anyone can dispel that core fear, it's birthparents. Only they can answer the burning questions: "Why wasn't I good enough to keep?" and "Who do I look like?" Only they can help clarify the muddy sense of self that so often mars adoptees' psychic tranquillity. Knowing original parents as flawed human beings also does away with the distorted fantasies that typically haunt kids who never meet their birthrelatives. No longer need they worry that mom was a hooker or wish dad was a rock star; they can deal, finally, with relieving or distressing news.

Many adoptees encounter more than the usual glitches in building close personal ties. "Having experienced an original loss—the loss of the first parents—trust in relationships and their permanence is shaken and difficult to develop."[16] For those kids suffering from a sense of primal rejection, the more stripped of mystery that defining event becomes, the less ill it bodes for their capacity to trust.

Ongoing contact adds another plus: access to what can be critical information. A sheet detailing a family's medical profile isn't good enough, especially when the information is self-reported, as it may overlook conditions not in evidence at adoption time. More dangerous, histories usually address the past in a limited way, perhaps excluding illnesses that run in families but skip a generation. Unknowing, an adoptee could be a carrier of a genetic time bomb.

What of birthparents? What does openness bring them? The consolation prize: the chance to have some, rather than no, link with their baby beyond birth. At the very least, it opens a window onto their child's development. Assuming s/he's loved and thriving, birthparents get proof that at least they didn't make a bad decision, or, better yet, that they made the best one. Because Andrea Hayward, for instance, got to know Spencer's adopters, "I knew he was going to a good home. [As a result] the whole experience wasn't as bad as everyone said giving him up would be." Even though birthparents sacrifice the irreplaceable parental role, they may yet assume a real and significant relationship with their child. Peace of mind, a rare and precious jewel for many a birthparent, may come with openness. Without it, serenity may slip through their fingers.

COMPLICATIONS AND SURPRISES, DISSENTERS AND FANS

What's the downside? Not only does open adoption demand intimate human rapport—challenging in the easiest of circumstances—but it is also culturally unscripted, complex kinship. More daunting, it holds a child at its heart, cherished by both sides. This weakness, of course, often proves its greatest strength, gluing together the most unlikely characters. Still, any number of factors can be its dissolution, or temporary undoing. What if birthparents abuse their babies before adoption, hurting the children adopters love? What if they aren't the most sympathetic types? What if adoptive parents don't empathize or treat them kindly? What if birthparents have adoption with access but don't use it? Or what if adoptive parents agree to openness, then get rattled and close their doors? The "what ifs" are endless.

Among families contributing their stories in this book, many have some degree of contact with their adoptee's birthfamily, or with significant early caregivers, such as foster parents. (Bear in mind, most of the families you'll meet here who adopted babies have still-young children, so you're getting a parental take on openness.) Some relationships, precious to all participants, are handled with such delicacy and work so smoothly they'd make you weep. Yet others, rockier, have not broken down. Marilyn Shinyei, whose Edmonton agency, Adoption Options, has mediated nearly 600 open adoptions in a decade, claims failure is rare. Most of her clients share in fully disclosed relationships; the agency functions as a mailbox for a handful only. She's had to troubleshoot in fewer than ten cases. Collapse, she has found, usually traces back to adoptive parents who can't accept any loss of control. So long as parties bring flexibility and a fair ability to express feelings to the table, major problems, she says, don't usually creep in.

The worst mishap, according to Shinyei? Adopters who make the mistake of becoming a birthmother's emotional bedrock. Interesting that she would nail this one, because I wondered if it was coincidence that I kept hearing this regret from adoptive parents. Judging from my small sample, when poor, unsupported women, especially younger or immature ones, place their newborns with older, well-off types, this risk multiplies. Why? Because the young mother may need mothering herself and the adopters are at the right age and stage of wisdom— and point of vulnerability—to provide it. The adoptive parents, per- haps guilt-ridden at taking another woman's baby, or grateful and feeling beholden, but also sensitive to the birthmother's plight, jump in—or unconsciously slip in. Suddenly they find themselves positioned as her main support.

That's what happened to Charlotte Meyer and David Glotzer in Berkeley, fortysomething professionals who adopted their first child, Aaron, from an impoverished woman. Charlotte and David were on the phone to her day and night, privy to details of a life held together by a thread. The birthmother looked to them for the parenting—and money—she needed. Her needs combined with their penitence and empathy to create a boundary problem, which they were struggling to resolve when we met. These adopters were ambushed into another boundary-setting snag when they and Aaron first got together with his birthmother. She tried to parent him, and, worse, in a style that included slapping, something they reject but she uses with the child she kept.

Margery Evans-Knapp and Melanie McClure, middle-aged lawyers, woke up one day to realize they'd fallen into a similar jackpot. Over several years, they'd adopted two siblings from a single mother who lives hand to mouth in South-Central Los Angeles. After Charlie came home, they were on the phone "faithfully every day," listening to his birthmother cry, not knowing what to do. They eventually timetabled a once-weekly call to discuss her problems as much as to talk about the children. Visits, in this case, go well. For the birthmother, who relates comfortably to the whole family as if she were a "distant rela- tive," Sacramento is a reprieve from helicopters overhead, gangs, and gunshots. "She says over and over how quiet it is."

At least the children in both these families have access to birthrela- tives. There are many cases, however, where families adopt more than one child, but not all in open arrangements. That situation can trigger sadness, as well as jealousy and rivalry, among siblings.

In the surprises department, two items always crop up. First, "permission to know one's heritage only makes the adoptee love his adoptive parents more—for giving him freedom and for trusting his love."[17] Second, those averse to openness have always claimed that birthparents would want too much, and might even try to get their baby back. (By the way, facilitators of open adoption report that a two-way street runs here, as some birthparents worry adopters might try to give the baby back.) Yet, in practice, it's more often the other way around: adoptive parents, seeing the benefits of contact, wish birthparents were more accessible. It's common to hear adoptive parents complain about birthparents "tapering off," especially in the early years, though many reappear later.

A research team recently asked adoptive parents how satisfied they were with their control over birthparents' involvement in their families. Most, across all levels of openness, were very pleased, but a minority weren't. When the investigators examined these cases more deeply, "in almost every instance the problem was that the adoptive parent wanted more contact with the birthparent rather than less."[18] Also, the more open the adoption, the less adoptive parents feared birthfamilies might try to reclaim. Both these findings—which, incidentally, concur with the anecdotal evidence—are the mirror opposite of predictions the fearful make.

Open adoption is still enough of an unknown to have new skeptics mouthing old misgivings. Frankly, many adoptive parents are so scared, they globe-hop to find adoptees with invisible parentage. Others, like adoptive dad Gale Allen, who lives near Pittsburgh, continue to believe it's too confusing for the children—"They need to know we're their family," he says—yet have no problem with post-childhood reunion. Indeed, Gale plans to help his sons find their kin.

Professionals, too are divided, though by no means evenly. These days, it's the exception for adoption specialists to question openness, though they do quibble over when, how to, and how much. *Kinship with Strangers* highlights the fact that opposition "represents more than selfishness on the part of adoptive parents who want a child 'of their own' or desperation on the part of birthparents who want to 'keep' the children they relinquish, or jealousy on the part of social workers who want to control the placement of children." These factors count, but what's really tugging at opponents? "Open adoption threatens deeply held assumptions about the American family. By dismantling the biological premise, open adoption exposes the entailments of that premise: biology represents permanence, stability, and exclusivity— the core of parenthood."[19] That's why the author, Judith Modell, calls openness "more subversive than even its opponents claim."[20]

If any slant on openness unifies members of the adoption triangle and professionals, it goes like this: open adoption isn't a happily-ever-after story. It's not the answer. There are no solutions in adoption, only better practices. "I know from mothering my kept children," writes Jan Waldron, "that the boundless strength of an unbroken tether is irreplaceable, and that, even under the best of circumstances, there is no substitute for it; there are only other ways."[21]

BOGEYMEN BIRTHFATHERS

Of other ways gaining momentum, Modell is right: openness is the most radical. But another rupture with past practice is, on the one hand, giving openness a boost, while, on the other, putting a damper on it—involved birthfathers. On the plus side, they complete the adoptee's family circle. But, on the minus side, depending on how and when they enter the picture, they might throw into turmoil the lives of everyone affected by the adoption.

The same societal mood that set the stage for lifting the veil of secrecy separating adoptees and birthmothers also brought birthfathers out of the shadows. They've finally burst onto the scene, but in the worst possible light. They've gone from one stereotype to another: from uncaring, craven fellows who abandoned mother and child, to heartless SOBs intent on nabbing preschoolers from the adoptive parents their progeny love. A spate of cases involving men, late to learn they have children and quick to demand them back, has resulted in high-profile interfamily wars, with kids caught in the crossfire. None is better known than the "baby Jessica" debacle, in which a birthfather, Dan Schmidt, reunited with Jessica's birthmother, fought tooth and nail for over two years to get his daughter back from the DeBoers, who were raising and in the process of adopting the girl. Though Schmidt initiated his claim when Jessica was an infant, by the time he won her through the courts, she was a young child attached to the only parents she'd known.

Birthfathers are unknown or unreported in 20 to 50 percent of all adoptions.[22] Yet they live in a cultural milieu where expectations of men as parents have changed drastically since the 1950s, when gender roles were carved in stone. Back then, someone could be considered a good father, yet get away with doing no more than handing over the pay packet and doling out the punishment. Today, men are invited— more than that, admonished—to be actively involved in parenting. We've come so far that we're blasé at hearing about a dad serving as primary or lone caregiver. It's little wonder, then, that even a man estranged from his child's mother—whether they'd been together long or only for a night of reckless partying—could imagine himself reclaiming and raising the child.

While there has hardly been a flood of such requests, the trickle has been steady. And putative fathers, though small in number, have already injected a major dose of fear into the adoption world. Some prospective parents worry so much about a father lurking in the bushes that, for this reason alone, however statistically farfetched, they look for adoptees offshore. What's the risk dad will show up here versus the chance of him muscling in on a family that adopts, say, from an orphanage in China? In the toss-up between some and nil, the latter, understandably, appeals more. While no parent I met adopted internationally out of fear of reclaimers, two families expressed relief that the dad factor was one less worry for them. This jibes with the general perception that missing males, who can reasonably be expected never to reappear, are a bonus tacked onto families built long-distance.

Latecomer-father cases typically involve a man belatedly aware of his paternity and that the child's mother signed away her maternal rights. The baby could be in foster care or at any stage of the adoption process. A combination of factors has, to date, made for almost-assured tragedy when dad shows up. The most disturbing thread: the utter failure of the courts to do better than wrangling adults when it comes to protecting a child's need for timely decisions. This, of course, is all of a piece with custody disputes generally.

But reclaiming birthfathers, the Johnnies-come-lately to this tug-of-war, particularly unhinge adopters. Why? Because there haven't been enough cases or enough history from which to discern a definite pattern of outcomes. Here's what adopters do know: the end result is impossible to predict, but they'll likely live with an ax over their head for several years. They know that the slow-moving, adversarial, winner-take-all judicial system will, in the end, skewer someone, possibly their child.

In the usual disaster, comeback birthfathers press for their baby's return when s/he's very little. The other parents fight like blazes to bar him, but don't exhaust all avenues of appeal until two or three years later. Whatever law or fairness might have been on the birthfather's side when the litigation started, by the time he assumes custody, if he does, hardly anyone would argue that switching families is best for the child.

The laws on paternal rights are a crazy-quilt in the United States, where the messy cases have surfaced. In some states, a man has to sign before parental entitlements vanish. In Pennsylvania, for example, an unknown father never loses his rights; he can show up at any time and assert them. In other states, courts require proof dad denied paternity, or was notified but did zip. Elsewhere, rights have time lines; if not exercised by the deadline, they're automatically zapped. In Canada, a father named on a birth certificate must give adoption consent. If an unnamed father discovers he has a placed child, he can petition the courts, though they're obliged to rule in the child's best interests— which sounds good, except that it hasn't been much tested.

Meanwhile, few litigants, unfortunately, take a page from the history of divorce. There, it's long been recognized that out-of-court settlements, using various intervenor models, play better for children and get to home plate faster. Mediators, unlike courtroom lawyers, try to cool rather than inflame overheated adversaries. The whole thing costs less, emotionally and financially. Custody arrangements that emerge tend to be less hard-edged about how children can maintain links with everyone who loves them, even if the adults barely tolerate each other.

A Vermont case a few years ago illustrated a more child-sensitive approach. The adoptive parents in the "baby Pete" case said from the beginning they'd sooner return the infant than risk a replay of the Schmidt/DeBoer fiasco. Instead, the adoptive mother and late-appearing biological father settled for joint legal custody. Pete resides with the adoptive family; his birthfather is entitled to visit and to contribute to key decisions about the child's upbringing. The adoptive dad became the stepfather.[23]

This still-rare story in adoption speaks of possibilities, and of newer understandings, especially of birthfathers as real people who hold their children dear. Although men have historically been left out of adoption—in many cases, doubtless happily so—mounting evidence suggests growing numbers of men no longer want to be off the hook. As personal testimonies in *Out of the Shadows: Birthfathers' Stories* by Mary Martin Mason illustrates, not all of them are the cold-hearted mooks they're made out to be. Being cut off from their kids can be emotionally harrowing for them. Just as many birthmothers ache permanently, so do some men, even if donating sperm was the full extent of their fatherhood.

Irrespective of what biological fathers want as individuals or as a group, their responsible involvement in adoption best serves their offspring, no matter if dad is a cad or a caring guy. On this subject, adoption professionals are of one mind: the sooner and more involved the birthfather—which requires that birthmothers not conceal pregnancy—the more aware of his rights and choices, the better the outcome for the child. Prospective adoptive parents, too, have a role here: not to let their eagerness to adopt blind them to details about dad. Any oversight could come back to haunt them, and to put their child's mental health seriously at risk.

Coming Soon to an Agency Near You

Like it or not, there's no getting away from the fact openness has taken the adoption world by storm. Though this type of adoption can no longer be considered experimental, the jury is still out on its long-term consequences for all parties. The first generation of children to grow up with both their families is only now approaching adulthood. It will take time and study for the unknowns to unravel. But, what's the consensus among professionals who've been in the middle of these controversial arrangements for more than a decade? Openness may not bring a Hollywood ending, but it's not the big drama outsiders imagine. What's more, it's not a fad; it's here to stay.

The anecdotal evidence, they say, is so compelling, and the alternative such a stinker, the question is not "Openness: yes or no?" but "How?" For example, should birthparents have the option, as most have had to date, of hiding their identity? Even if very few would go for this—as the evidence suggests—should new laws cover the exceptions? What of adopters like Gale Allen, who are gung-ho for reunion but reticent about no-holds-barred openness? Must the "when" of contact be by mutual agreement of those affected? Or should Gale have legal assurance that his family can meet relatives—assuming they don't veto it—when, at his house, the time seems right?

Except for adoption professionals and stakeholders who favor openness, plain and simple, no legal strings attached—and there are significant numbers in this camp—many working this virgin territory still struggle with the answers. They reckon the research, as it breaks, will provide guidance for fine-tuning what they regard as a practice that has come of age. More accurately, one that has come full circle, returning to the original open-door state of customary adoption. As Modell highlights, "for those who support it, openness is not a breakdown but a restoration of values—putting adoption back on course, away from the commerce and calculation that have come to characterize this transaction in kinship."[24]

For those of us sick of the obsession with shared genetic material as the only progenitor of true families, adoption with contact clears the air. It expunges the "as if" scent that fouls the authenticity of adoptive families. So long as relatedness can be real and right only if it pretends to be something else, adoptive families will continue to languish in the ranks of the also-rans.

Double Daddies
or Mommies

... our essential human bonds transcend any particular family structure and exist in many forms.

—*Laura Benkov*, Reinventing the Family

One steamy July evening, while wilting around a kitchen table in a leafy Midwest suburb, sipping ice tea, Jo and Kathryn tell me their "miracle" story. Distracted by their glaring personality differences, I only half-hear their words and have to check details on the cassette later. Jo, a French Canadian, thinks quick and talks fast. She's glib, blunt, upbeat. Kathryn, from California, picks over her words as if buying diamonds. She's pensive, cautious, down-tempo.

The miracle happened in Seattle. Kathryn, a pediatrician pushing forty, had just bid goodnight to patients in a support group. A teenager approached. "Do you want a baby?" she asked, just like that. Kathryn didn't skip a beat. "Sure," she said, even though she and Jo, her longtime lover, a pediatric nurse, had no such plans. The infant on offer was due six months hence to a bisexual eighteen-year-old named Cathy. She wanted to give her baby to a bisexual, lesbian, or gay couple because she felt it unfair that the adoption system is rigged against them.

Kathryn raced home with the news. Jo didn't miss a beat either: "Yes!" Within days, Cathy came to check them out. Her concerns: that her child would not be raised in a fundamentalist religion and would be given a chance to go to college. Once she saw her priorities were safe with this Unitarian couple, Cathy committed to them as the adopters. That didn't stop Jo and Kathryn from anguishing that the birthmother, seemingly clearheaded about her decision, might waver. She never did. Despite the protests of her boyfriend, who wanted to marry her, she was going to be a shipbuilder, not a mother, thank you very much.

Given the special wrongs gays and lesbians endure when trying to adopt, Jo and Kathryn initially found the gift of an unsolicited newborn too good to be true. It was still hard to believe on that night five years ago, at a restaurant where the three women had gathered, when, over sushi, Cathy's contractions began. The next morning, Jordan was delivered, team-assisted by her birthfather, Jo, and Kathryn. Cathy presented the new parents with a quilt she'd hand-stitched: "I don't," she said, "want Jordan to go into the world naked." Jordan, a spunky nymph with dark eyes and shiny hair, prizes the present from the person she knows as "the woman who gave birth to you to make a family for us."

No guardian angel visited Sacramento lawyers Margery Evans-Knapp and Melanie McClure. A bit of an odd duo—odd for the absence of coupledom's little japes and jibes—these two finish each other's sentences. Not to get metaphysical, but with Margery you know you're in the presence of someone who has suffered. Turns out she's a recovering alcoholic.

Their adoption story? The typical jeremiad. Margery was forty-five, Melanie thirty-nine, when they started looking. From the system's perspective, they were *personae non grata*. Though no one said it, they got the message: old dykes need not apply. The worker at the county office, for example, opened with "We don't discriminate." Two sentences later: "But any healthy baby would go to a married couple." Realizing they'd be in their dotage before the county helped them—even though they weren't stuck on having a perfect newborn—they turned to private adoption, where anything seemed possible for a price.

A high-profile lawyer, her office walls papered with pictures of "all these happy families she'd made," included Margery and Melanie in a group ad that ran in *People Weekly* and *USA Today*. One birthmother chose them, but, as they would learn too late, she also chose four other families, all of which, M and M included, contributed to her kitty during pregnancy. She kept her child. Another pregnant teen who picked them, and with whom they built a telephone friendship, went through a postpartum change of heart. They were in Manhattan for the birth, bearing shower gifts, when the turnaround happened. Two years later, they still had big bills but no baby.

Onto their own advertising—"Two professional women offer a loving home …" etc. From that, a few phone interviews. "We kind of got the impression," Melanie recalls, "that [some were] looking for a 'white picket fence' … and you can't blame them." Others seemed not to care about M and M's sexual orientation or their age. Still, no child. Then they got a tip on Pact, a San Francisco adoption alliance for children of color. Within six months, and just weeks after the Rodney King episode, they were in "surreal" South-Central Los Angeles picking up newborn Charlie from his thirty-year-old mother, originally from Belize. Later they would adopt Libby, her next-born. Now, they are deep in the thrall of parenthood, and in the maw of a tricky, but viable open adoption.

Adopting was no cakewalk for Gale Allen either. He and his mate of eighteen years, Gil Cowan, who live near Pittsburgh, sporadically discussed adopting. They knew their desire to do it legally as a couple was a lost cause. They were both past forty, the adoption clock ticking into overtime, when it hit Gale: "I don't want to reach old age and wonder what might have been." If he and Gil could nurture their bond without the glue of convention, so, too, could they extend their family without the formality of a legally binding relationship.

Decision made, Gale went into overdrive. It's easy to imagine him in high gear; he's a loquacious type who gobbles up psychological space. (Opposites attract again; Gil, quiet and contemplative, goes along.) From the first phone call—to a TV talk show featuring adoption, with county reps on the panel—Gale butted up against the predictable bull. You're male, gay, and going gray? Get a dog. Though no one said it outright, the message was loud and clear.

More inquiries and Gale got the picture. The most hassle-free, affordable route for ostracized applicants: a "hard-to-place" child through a specialty agency. Gale, an administrator in the disabilities field, was choosy about special needs. "It sounds cold, but it's what I do for a living and it's not what I want to deal with when I get home." Enter Project Star. Though no one uttered the "g" word, the worker "could accept our lifestyle." The agency put him and Gil through the same homestudy paces as other hopefuls. But every time their social worker got a lead on a possible adoptee (Star has no children; they place for other organizations), the child's worker would reject them, saying something like "a two-parent family is more suitable in this case." Code for "no fags welcome."

Finally, Gale found a back door. He persuaded a friend who has some pull with child services to run interference. Soon Gale adopted Douglas, an African-American toddler in foster care from birth. Since Gil, the coparent, is black, the couple didn't get caught in the transracial adoption wars. Not long after Douglas came home, year-old Trent, also African American, joined the family. Both boys, four and two when I visited, busy as beavers and angling to get their mitts on my tape recorder, came with a roster of psychomedical labels, all of which so far appear to be nonsense. "Just look at Douglas [who is supposedly developmentally delayed]. He's brilliant. He's charming. He's funny. He's going to make us rich old men." Gale chuckles as the boy clambers onto his lap.

THE GOD SQUAD

Ten percent, or about 25 million Americans—and by the same measure, about 3 million Canadians—are thought to be homosexual. Right now, in the United States, 6 to 14 million children are living with 1.5 to 5 million lesbian mothers, and 1 to 3 million gay fathers.[1] These generally accepted estimates rile those who make a fetish of the nuclear family; conservatives peg the prevalence of homosexuality at about 1 percent. Most children involved are biological offspring, primarily from previous marriages, or from donor-insemination and coparenting arrangements. A growing, but unmeasured, segment involves adoptees.

Gays and lesbians have been coming out and speaking up as parents, defending the families they make, often through unconventional methods, including adoption. That has brought the homophobes out of the woodwork. It has also made the uneasy but undecided prick up their ears. Indeed, of family types that hit a nerve somewhere in the population, few trigger more spasms of outrage than gay- and lesbian-led adoptive units, especially if the child in question is a stranger.

Homophobia is an old hack, going back to biblical shibboleths of sin. The "language of sin" was later recast as "the language of sickness" by the "modern-day religion of psychiatry," writes psychologist Laura Benkov in *Reinventing the Family*. The double whammy, scriptural plus medical, gained legitimacy through sodomy statutes—a few still exist—and state-sanctioned curbs on equal rights. Historically, gay sexuality, painted as unnatural, perverted, and promiscuous, has held the almighty focus in the long campaign.

Melanie McClure chuckles about the voyeuristic mania over the "gay lifestyle." What does that mean? she wonders. The campy guys in drag on Pride Day? The bathhouse scene, which homophobes equate with homosexuality? The man–boy love club, reviled by practically everyone? She reckons it can't mean her family, because, as she says, "we live in the suburbs, we go to church on Sundays, take the kids to the park.... We know lots of families like us who just live ordinary—go to work, come home, take care of the kids, sometimes hire a babysitter and go to a movie."

As gays came out as parents, the spotlight of anxiety shifted from the bedroom to the playroom. Benkov says the panic over gay parenting derives from an errant belief, based in the sinner–sickness axis, that "homosexuals and children don't mix." When it comes to kinship with kids, she notes, even anti-discrimination activists may draw the line: gays and lesbians on one side, families and children on the other. The basic fear? Homosexuals are bogeymen out to wreck the family. The hysterical rendition? They're "stalkers" and "pedophiles out to recruit the next generation." These gems, she says, usually come from lathered-up types who talk about "homosexual pedophiles" as if they were one and the same, a theory long ago debunked. Research has repeatedly shown pedophiles either aren't choosy or have a predilection for heterosexuality.

I ask Kathryn in her Midwest kitchen for her take on the hysteria. The population, she estimates, divides into three parts: a sliver of "irrational, homophobic, hating kind of people"; a middle bulk who haven't been exposed—"they just live their lives and don't really think about [homosexuality]"; and a slip of supportive straight people.

It's the evangelists patrolling the borders of the so-called traditional family that make her skin crawl. They're the reason she and Jo chose to stick with first names in this book. You can't blame them for fearing a brick through the window when you hear the neo-conservatives' line. Listen, for example, to David Frum, a Canadian ideologue based in Washington. He makes no bones about it: all bids to normalize gay and lesbian families should be obstructed.

> Civilization rests on two fundamental institutions, private property and the nuclear family.... Canada faces no social problem more urgent and important than the strengthening of

the family.... In order to achieve that aim, it must revitalize the institution of marriage. How? Exactly as the Victorians did it when they faced a similar social crisis: by ensuring that the laws and customs favor ... not "partnerships," but ... real marriages, between fathers and mothers, lasting for life.... [That] necessarily precludes—and excludes—almost every single item on the gay-rights agenda.[2]

A LEGAL MUDDLE

Frum's take is enlightened compared with that of the zealots of the mostly religious right, who prefer veritable jihads against homosexual parents. Readers will remember "Save Our Children," for example, singer Anita Bryant's crusade, launched in the late 1970s. It inspired anti-gay legislation in Florida, followed by copycat statutes in two other states. As things stand, only Florida and New Hampshire explicitly prohibit gay adoptions. New Hampshire forbids gay fostering as well. By contrast, New York and California shield gays and lesbians from adoption discrimination in certain circumstances. Indeed, New York's highest court has ruled that unmarried couples, regardless of sexual preference, can legally adopt. Lower courts in at least eleven other states have ruled similarly.

In Canada, only British Columbia permits gays and lesbians to adopt, thanks to a new law opening adoption to "one adult or two adults jointly." (Straight unmarried couples, traditionally among the unwelcome, will also benefit from the new rules.) A similar legislative proposal was defeated in Ontario. In the rest of the country, gays and lesbians can try to adopt, but as singles only, entitling their children to only one legally recognized parent. When it comes to foster parenting, some provincial social service agencies quietly permit while others quietly prohibit gays and lesbians. Alberta, however, went loudly on record in 1997, declaring that heterosexual couples make the best parents and that, forthwith, gays and lesbians in particular were finished as fosterers. The announcement followed a challenge from a longtime foster parent whose foster children were removed when Children's Aid belatedly realized she was a lesbian.

Though it isn't illegal for homosexuals to create families, those they create don't enjoy the same safeguards as their conventional cousins.

Non-status leads to a field day for men (mostly) in black robes, who interpret laws as they see fit. And since many judges are still card-carrying members of the Old Boys' Club, rulings often lag behind the pace of societal change. However, the more the bench begins to look like the body politic, the more flexible it may become. In the current void, meanwhile, everything goes, from the attitude "no homos get kids while I'm reading the law" to "let's stop these anthems to the family that hardly exists anymore and start validating the ones that do."

So, in recent years, you get Virginia's Supreme Court ruling 4–3 for a grandmother seeking custody of her three-year-old grandson, the court calling the natural mother "unfit" because her lesbianism would bring "social condemnation" on her child. Around the same time, you get the DC Court of Appeals ruling that unmarried couples, straight or gay, in "committed relationships" could adopt. Hardly a monthly newsletter from any adoption advocacy group on either side of the border goes by without mention of schizophrenic verdicts like these. Judges, on one side, screening the law through their Victorian values; on the other side, screening it through an impersonal human-rights gauze.

Family law supposedly reveres "the best interests" of children above all. And what's best, no dispute, according to the experts? Permanent loving parents, or stand-ins to whom the child grows attached. Despite this child-rearing rudiment, judges continue to flex their morality by muscling in on nurturing, stable families that happen not to be traditional. And judges who do so are operating well within the room the law gives them. That is, the room to wrench a child from a competent caregiver, who may or may not be biologically related, because they believe homosexual parenting is tantamount to what could be called moral abuse.

In the most common scenario leading to lawful raids on the family, the biological parent, usually the mother, dies. Her lover, a coparent but lacking legal sanction, continues her role, just as the other parent would were a couple married or cohabiting. Relatives, probably the deceased's parents, seeing their chance to "save" their grandchild, apply for custody—and sometimes win. In the worst cases, the courts further cheapen the surviving parent's relationship with the youngster by referring to her as a "biological stranger."

It's heartbreaking to think what this does to a child already dealing with the death of one parent. Now the second is spirited away. Why? So the minor can seek the comfort of connections with septuagenarians who hate homosexuals, that is, the kid's own parents. As if this weren't bad enough, the elderly saviors will probably make their final exit during the tumultuous teenage years.

The more you think about this plot line, the more flabbergasting it gets.

Failure to recognize and protect in law family bonds *as they exist* spurs discrimination down the line. Everywhere they turn, gays and lesbians find the system ranged against them: health insurance, employment, workplace benefits, taxes, inheritance (especially if there's no will), housing rights, child-care leaves, bereavement entitlements, support provisions when couples split. All of these, predictably, are facing court challenges. Not long ago in Toronto, for example, a judge in effect rewrote Ontario's Family Law Act to entitle same-sex couples to sue each other for support.

Meanwhile, Tammy Duffey, in Monroe, Michigan, can't get a cent from her adopted children's other parent. Tammy complains, "I can't get my ex court-ordered to do anything." While deadbeat dads top today's most-wanted list in family courts, and get bad-mouthed for abandoning the kids, authorities don't utter a peep about the plight of children in broken homosexual households.

It doesn't take a child whose family risks financial ruin—or, worse, rupture—to see the ways in which definitions of "family" and "parent" hobble the law. That's why everyone lobbying for new legislation focuses on family roles, not on formal ties. By the time broad-minded ideas do make it onto the books, the rights of whomever a legal parent intends as coparent, regardless of gender, will outrank those of a relative with a homophobic agenda.

In the meantime, gays and lesbians who turn to agencies to build their families can, at best, hope for an adoption order naming them as "parent and parent." The billing doesn't recognize their union or their legitimacy as a family, but does acknowledge their parity as parents. And couples will get this far only if they track down an avant-garde agency, an uncommon lawyer, and a leading-edge judge in a new-wave jurisdiction like California, where they can get away with it. Two couples I met pulled it off. The rest, among the minority who manage to sidestep the single-adopter snare, work other angles for legal or quasi-legal standing. They either go for stepparent adoption—a long shot— or for "guardian" designation in the legal parent's will.

In short, the chance of becoming two legal parents is slim. But while legislatures muddle alongside judges up to their gavels in contradictory decisions, most roads are leading to more legal largesse with respect to two of society's mainstays: families and parenting.

ALL-POWERFUL AGENCIES

Laws aren't the gospel when it comes to stopping gays from adopting a child they've never met before, as opposed to adopting a partner's birthchild, where laws count. In the hazy adoption world, if there's a will to facilitate, or to quash, a bid for a baby, there's usually a way. Because adoption outfits function on low-visibility decisions, it barely matters whether a policy manual favors or frowns on gay adoptions. What does count? What adoption workers think about homosexuals.

There's no reason to believe the average social worker is any more at home with the idea of gay parents than is the guy on the street. In Canada's 1993 national adoption study, 81 percent of service providers expressed greatest concern about placing both infants and special-needs children with gays and lesbians. So much for social work's liberal reputation! By contrast, respondents were only moderately anxious about adoptees going to single, racially different, or middle-aged parents.[3]

That most resist giving newborns, presuming they're healthy, to gays doesn't surprise. It goes with the flow: reserve babies for pick-of-the-crop adopters, meaning conventional couples. But that so many adoption arrangers hesitate about older kids does surprise, since it bucks the trend—namely, matching depreciated kids with like adopters. Many up-front homosexuals who've approached the system will tell you they were refused an infant flat out. But, if they persisted, some were eventually offered the most fragile kids. Herein lies a paradox of modern adoptions: applicants, however wrongly dubbed inferior as parents, matched with children who need superior parenting. Tony Mello, single gay adoptive father to two boys, makes a telling comment about one of his sons: "The Department of Social Services has no idea how wonderful Paul is—if they did, they might have selected a straight, two-parent family for him."[4]

What about straight adopters? Were they in the driver's seat, would they select gays and lesbians as adoptive parents? When I put this question to my sample, no one insisted "under no circumstances should they get kids," but some expressed reservations. Pam Soden, for example, a management trainer in Manhattan, admitted she's "betwixt and between on [gay adoptions].... They're some of the most loving couples ... and, in some instances, the love ... manages to insulate the child from whatever they might have to deal with.... On the other hand, [having homosexual parents] also gives the child an additional battle."

It's probably a fluke, but when I look at who in my sample is betwixt and between, what do I find? People who crossed traditional lines themselves in their own adoptions. People like Pam—single, almost fifty when she adopted—and like Jesse Williams, who was forty-five and on his own when he adopted his first of five boys. Another curious twist in reactions: only one among the few die-hard Christian couples I met objects to gays adopting.

Attitudes are changing. On the rocky transition road, however, many helping professionals cleave to the idea that, as parents, gays are contaminated. The thinking seems to go: except for screaming queens, they may seem like regular folks, but who knows what latent tendencies and covert acts lurk behind the mask and the closed door? One psychiatrist, for example, argued that permitting gender-identical partners to adopt was "less than the best." Why? "Because all the psychological understandings of the past hundred years have demonstrated to us that the best environment for a child to grow up in is a home with two parents, one of each sex, living together in a committed, loving relationship."[5]

While the psychiatrist undoubtedly has lots of company in holding those views—though less social science than he claims—unless he's clairvoyant, how can he be sure only a mom-and-pop combo is paradise? No historical precedent exists, no societies in which gays and lesbians have raised and ruined children, for declaring them less than the best parents. Planned gay and lesbian families are only now coming under scrutiny. Preliminary findings will disappoint the good doctor: the kids don't appear to be any more screwed-up than the norm. More about that later.

A growing number of adoption agencies bet the psychiatrist is wrong. They wager gays and lesbians will turn out to be no more or less spectacular parents than their lionized competitors. To help make the case, the gamblers cut these applicants some slack, though usually on the QT. Quasi–closet adoptions, where candidates are coached in how to present themselves on paper to birthparents, to lawyers, and to judges, exist wherever gay adoptions do. Governing the tips couples receive: one of you apply as a single person, and make "the less said, the better" your motto. As for the other partner, do a vanishing act.

The advice poses a dilemma: refuse it and risk missing out on parenthood, or capitulate to bolster the chances of having children? However and whenever this double bind sneaks up on would-be adopters, applicants can be sure the system will test their internal tension between political and personal ambitions. At some point, they will have to self-interrogate. Should I raise a banner here, maybe get tied up in litigation? Or should I eat humble pie since I'd prefer to get tied up in parenting?

To make their family fantasy come true, some child-seekers take in stride the demeaning rituals of going back to silence. Candidates who can stomach the enforced invisibility decide who'll be the front person and who'll take the back seat, which, for the homestudy, may even entail burying proof that the coparent lives on the premises. But the hiding, lying, and tongue-biting can exact a heavy price. For one legally nonexistent adoptive mother, playing the ghost "forced open some of my raw childhood wounds. . . . Any feelings of inferiority or inadequacy tucked away inside me again appeared. I felt as if I were being scolded by a critical parent who kept reminding me of my rightful place."[6]

Except for Jo and Kathryn, couples in these pages had the riot act read to them by someone during their adoption odyssey: do it this way—one of you go it alone and shut up about your proclivities—or there's no way. And, interestingly in Jo and Kathryn's case, they didn't locate a birthmother through an agency, but connected with her themselves. Then, for the mandatory homestudy, they entered the system. Although theirs was the first such case the agency handled, their worker took a risk: be aboveboard about your domestic partnership, she advised. The agency's lawyer disagreed. Go the single route, he urged. Surprisingly, the agency stood firm: there'd be no subterfuge. The lawyer relented, investigated case law, but couldn't find one precedent to help them in court. Karma, however, was with Kathryn and Jo. Seeing two female applicants, the judge announced she'd assess their bid on parenting merits and nothing else. From the top, their adoption was a series of lucky breaks. Rare stuff.

What happened to Margery and Melanie is more typical. When they tried to adopt a youngish, moderately healthy child, they got the message: fat chance, unless you're open to an HIV-infected baby, which they weren't. So the duo turned to international agencies, cross-ing their fingers that there they wouldn't be treated as the all-American damned. They approached three organizations. Their contact at the only one not to reject them told Melanie right off the bat, "You'll have to lie about your relationship." Unwilling to start a family on a foun-dation of fibs, the women declined.

Gale Allen was a quick study. It took him one dust-up with the pub-lic system to get his priorities straight. If you want to find a child, don't "wave flags or raise things that don't need to be raised." Take your lead from the worker, who, after one home visit, will realize there's a spouse in the house. If s/he opts for conspiratorial silence, it doesn't mean no one understands what's what. It only means that's how we're going to play the game if we want to pass "go."

Were the gays and lesbians interviewed for this book not to announce their bent, few who met them would automatically wonder about it. Nothing superficial distinguishes them from the crowd. Hence, if they kept their partners undercover, they could probably slip through the adoption rigmarole as singles. Not Tammy Duffey. Maybe you can't always judge a book by its cover, but this one is easy to read from the moment I spot the petite figure in working denims at our ren-dezvous in Detroit. The masculine gait, the short bob and rattail, the rolled-up shirt sleeves, tattoos on display—a rainbow on one arm, a medicine wheel on the other—keys jangling from the belt loop, this is not David Frum's dream mother.

All confidence and candor, with blue eyes Paul Newman would envy, she's one of those instantly likable people. Tammy, now thirty-six, adopted two young birthsisters. In applying first to foster, and later to adopt, she didn't try to hide her live-in. Indeed, the two attended training classes together. All authorities throughout the process knew the girls were going to two parents. Beyond one bit of advice to keep her love life to herself, however, no one whispered a word. Everyone played the solo-applicant game. Even the judge, who knew the score—when he asked Tammy's lawyer what the plan was should she not be able to care for the girls, the lawyer jabbered her way through an answer without acknowledging Tammy's partner of six years.

There are different ways of viewing the dance of deceit. You can see it as adoption insiders siding with gays by helping them get over on a system that all but outlaws them. Or, you can see it as cowardice all down the line when it comes to challenging moribund policies and laws. However you regard it, lies are becoming an increasingly visible sore spot in these adoptions. The 1994 Peirce–Warwick Adoption Symposium—an annual conference that tackles cutting-edge controversies—spotlighted issues in homosexual adoptions. It found that agencies willing to forge gay families nonetheless downplay them for fear of reprisals from funders and directors. There's a lot of this brand of thinking going around, but there's no epidemic in principled stands.

Despite clandestine adoptions, word is getting out that "we are good parents," claims psychologist/author April Martin, in *The Lesbian and Gay Parenting Handbook*. She says many agencies which wouldn't have dreamed of placing with people like her even a decade ago have reversed themselves in recent years. Even birthparents, always depicted as the least likely to accept gay parents, now sometimes select such adopters.

This is especially intriguing news. Why? Because adoption lore has long held that birthparents are a squabble of conservatives in search of young brain surgeons with stay-at-home wives. Paul Conlin, a Canadian adoption lawyer, for instance, was quoted as saying: "In my 20 years of practice I've never run into a girl who would give her baby to a single parent, let alone to a homosexual. Most prefer intact families."[7] Some questions go begging here. When parents outline their ideal adopters—listing such things as education, religion, child-rearing style, etc.—do they specify married couples only? Or do intermediaries, based on their own biases, prejudge their clients' meaning? And when the bio parents' list fits a nontraditional adopter, do facilitators eagerly fetch the profile from the bottom of their pile? How do they then present other-than-"intact" families, especially to young mothers with limited life experience?

Doubtless the typical gen-Xer raised on *Seventeen* magazine thinks good family equals mom/dad/bungalow. She doesn't traipse into an adoption office insisting on a gay man as ideal dad for her unborn child. I suspect, however, that, since birthmothers live in the real world and it has changed, some walk into agencies with far less rigid proscriptions than Conlin claims. Maybe even an open mind. The question is: What happens next? Is the script already narrowed by agency policy and counselor values? It's time to ask: Is it really birthparents who are putting the kibosh on gay adoptions?

ALL IN THE FAMILY

Families have always been regrouping, and the old guard has always been in a snit about it. Today they're sending up flares about fatherless families and about homosexual-headed households. In fairness, the worriers are not all wrong. Stalwart supporters of the good old family do have reason to fear that experiments in reconfiguring society's basic cell will fan out. The community, clearly in the mood for home-front changes, picks and chooses from every available innovation.

Rigid gender roles may be biting the dust in all types of families, including the nuclear icon. But, the division of power and the duty roster are up for grabs even more so in gay and lesbian units. Hence, their family remakes do deserve to be up there with the major social tremblers. This is not to warn of a mass exodus from heterosexuality, or to alert the family next door that it's an endangered species. Rather, it is to suggest that gay and lesbian pathfinders may have something to teach the rest of us about gender-bending in domestic life. Let's not kid ourselves: their families don't start from ground-zero. The adults who form them carry the ghost of tradition on their shoulders. Nevertheless, they do have to break new ground. From that project, more egalitarian family relationships may emerge.

Gender-same parents must, for example, puzzle out parenting day by day. In lesbian households, who'll be the "real" mommy? How about two equal ones? What about dad? If he isn't a sperm bank, how might he relate to child and coparents? If he is a donor, but not anonymous, how should he figure into the family? If there's no biological father around, should someone be recruited to approximate the role? In the male household, parallel questions are asked—about parental parts to be played, and about formative female figures. As well, questions about surrogate mothers, who may even be a friend doing a favor. Should she be a parent as well?

There are no easy or universal answers. Indeed, the questions themselves merely hint at the complexities involved in recasting an institution with a centuries-long script. While every family must make its own mold, each picks up imprints from others. Margery and Melanie, for instance, in Sacramento, which they call a "provincial little city," stumbled onto four other households like theirs: white, middle-aged lesbians raising adopted children of color. The group gives them a reference point for issues unique to their newfangled family.

Not surprisingly, language is a bugbear. What's in a name? What will the kids call us? Gale and Gil decided the legal father, Gale, should be "Dad," while Gil would be "Uncle." Jo and Kathryn chose "Mommy" and "Mama," which drives the critics crazy. How can children, who like things simple, accept dual mommies, let alone two who go by virtually the same ticket? Easily, if Jordan's any evidence. She uses the names comfortably, unconfused about which goes where.

And even if kids can cope, how can the outside world relate to this kind of cockeyed unit? Margery and Melanie have found that, though it may startle outsiders initially, "people work it out." They picked grandmother monikers, "Nana" and "Meema." Other kids at the play group readily cottoned onto the fact that Charlie has two moms with non-mom names. The attitude from the peanut gallery in general? Somewhere between indifferent and "that's cool." Staff hopped to it as quickly. Come Mother's Day, they help Charlie make two cards. It's just not that complicated.

The name game, however, as Benkov laments, is larded with meaning:

> People struggle with homophobia—both their own and the world's—as they choose how much of their stories to reveal through the shorthand of a child's hyphenated last name, or the delineation of two mommies. They puzzle over the complexities of parent–child negotiations in a homophobic environment, as they decide how much space developing children need to choose their own presentation, and how that space will be determined by the choice of names.... Is it more important for children to be able to join with mainstream culture through conventional language or more important for children's language to reflect their particular realities, and thereby challenge cultural conventions?[8]

Jo and Kathryn would answer that there's no hiding behind names, that no matter how neutral they seem, the truth will out. Jo recalls a train trip with Jordan. They were going to meet "Mommy," Jordan explained to her little playmate, while calling Jo "Mama." Jo caught the flicker of recognition in the eyes of the playmate's mother. For Jo, it was a moment of epiphany. She thought to herself: "Being out is no longer a choice. It's out of my hands."

Whether or not children take the choice out of going public, some parents, even if they flaunted their lifestyle when single, try to recloister. Like Rene and Roger, whose story is coming up, they feel compelled to protect their kids from potential cruelties lurking outside the home. For others, previously more closeted, parenting casts them as reluctant crusaders. For yet others, becoming mom or dad triggers "a deeper courage to move boldly where they would previously have retreated."[9]

RENE,* ROGER,* AND BRIAN*
Ultra-conservatives have really been sticking it to gays and lesbians. Just how much fear they've infused in some people I couldn't have fathomed until I tracked down an old acquaintance, Rene. Last I saw him, he and his life partner, Roger, were bringing a boy named Brian home for weekend respite from his group home. Later, I heard they'd adopted the child. With his kitbag of differences from typical kids, Brian could be the poster boy for children often dubbed "unadoptable" by the system. I found Rene and company snugged into a suburban bungalow near Halifax–Dartmouth. We'd barely hugged "hello" before the urgency around anonymity I'd heard over the phone asserted itself. I reassured him, as I'd done long distance: Don't worry, I'll fudge revealing details.

Why is he shaking in his boots? "There's too much at stake, and it only takes one idiot ... [from] the self-righteous groups ... out there." Rene explains that, because Brian needs an assistive device to communicate, opponents of gay adoptions might target their family as a child-abuse setup. He's heard it all before. Two men parenting a mute boy? Perverts, no doubt. Because Rene and Roger live in the margins of social approval, the media are fascinated. A few of the freak shows—*Geraldo* et al.—have tried to lure them on the air. Though Rene knows public education is a crying need, he shuns publicity. "We're just too vulnerable."

There's the school to worry about. Brian attends a regular class in the Catholic system. Given the Church's cold-blooded attitude toward homosexuals—condemn the sin, love the sinner—Rene prefers to keep his family under wraps. Why draw attention to anything that moral hicks construe as a disability? When interacting with teachers, indeed with anyone outside their trusted circle, Rene presents himself as a single father. Roger poses as Brian's godfather, who, if anyone asks, happens to share housekeeping with father and son. Sounds pretty flimsy, and I can't imagine any Nosy Parker who'd buy it. But Rene and Roger go the distance on camouflage. For Brian's safety, and to keep his small world as open as possible, they feel they must.

Rene is also on pins and needles about jeopardizing benefits he gets as a single parent of a special-needs minor. Money is a major-league worry in this household. "The [social services] ministry already makes us feel like we're welfare cheats and don't deserve what we're getting." So they can't risk anyone sniffing around. Sniffing around? A social worker in this day and age so wigged out over gay adopters of a child few apparently want that s/he'd try to rescind subsidies? It could happen, Rene believes. I don't, but then no one made me run the child-welfare gauntlet to get Brian in the first place.

I'm wondering if Rene's gone a little mid-life paranoid when he begins his social-services saga. By the time he finishes, however, I've abandoned my line of thinking. First, Children's Aid got wind of the rumor. Roger, doing volunteer work as Brian's classroom attendant, had befriended the boy to the point of taking him to his home for weekend visits. Problem was, Brian's new adult friend might be "queer." A worker showed up at Roger and Rene's flat: "If this is a gay relationship," he announced, "we have to be concerned about child abuse." Next, the director called Roger. He didn't mince words: You and Brian are kaput. Our policy says no homosexuals as volunteer, foster, or adoptive parents. "Can you believe it?" Rene asks rhetorically. They were ready to sever Brian's only tie to caring adults, the only unpaid people in his life? No investigation, just butt out.

Rene is a small-framed, soft-spoken, modest man of Ojibwa and French—Métis—heritage, but there's a lot of passion behind his unassuming style. He mobilized an avalanche of protest letters. The upshot? He and Roger were granted an exemption from the policy, but day trips only, no overnights. Meanwhile, Brian was freed for adoption. Rene and Roger, by then irredeemably committed to the child, determined they'd adopt no matter what it took. It took a lot.

A homestudy, conducted by a parade of workers, focused obsessively on their sexual habits. "Will you be 'performing' in front of him?"

questions like that, Rene chafes. He can barely bring himself to revisit the inquisition. The men endured, however, and in the end, with the help of one sympathetic worker, brought Brian home. Here's the kicker, Rene summarizes: The state cries crocodile tears over some hideous fate it concocts for a child, just because we're gay, when the inventors would have back-warded Brian without a second thought. Indeed, the boy was slated for a rural, chronic-care institution (read: deep end of system, no escape) when the guys befriended him.

As Rene, Roger, and I chat over tea in their cozy living room, Brian sits in gray sweats, propped up in his wheelchair. He's seventeen now, seventy-four pounds, with flawless, porcelain skin like a baby's. He wears a Walkman-type gizmo with foam pads near his ears. A signature is inked across one of the discs—Pat Borders, MVP (most valuable player) for the Toronto Blue Jays World Series win. By banging left or right with his head, Brian sets off a voice signal on his communication device: "Yes" or "No." Is he a baseball nut? Much banging to the affirmative side.

Every twenty minutes or so, he coughs convulsively, his frail frame rocking from the attempt to clear his throat. His parents move swiftly and surely through their routine. Roger puts tissues to Brian's mouth to catch the gunk. Rene taps Brian's chest to help him get it out. Brian's head gets dislodged by the effort. Roger gently moves it back. Brian copes with a cafeteria of conditions: cerebral palsy, developmental delays, spastic quadriplegia, cortical blindness. But he is not deaf, totally blind, or stuck in six-months-old mode, as his Children's Aid rapsheet claims.

He does miss oodles of school. Sadly, Brian's health is so fragile Rene may have to quit his job to stay home and care for his son. He can't bear the thought of severing Brian from his school buddies. Like any proud parents, these fathers boast about their child's accomplishments: pals he has drawn to him, pleasure he takes in math class counting money with help from his aide. I watch the two dads fawn over their child, catering to his every need and comfort. Rene notices my misty eyes. He smiles. "See," he says, "this remarkable young man has made us into more responsible, stronger adults."

THE POOR THINGS

Aren't kids who are raised by gender twins, or by a single lesbian or gay male, bound to be mixed-up misfits? Surely adolescence will be intolerable, given what peers will strafe them with? Won't the kids face a heightened risk of sexual abuse from their parents or family friends? Any bets they'll grow up to be homosexual? These questions and fears continue to surround gay families. While few claim dysfunctional outcomes are certain, they contend that the unknowns ought to deter society from allowing gays and lesbians to adopt, especially children with whom they lack any prior connection.

A report on the published and unpublished research from the Child Welfare League of America—hardly a gay-rights mouthpiece—should lay to rest fears that homosexual parents harm or handicap children. As the doom watch likes to highlight, the number and scope of existing studies is limited, even minuscule, on the subject of adoptees in planned gay and lesbian families. Though adolescent and young-adult data do exist, more information abounds about younger children. And most inquiries look at kids raised by divorced lesbian mothers, kids, who as the gay-adoption naysayers would put it, had the advantage of a father during their formative years.

That said, what are the findings? Compared with hetero parents, homosexuals do not compromise children in any discernible fashion. In other words, kids from suspect households accomplish developmental tasks indistinguishably from kids who have mothers and fathers, or a divorced straight mother. Some newer fact-finding, focused on planned lesbian families, including adoptive ones, has so far failed to find any quirks peculiar to their kids. Again, the body of research is small.

All the apparent normalcy probably occurs because craziness doesn't pop up more frequently among gay than among straight parents. A large body of research on adult psychosocial adjustment shows few differences between the two groups. Studies on parental skills, again, turn up no significant contrasts. And despite the media feeding frenzy on the wild side of homosexual lifestyles, gays and lesbians, it seems, are as tame as the rest of us. Surveys have found that 45 to 80 percent of lesbians, and 40 to 70 percent of gay males, are in steady couples at any given time, and that their relationships last as long as straight unions.[10]

According to the few existing studies, the kids demonstrate conventional gender behavior as youngsters and as teens. As adults, they are no more likely to be homosexual than children of straight parents. (And what if they were? Would this be a legitimate reason to curtail human rights?) Most now-adult homosexuals, remember, have straight parents, most of whom we can safely presume would prefer their offspring had turned out like them. According to the research, however, gay and lesbian parents do not expressly prefer that their kids share their sexual direction. Finally, no evidence supports the claim that these parents are unusually prone to molesting their kids. On the contrary, the well-established fact holds: straight and bisexual men perpetrate most sex crimes.

None of this good news nullifies the unique challenges facing the children involved. The biggest obstacle: living in families with nonentity status. With good luck, the cost of legal limbo confines itself to lost economic benefits accessible to other families. With rotten luck, like disabling illness or death of the legal parent, the full impact can turn a family upside down. Worst case—child loses his other parent. Though a rare occurrence nowadays, it can happen.

At other levels, the lack of legitimacy also stings. We all know how adolescence can hypnotize kids into a kind of stupor of conformity, making this passage hideous for the outcasts. Stephan Lynch, who is in his twenties and has a gay dad and lesbian mom, knows all about the schoolyard scourge. Executive director of Children of Lesbians and Gays Everywhere (COLAGE), out of San Francisco, Lynch says youth don't get "messed up" by their parents' sexual identities. But they get grief because "'faggot' is the most prominent and hurtful epithet in the playground; they attend churches where their families are berated from the pulpit; and they turn on the TV and see little or no positive representations of their lives."[11] However, studies have shown that sticks and stones and names don't overly damage, because parents prepare kids and help them handle the attacks. Preparation also shows up in the discretion children use from an early age, especially if they have a gay father.

Still, there's no getting around it. These kids, whether homemade or adopted, live in families pigeonholed as a detested minority by a powerful lobby. Enough preachers, politicians, professionals, and even voxpop plebs would still sooner lock them up than let them adopt children. Living amid currents of fear and hatred, no matter how obviously based in ignorance, has to take its toll.

CATHY AND JENN HALKETT

Going by the "difference equals disaster" school of thought, seventeen-year-old Jenn Halkett should be a head case. She was born in Inuvik,

Northwest Territories, and spent her first twenty-seven days of life on earth detained in detox. Next, she lived at the mercy of a mother lost in a bottle. Jenn's father, a trapper, was mostly absent. Sometimes she was left in the care of her big brother, four years old. After a revolving-door year, neglect-hospital-home, Jenn ended up a state ward "down south," in a Calgary foster home. Her older sister, Dory, was already there.

Why didn't Jenn stay in her community, tucked into another Inuit family? After all, customary adoption, where relatives raise kids from incapacitated families, was and still is the rage in the NWT. Cathy Halkett, Jenn's forty-four-year-old adoptive mother, was told the girl's paternal grandparents chose to get her out of the North, away from its numbing poverty and alcohol.

Cathy, then a college phys-ed instructor in her late twenties, though not fully out, was living with her lover, Barb, when she decided to adopt. Social services met her *chutzpah* with disbelief. But after one intake worker, no liberal—take a hike, lady, he told her; better foster care than an adopter like you—Cathy lucked into a supportive social worker. Supportive, provided that Cathy had no illusions about healthy newborns. No, she didn't. She knew they go to "proper" families.

Enter Jenn. For Cathy, it was love at first visit with the little eighteen-pound, two-year-old, suffering from fetal alcohol effect (FAE). Growing up, Jenn had a lot to face. Geographical and cultural displacement. Lost connections to her original family, except for Dory. A litany of debilitating medical problems, including a correctable hearing impairment brought on by the booze. "She spent her first five years like she was in a swimming pool, underwater," Cathy explains. Doctors, who automatically equated "Native" with "underachiever," wrote off Jenn's muffled speech. It took four years of racism before the child was finally diagnosed and treated.

Jenn had yet more to grapple with. Barb's death, from leukemia. "She was one of the best persons I've ever known, besides you," Jenn says tearfully to her mom as Cathy tells me the story of her lover's decline. Then there was her mother's sexuality to absorb, and not just lesbianism. After Barb died, Cathy married and gave birth to a daughter, now eight. Why marriage? "Last attempt maybe to gain some sort of approval [from my parents by doing] . . . what a girl's supposed to do. . . . [It seems] stupid now, but it wasn't then." Cathy laughs.

Jenn looks thirteen, tops, thanks to FAE, which stunts growth.

Because of her fine features, she is often mistaken as Southeast Asian. Cathy certainly isn't; she's a tall, heavy blonde. These two could not look less like DNA sharers. More for Jenn to handle. Yet, she is thriving. Passionate about horses, busy with friends and pursuits, she made the grade 11 honor roll at school and respects the honor system at home. Yes, she has issues, right out of an adoption textbook. Occasional twinges of not feeling a fit with her family. Jealousy over her sister's blood bond with Mom. Curiosity about her birth culture and family, though tinged with worry that birthrelatives might somehow whisk her away from Cathy. Jenn, who clearly adores her mom, was candid about her comfort with her mother's sexual persona. For all her differences, for all the digressions of Jenn's family from the neighbors', she seems more grounded than many peers in the family type still perched on society's pedestal.

JUST ANOTHER NORMAL WAY TO BE

The option of plunging into parenthood impulsively will not, as it does for most people, come overnight for gays and lesbians. But society is in striking distance of laws and social policies that will reflect and protect the plurality of real families. "Good Christian hatred," as one contributor put it, may not loosen its grip in a hurry, but it will lose its punch. Looking through the eyes of defiant families, creating new templates for intimate attachment, it's easy to believe in progress even in these days of living dangerously. In the contest between the myopic morality of yore and the broad human-rights vista of today, homosexuals and their sympathizers have little doubt about the ultimate victor. They take Tammy Duffey's view: "You have certain rights because you are here, not because of what color you are, who you worship, or who you sleep with."

I found myself among people who believe in their power as social transformers. Parents talk up their domestic lives as a locus for revitalized citizenship. Family life as a school for learning to celebrate diversity, not as something "out there," but as something in which you have a stake. Households like theirs, say Jo and Kathryn, by their very existence teach children that "normal" has many newly minted meanings, and hurrah for that.

As for jeers, yes, parents acknowledge their kids may be subjected to a few. But "the amazing thing I've found," says Kathryn, "is that I'm expecting people ... to react in a way that's really negative because of all the right-wing stuff going on. But the reality for our lives is that when we touch [other people] we get a very positive response.... If you're out there creating a positive atmosphere, you get it back."

Families all say the nicest feedback is none at all. They take heart from the small transactions of daily life between them and others, who are clued in to their family format, but who "forget." Jo delights in recalling the time their accountant, who has the picture, advised her and Kathryn to file their tax return jointly for the best benefits. "Then he remembered we can't.... It's really nice when things like that happen."

I think back to my interview with Gale Allen and Gil Cowan. It was winding down none too soon because their kids, Douglas and Trent, had traded sweet and patient curiosity with a stranger and her mini-corder for behavior designed to drive an intruder out. It was bath and story time, and they weren't about to get shortchanged. Gale read my mind: "Were you to ask, 'What's different about this family from the one next door? What's the same?' you'd have a very long list for 'same,' and very short for 'different.' ... Every night after work: dinner, fighting, arguing, kissing, loving, hugging, bath time, more fighting, stories, dirty diapers, laundry." As I beetled out, catching glimpses of bedtime bliss and bedlam, I wondered how observers of this scene could see anything but another normal way to be.

FIVE

Flying Solo: The Single Parent

There is still the belief that single people should adopt only the children no one else wants: the oldest, the most difficult to deal with. But that is wrong. Who will be the best parent should be the basis of the decision.

—*Elmy Martinez, who adopted five older boys*

This is a good news/bad news chapter. First, the heartening stuff. Single women, provided they're university graduates and attracted to the opposite sex, have inched their way up the ladder of acceptable adopters. Women have come a long way since the 1970s, when a young professional stoked up her courage to ask a Toronto Children's Aid office for a healthy newborn. They made her feel she "had some nerve, turning up here without a husband and asking for the same thing as everybody else."[1] Today, by comparison, few North American agencies would blink about her missing mate. On the contrary, some would welcome her with open arms, so long as she'd ditch all hopes for a baby and switch to an older child.

The discouraging dispatch: single men are barely out of the blocks. Though more and more of them are taking a shine to solo parenting, the prospect makes the system squirm. There's an entrenched belief that guys can't meet children's emotional or practical needs. But the heebie-jeebies go deeper: any male planning to go alone into parenting must be gay, and therefore, *ipso facto*, a molester.[2] Of course, not all adoption arrangers think like this, and of course, some men, including a few of those you'll meet in coming pages, were treated civilly. It's no accident, however, that almost all the children came to them through private and specialty, not public, agencies, which, on this front, remain a bastion of conservatism.

Keep in mind while reading this chapter that the adoption world runs on an unadmitted pecking order. All children needing homes and all families wanting to provide one are not equal, as this book argues they should be. Certainly single women—and overachievers, in particular—have, in theory, made giant steps, though smaller ones in practice. How do we know words have improved more than deeds? Because, unless they have inordinate amounts of money and time, singles almost never access the most sought-after babies.

Nonetheless, in adoption overall, "single parent" has a better ring than ever before—certainly better than in the world beyond adoption—but it's still toting plenty of cultural baggage. It's hard to shake off everything that sticks to the lone-parent image: a barely literate girl, scraping by, raising ragamuffins destined to rear another wave of welfare waifs while still babies themselves. Solo parenting also brings to mind the legions of women dispossessed by separation and divorce. Often depicted as doing their darnedest, despite deadbeat dads and puny earnings, to raise their kids right, they nonetheless get blamed for turning out latchkey demons: dropouts, dopers, and delinquents. At its most benign, the image of an only parent suggests a career woman with lots of disposable income but no time for her kids.

Single adoptive parent, though a less-familiar image, is nonetheless a definite picture: a woman past her prime, successful in her profession, but disappointed in her personal life, seeks baby to find meaning.

Were a roving reporter to ask the man on the street "What kind of single person would adopt?" any bets how he'd answer? Would he say "lonely schoolmarms," "psychos and saints," or "regular blokes, like me"? What are the chances Joe Blow might think of a hip thirty-three-year-old Italian accountant who bustled over to Guatemala to build his family; an eligible African-American male who, at forty-five, traded in a white-collar job for five older boys riddled with psychoemotional scars; a woman in her twenties, just launching her career, who poured her income and energy into cobbling together an international family of kids who have heavy-duty challenges?

In response to the idea of single-parenting itself, never mind getting there through adoption, the reporter would likely evoke more shudders than cheers. Everyone knows, after all, that the very existence of one-header households only goes to show how far the family has decayed. Why such pessimism? How come so many of us know that kids raised by single mothers have more emotional and behavior problems than peers in two-parent situations, whether or not families are poor? Yet how come so few know that boys who grow up with a mother alone are much more likely than men raised by mom and dad to establish good and lasting relationships with women?[3]

Why don't happy throngs of sole-support families crowd into the mind's eye? Because belief in family as holy trinity, though out of sync with reality, is still the gospel. Hence, it isn't on the tip of the tongue to say that single-parent households might be more of a breakthrough than a breakdown for some people; that this domestic setup might be exactly what the doctor should order for a whole slew of unattached adults and children craving one solid attachment.

To this day, a home lacking any element of the trinity—and especially dad—still rates as a pretend version of the desirable product. Because they've done such a formidable job for so long, African-American women command more respect as solo family heads than do their sisters from other backgrounds. But even with 63 percent of black homes in the United States anchored by one adult, mostly women, even their families get short shrift for having missing parts.[4]

Sexism, which helps stir up nostalgia for the male-breadwinner family, inflates the bad-news billing. But so does poverty, which female-steered households endure disproportionately. Family-valuists have created the myth that women who try to manage without men are a pox on their kids, the poor little screw-ups. The myth leaves little room for the facts: two-parent homes aren't always havens of mental health for the coming generation, while one-parent replicas sometimes are. Besides, it's not normally mom who messes up Johnny's life—if it goes off the rails—but the debilitating cultural and economic forces stacked against them both. With most women consigned to low-wage ghettoes and exhausted from work, little wonder they plod uphill to mind and guide their daughters and sons. The problem is, single moms and their sometimes off-track kids get a bum rap, while the forces that derail them get off scot-free.

In a climate hostile to one-parent families and in an economy that makes most uncoupled women lifetime members of the poverty club, it's amazing that some choose single-parenthood. But these days they do, and in increasing numbers. Remember, however, that the Grand Canyon divides those who fall by circumstance into a slot they wouldn't choose, and adults who, without a mate, strive for years to bring dependent children into their lives. Accidental single parents may make the best of what they consider a bad situation, maybe even grow to prefer it over the gossamer ideal. But deliberate single parents, like the adoptive ones you meet here, generally want kids more than they want an adult companion—if they want a partner at all. They don't buy into what "comes naturally" in the culture: love, marriage, baby carriage.

Though you'd guess from the vilification that mother–child families must have been invented *circa* 1990, in fact they're ancient. They dominated prehistory and matriarchal societies, and accompanied patriarchy from the beginning. While ever there, their presence ebbs and flows. In Canada, they now comprise about 16 percent of the population; in the United States, about 25 percent of white families. Indeed, more than half the children born these days in both countries will, sometime before they hit eighteen, live with a sole parent, likely mom, though perhaps dad, since he leads one in thirty-five American families.[5]

But single-parenthood tells a different story in this generation than it did in the previous one. No longer is it only about lack of access to birth control and abortion, or abandonment and widowhood. Now, separation and divorce spike the rate. Young motherhood, especially, drives up the numbers.

The most startling new factor? Freely exercised choice. Women mostly, but growing numbers of men, either consciously or circumstantially bypass long-term coupledom and go directly to parenthood. Pairing and parenting, they contend, can be done in tandem or can be mutually exclusive. While some turn to mother nature, with or without help from test tubes, to get a baby, others opt for adopting. Not that many in Canada though. In the 1980s, married couples still accounted for all but 2 percent of applicants who approached adoption agencies.[6] In the United States, however, even ten years ago, half as many singles as couples—1 million versus 2 million—sought to adopt.[7]

Who are these brave—some would say foolhardy—souls? The Committee for Single Adoptive Parents, based in Maryland, tracked their members for a decade to find out. Most are between thirty-five and forty, college grads, primarily from the helping professions. There's no reason to believe the Canadian profile differs. Adopters who share their stories here are true to form, but some come from newer constituencies as well: people past forty, for instance, and fost/adopters, as well as working- and welfare-poor women.

The gladdest tidings about single adopters: they bring home an estimated 25 percent of special-needs children who get placed.[8] Though some go looking for the neediest kids, most don't. The system, however, which still dotes on the mom-and-dad duo, tends to reserve kids who've been kicked around longest and hardest for least-preferred comers, including singles. Luckily, many leap at the chance to raise a child different from the one they'd imagined when they began searching.

Here's what the studies show: lone adults, more than couples, adopt teenagers. Sixty-nine percent of singles compared with 31 percent of pairs adopt nonwhite children, and 16 against 9 percent embrace youngsters with mental delays. The racial discrepancy reflects the fact that more than half of single adoptive mothers in the United States are black, while about a third of adoptive fathers are as well.[9] Though research is contradictory on this point, apparently single adopters, and particularly males, prefer children of their same gender. This "preference," however, may reflect agency antipathy to matching girls with lone guys.

Deciding to parent without a partner is daunting enough without added disincentives, like a system determined to dodge you. Most parents I met ran an obstacle course in the inhospitable world of adoption agencies and in their personal worlds peopled with doubters and discouragers. The Committee for Single Adoptive Parents has found that their members do indeed get more aggravation, even from family and friends, than would-be adoptive couples do when they announce their plans.

Singles also go through quite a process within the privacy of their own hearts. David Aiello, for example, the Toronto accountant of Italian descent, always pictured himself married with children. Still does. But when Ms. Right didn't show up after a "series of two- or three-year things, and a couple of one-year things," by the time he was in his late twenties David felt he was missing out on parenting.

It's a sign of the times that adopting even crossed his mind. Men in noticeable numbers have only recently found the moxie to imagine they're up to parenting alone and liking it. Personal experience with joint or sole custody, or with watching other males manage, now emboldens guys like David. Possibility is in the air, partly a payoff from the feminist ferment that has been pushing men to pick up their share of domestic work.

When, to his buddies, David broached the subject of adopting, they said things like "You think you're going to attract all these women and it's all going to be so fun," and "Oh, Dave, you're fine. You just broke up with this girl," intimating that he'd build a family the normal way, as if normal has only one way. He didn't drop any hints to his family because "they would have definitely thought I was crazy." After his next romance, a "nine-month thing," ended, he decided "That's it." He was ready to adopt. He knew enough to steer clear of the standard channels, and instead worked through lawyers.

Unlike David, Pam Soden was no pup when she got the parenting bug. She was forty, post-hysterectomy, and long past knowing "that having biological children was not something critical to me." Every inch the high-powered—and slightly intimidating—big-city business-management trainer she is, Pam took it one step at a time. Collect information from the New York Council on Adoptable Children (COAC). Assess it. Attend orientation sessions. Interview the interviewers. Five years later, she called COAC back. "Okay, I'm ready."

Whereas a single nonparent of menopausal age and not of color can pretty much predict a runaround from the public system, Pam had a better chance of being treated, comparatively speaking, like royalty. Because she's black and a good earner, because mature African-American women are famous as family heads, and because so many minority kids are aching for homes, she had a few things in her favor. Her biggest selling point: she definitely *did not* want a newborn, which most searchers prefer. Pam wanted to skip diapers and daycare and go straight to school, which she was able to do with six-year-old Monique, whose mother had died and who'd been in foster homes for over two years.

Pat O'Brien, who runs You Gotta Believe! The Older Child Adoption and Permanency Movement, from Coney Island, wouldn't be surprised to hear that Pam and Monique are going strong. Yet, he's downright gloomy about single professionals as adopters for waiting children, who are, by definition, troubled. Gloomy, that is, if adopters are white, have never been married, and have never parented. O'Brien's cynicism comes from experience working in an agency where not one of twenty-four such placements in progress went through. However, change even one factor (Pam, remember, is black), and O'Brien says the prognosis jumps from grim to great. His theory about why?

If you put very privileged adults, especially those who've never been in the trenches of parenthood, together with very underprivileged kids, their planets prove to be too far apart. O'Brien found the would-be adopters' heads were up in the clouds, their expectations for their adoptees too high. From what he's seen, people who've had a lot of hard knocks—racial victimization, for example—and who've survived the rigors of long-term relationships and/or parenting, more likely make it with kids who've not had fairytale lives.

While it's refreshing to meet a child-placer who doesn't idealize white yuppies in a world that slavers over them, you can't safely extrapolate from O'Brien's experience. Indeed, Phyllis Rogers would probably think O'Brien is full of malarkey. Phyllis is the kind of adopter O'Brien would doubt: a young white professional, always single, and never a parent until she adopted.

She wasn't yet thirty when she became determined to adopt a deaf child. While other coeds were getting their MRSs along with their BAs, Phyllis, who claims she has a one-track mind, was pursuing "acculturation in the deaf community," not an easy task. Getting a Masters in deaf-ed from Gallaudet in Washington, DC, left little time for socializing, and, besides, marriage was a maybe "if things sort of fell in that direction," while having children was a must. She was twenty-five when one of her housemates, who worked for an adoption referral service, threw some interpreting gigs her way. Before long, Phyllis started on her costly seven-year slog to bringing home the first of her three children, one of them paraplegic, two of them deaf. When I met her, she was packing for China, hoping to adopt one and possibly two deaf girls.

HOMES OF LAST RESORT

Single professional women were the pioneers of nontraditional adopters. In the 1970s, when the trend started, the system rebuffed most newcomers, either rejecting them outright or wearing them down until they gave up. Females on their own were regarded as a last resort for supposedly least-placeable children. Unmarried women have since risen in the hierarchy; the system has relaxed considerably about placing waiting children with them. But, as the single adopters' committee laments, it's still "almost unheard-of" for their members to adopt healthy infants.

"Almost" is an important word here. In all adoptions, irrespective of family form, income is the basic breach between two groups of wannabes: haves and have-nots. If money is no obstacle, singles can sometimes buy their way around misgivings about their suitability as parents for babies just born. In the preceding chapter, you even met homosexuals, the most disfavored of all adopters, who managed to find healthy newborns, the most preferred of all adoptees. So, it is possible.

Affluence will do it some of the time, so long as the seeker doesn't expect fast delivery. Take David Aiello's case. A professional who owns a suburban dream house—compared with most working stiffs, he's obviously not hurting for money. Yet, it took about a year and a half from the time David first met the eighteen-month-old in Guatemala he wanted to adopt until he was able to bring the boy home. The delay had nothing to do with David's marital status or gender; it had to do with the labyrinthine mechanics and snail's pace of many international adoptions.

Lest anyone imagine that even domestic "hard-to-place" kids come easily to singles, Elmy Martinez will disabuse you of the notion. Single adoptive father to one Cambodian war orphan and four Latino foster-care veterans, Elmy founded the Adoption Resource Exchange for Single Parents (ARESP) in Springfield, Virginia, where he lives with his sons. An advocate for waiting kids and those, especially single men, in pursuit of them, Elmy knows the score. If adopting is easy, he says, it's a fluke.

Though Elmy had a relatively painless journey to completing his family, the infuriating prejudices that still greet many solo applicants did affect him. He recalls one older child he wanted. The system said "No," this one needs two parents. Eventually, the boy got two parents, who abused him. The adoption disintegrated. The child cycled back into care. Elmy tried a second time. Again, "No." Why not, especially after the failed family? Because you're male and single. Will the system ever get it? Elmy asks in anger. Will it ever grasp this one simple principle: The best family is the one that wants the child?

Among common themes emerging from the diverse contributors throughout this book, none stands out more than the biases faced on agency row. It's baffling, actually. You'd figure adoption fixers would feel relieved to see anyone coming forward. So what if they're solo applicants? Who cares? Half the kids out there live with parents like them anyway, or with some other modern variant. You'd expect that the workers, mostly mothers themselves, would think "Great." Instead, up go the barriers.

It's the kind of response that makes Claudette LaMelle bristle. She's in a unique position to know what's going on. A social worker herself, she teaches a social-welfare policy class at NYU (New York University) as well as having an executive-level day job in juvenile justice. Then she goes home to Evan, her five-year-old, who'd already been shuffled through three foster homes by the time she got him, not yet a year old. Claudette was forty then and waving the daughter she'd raised alone—like so many of her African-American sisters—off to college. Now, she's flying solo again. And finding time to run a small private practice homestudying foster and adoptive hopefuls.

Just hearing about her whirlwind days makes me dizzy. How she manages to juggle so many balls and be so coolly glamorous at the same time beats me. Tall and svelte, with caramel skin and fine features, she's impeccably dressed in a fashionably subdued business suit, looking like an ad for designer something-or-other.

Irritation cancels her cool when I ask how the system treats singles. "You have to muster up so much strength to get the kid you want.... There are so many contradictory things going on. They behave as if they were doing you a favor by letting you adopt. They don't listen to the profile of the child you want. They try to railroad you into accepting the child they happen to want to place that week."

Whoa. "Wait a minute," I say. "You call yourself an advocate for waiting kids. Shouldn't workers at least feel you out about accepting a wingier kid than the one you came in the door wanting? Aren't they doing a good job if they at least try?"

Yes, they should push harder for the hard cases, Claudette agrees, but without a this-child-or-no-child attitude, which least-welcome applicants often hear. Placers, she says, should bend over backwards not only to entice every reasonable comer to walk in the door and to leave with an older child, but also with a match that won't backfire.

Mary and Cookie Backodi, thirty-nine- and fifty-two-year-old sisters living in Pittsburgh, know how tough it can be to get even the most challenging child if you aren't on the unofficial "A" list. Mary, the legal parent, by happenstance found Project Star, an agency that does bend over backwards to bring not-your-usual-adopters and not-your-typical-kids together. Rather than discouraging Mary, a single woman with health and weight problems, working a low-wage job and sharing a house with her middle-aged sibling, when she rang up, staff latched onto her. In an eight-week course, designed to prepare families to parent kids with horrid histories, Mary got the straight goods on what kind of youngster to expect. No problem. She and Cookie, slated to play a major parenting role, were open to a child who'd bring a thorny past. Yet, Cookie complains, their home was always last on the block for kids whose trial visits broke down with two-parent prospects.

"That's not right," Cookie emphasizes. "Nowadays a lot of single mothers are raising kids. It's not against the fathers or anything. But a lot of kids are happy with just their mothers." After a series of lost leads, Mary adopted Amy. The child had been a battering ram for her birth- and foster-parents and came with more labels than the Campbell's Soup company. Although Amy does have more than her share of developmental and medical miseries, most were overblown.

If unmarried, working-class females like Mary angling to adopt still turn some child-placers off, nothing leaves them colder than single males with the same agenda. A 1985 survey of successful and prospective adopters tells the story. The men reported that agencies were jittery about accepting them even for kids no one else seemed to want. Elmy Martinez shakes his head in frustration and disgust. He hears regularly from men who get halted by the tired old assumptions. His most recent caller? A heterosexual with a signed homestudy in hand contacted an agency. Their first question to him: "Are you gay?"

JESSE WILLIAMS AND SONS

Memorial Day. Jesse Williams's house in the Woodbridge historical area, a district on the comeback near downtown Detroit, is jumping. Jesse's five sons, three of them age fifteen, plus a nine- and a seventeen-year-old, cavort with girlfriends and assorted visitors. The younger set congregates in a jerry-built clubhouse out back, surrounded by a large, lush yard—no crabgrass here—and a gorgeous garden of flowers, Jesse's labor of love. The older guys hustle the girls to a basement rec room, away from Dad's eagle eyes. The boys surface only to get several helpings of lunch, their plates piled with goodies Jesse cooked in his cramped kitchen: barbecue chicken and ribs, homemade sauce, collard greens, cornbread, and salads. Not to mention several desserts.

Keeping the crowd, which also includes neighbors and friends, fed and happy, while keeping the chaos and kitchen clutter down, would daunt your average host. Not Jesse. Unfazed, he exerts a quiet but precise control over the proceedings. He prepared the food in advance, everything's ready, he's got a cousin helping out in the kitchen, the boys know their chores and how to behave for company—what's to fret about?

His grace amid the flurry was no surprise. I knew from the minute Jesse greeted me at his door that this was one very in-charge guy. He even looks the part. Tall, lean, and, as they say, well preserved for his fifty years, with a freckled face that adds youth, his straight-backed but affable style is right there. Watching him orchestrate the people and the flow of the day's events will reveal more clues about how Jesse manages his clan, not an easy lot to fit into a family container.

Jesse adopted the boys, two sets of brothers plus one, when they were between the ages of seven and twelve. Over the years, he has also fostered others. All came with unspeakable memories of birth-families, like a father who shook a baby sister so violently she died and a heroin-addicted mother who murdered her infant twins. His sons also brought everlasting pain from abuse the child-protection system heaped on them. Two boys, for example, will have lifelong scars from psychic wounds accumulated in fourteen foster homes before age six!

What made Jesse think he could handle so many boys and their boodle of heartaches? Starting out, he was a bit cocky, he admits. "I was always criticizing how kids were being raised and I thought I could do better." He chose boys because he feels that, when women raise them alone, they don't get the "right imprint." Jesse was forty-five when he got the urge to put his life where his mouth had long been. He'd just taken early retirement from his job as an accountant for Ford to nurse his ailing mother. There was lots of room in their three-story, five-bedroom brick semi, all hardwood floors and wainscoting, lovingly restored by Jesse.

And there was room in his heart for a family. After a long relationship ended, he found himself aging and not where he wanted to be: married and with children. No thoughts of adopting, he became a foster parent, first to one set of siblings, then another. They were hurt kids. It was hard work. Even basics like getting them to eat decent food was a battle because they'd grown up at Burger King. But he liked the challenge and discovered he wasn't half-bad at helping them turn things around.

Before long, he couldn't bear the thought of the boys scattering into group homes. At the same time, "they would sometimes get really wild" and he'd question his ability to parent them. But if he couldn't, who could? Who would? With encouragement from specialty agencies, he adopted all four, and later his youngest son. There was one fosteree, however, to whom Jesse said "No" when the child pleaded to join the family. This boy's mother, a prostitute, had nine children by as many different men. The home and the kids were disasters. The boy Jesse fostered had raped one of his sisters before he was ten. "He set this house in an uproar, and I just couldn't keep him." Jesse felt the hell-raiser needed the focus of a one-child household, not competition with a bunch of brothers. There's hope for every kid, even seeming "incorrigibles," Jesse stresses, but the match must be right.

The research backs up what Jesse is saying. It's worth quoting Barbara Tremitiere at length here. She's the head of a large, mostly adoptive household and a ground-breaking adoption agency.

> Agencies may well look to place certain children, deliberately, into large family systems. Deprived children who need socialization, structure, and cultural enrichment could do well here. Many handicapped children thrive in such consistently stimulating family settings. Sibling groups seem to fit in, with preparation and supports. Children with attachment problems usually find this to be a comfortable, non-pressure situation where they can take their time learning to trust and relate to parent figures. *Emotionally handicapped children with severe behavioral problems, however, need to be considered carefully, as some difficult behaviors can have a contagious effect on the other children in the family.* Also, a combination of severely physically challenged children and emotionally disturbed children ... tends to be very problematic (my emphasis).[10]

Back to the Williams clan ... Jesse didn't mean to suggest his sons aren't capable of an occasional uproar. It comes with the territory. At first, for example, some of them routinely stole what they wanted. He cracked down, even embarrassing one boy by forcing him to return baseball cards he'd lifted. Jesse, whose former military training meets his conservative Christianity in his parenting style, runs a bit of a tough-love bootcamp. Some say that older kids who've known neither love nor limits thrive when lavished with both. If that's true, the boys have found the right family: love aplenty and more limits than most teenagers could accept. No rap music because it represents "black demoralization." "No earrings unless you wear a dress." No condoms, at least not from Jesse, who won't be party to "promoting promiscuity." No drugs. The cousin in the kitchen tells me Jesse springs surprise tests on the guys to ensure they're drug-free.

"I'm glad you're not my father; no Dr. Spock in this house," I rib Jesse. Luckily, he has a sense of humor about his rigidity, and laughs up a storm before barking orders over the kitchen intercom. I'm waiting to see what action he'll get. In a flash, the guys hop to it. Do they jump from fear or from respect? Jesse claims the latter. How can he tell? Because the boys turn to him for help, and openly share their problems. I could be wrong, but I, too, sense they comply more from respect, though a dose of scared mixes in.

As a visitor on a busy holiday, it's hard for me to take any soundings from the younger crowd. At one point, we do sit around the dining-room table and gab. Light chatter till I mention foster homes, which makes them giddy. Terrible terrain they can approach only with jokes. There's no time, and the circumstances are wrong for individual characters to make an impression. I don't get much beyond the visuals: guys buried in fashionably baggy clothes, awkward in their skins, and edgy to be somewhere else.

Jesse tells me about some of the baggage they're sorting through. One son has ADHD (attention-deficit hyperactivity disorder), initials that roll easily off the tongue of many parents who adopt older kids. Jesse's son is sometimes off the wall. He can't sit still or concentrate, which affects the climate at home and in the classroom. His behavior got so hinky at one point that six months in residential treatment was in order. But Jesse describes this son, in counseling from age four, as "therapy-proof."

The family as a whole, however, profits from sporadic therapy sessions. Jesse's afraid I'll get the wrong impression if we focus on what needs fixing. Mostly, he reminds me, his family is a success story, proof that one committed adult can profoundly alter older children's lives no matter what chilling experiences came before. That four out of five kids with his brood's histories now do well in school hints at the healing power of love and discipline. "I spend 90 percent of my time in the schools. That helps," Jesse says, exaggerating only a little.

Is this gang as good as it looks? Are the young men as well on their way to rounding the corner, as their dad claims? I have no idea. But it would be hard even for a skeptic not to walk away from Jesse's door brimming with optimism. And whatever setbacks might befall this family, one thing I do know for sure: without Jesse or someone like him, these guys, as far as having a good life goes, would have been toast.

Pros and Cons

What makes singles suitable adopters for the most-upset youngsters? First, their extraordinary commitment to parenting. Anyone who gets through the assessment screen—more like a wall—probably possesses the superior stick-to-it-iveness they'll need. Don't forget; they'll probably take home a trauma victim. Second, without the demands and distractions of the parent–parent jig, singles can fixate on the parent–child bond. Third, kids who survive the loss of original family, the cruelties of the system, and God knows what birth defects and disadvantages, usually come from unthinkably cluttered and chaotic backgrounds. One-on-one simplicity can be just the savior they need.

Linda Miles, forty-one, has seen what the intense focus of "becoming everything for each other" can do for an emotionally lacerated child. To see seven-year-old Wendy now, sweet as they come, self-possessed, outgoing, showing off her stuffed-animal menagerie, and trying to wrangle a late bedtime out of my visit, you can't imagine the child Linda describes. When Wendy first came as a foster child, however, she was so petrified that she was "buried in her own body." Not surprising, Linda says, after spending the first half of her life in a string of foster homes, which were indifferent at best—"no one had loved her, hugged her"—and abusive at worst. Even before Wendy confided the horrors, Linda knew the girl had suffered the lash. "When she'd do something wrong, she'd go into a corner and stand with her face to the wall" while pretzeling her body into a self-protective stance.

To help Wendy compensate for her nightmarish beginnings, Linda gave up everything and devoted herself to the child for six months. Mom number three for Wendy, Linda knew she had to do something to show the girl she was different from others, who'd abused and left her. She knew she couldn't amble off to work every day, leaving Wendy to wonder if this mom would come back that night. Staying home sounds like the right move to help Wendy stabilize and attach, except that Linda doesn't live on easy street in the world of paid sabbaticals. She didn't leave a plum job, a plush office, and a padded pay packet for the comfort of home. Nevertheless, she took leave, without pay, from her job as a patients' advocate at Harlem Hospital to hole up with Wendy in her one-bedroom, third-floor flat—no elevator—in a decaying co-op in the Bronx. They survived on savings and Wendy's small special-needs adoption subsidy.

I say "hole up" because Linda, who is African American, lives on a street where it's too risky for Wendy to play hopscotch even at noon. Occasionally, in the blistering summer heat, Linda lets the child join the other kids, but only for an hour, and only on a short stretch of sidewalk opposite their building. It has to be the other side of the street, Linda explains, so she can supervise from a window. Wendy knows the rules. Keep within your boundaries. Stay outside; don't enter your playmates' apartment buildings, because you can't be sure it's safe. Hearing the odd gunshot and witnessing frequent drug deals is standard for her neighborhood.

I'd spent only one hour roaming in the Fordham Road area, near Linda's place, before I saw two such exchanges myself. I'd stopped for supper at a fast-food joint and sat at a booth with an unobstructed view of the street. Within a space of ten minutes, two twitchy, glazed-looking young women openly handed cash through a car window—two different cars—and carried away small parcels. The rest of what I saw in my walking tour was exactly what you'd predict in America's poorest congressional district: almost no anglo faces or green spaces, an endless parade of girls pushing prams, lots of beggars and homeless mumblers *schlepping* their worldly goods in shopping carts, spent-looking women bent by the weight of plastic shopping bags, aggressive street hawkers pushing glitzy junk, and all of this against a background of graffiti galore, garbage, neon, and noise.

How do you protect whatever innocence Wendy has left? I ask Linda. Physical security comes first. That's why Linda is so strict about such an ordinary childhood routine as playing outdoors. Here, "ordinary" is not what most readers visualize. But there's also psychic protection. In the midst of their reality, Linda struggles to cocoon Wendy a while longer by telling her as little as possible about the world outside their door. Linda's dream? To move someplace where Wendy could have a room of her own and play freely and safely outside.

Even after four years, Linda still has layers of damage to help her child unpeel. But this mom wasn't up against one sophistication many mistreated children like Wendy bring: manipulation. You might not think a preschooler could be so messed up or so clever that s/he could pit two parents against each other. In fact, kids who've been yanked around by the twins of child abuse—fractured families and failed child-protection services—can be little experts. As Pat O'Brien says, "Playing adults off each other is a sport in which [system kids] have PhDs." Here's where having a sole parent can help. One disciplinarian can assert a more consistent message in place of the split decisions or mixed strategies kids can mine from a couple.

O'Brien raves about parents like Linda who are on intimate terms with hardship and who have an old-timer's intuition about what their kids need. But even singles who've had a cushier life, yet adopt kids with tougher histories, quickly understand the value of an only parent from their children's perspective. "They don't have to deal with adult battles that go on in a two-parent home," says Phyllis Rogers, "and that is a good thing, I think, for children."

Another potential plus in one-parent homes has to do with gender. Take the case of a little girl who has had horrendous experiences with men; say, her father raped her. She may fear and loathe males. Yet, she could thrive in the care of a single female. Another boy or girl, who has lived at the mercy of a cold, strict foster mother, might more readily glom onto a caring male. A wild teenager, used to running roughshod over female authority figures, may rein in more for a male.

The point? Solo parents are tailor-made for particular kids. Admittedly, the benefits of having only one parent can come at a price. The girl, for example, who distrusts men may never learn they're not all facsimiles of her father. She may be left with mistaken ideas about men and adult relationships—explosives to carry into whatever family she may create.

You Can't Do It Alone

This brings us to the unique challenges of parenting solo, such as how to create conditions for a positive, significant adult male in the girl's life. Single adopters, as it happens, tend to be very savvy when it comes to the opposite-sex, role-modeling department. It just makes common sense, they say, to compensate for the absence of a woman or a man in the home. But in many cases, the wisdom goes deeper. It goes to the unique needs of each individual child, and to the parents' measure, as they get to know their adoptee, of how best to make up for deficits.

For example, when Elmy Martinez brought home brothers Luis and Juan, who'd grown up, hard, in government hands in the East Bronx, Elmy was relieved to be prying them from the system's clutches. The boys were as eager to shake free. Everyone was looking ahead, not back. Elmy, who took it for granted that godmothers would bring needed balance to their all-male household, found among his circle women who wanted the role.

But as time wore on, Luis and Juan shared memories of important people they'd left behind, especially their first foster mother. Once Elmy realized the brothers were already attached to a female mentor, he worked to bring the woman back into their lives. Now she and the boys stay in touch, and get together occasionally in New York.

Not all kids come with kinlike ties or affection for past parents or guardians. So their new parents try to craft those connections for them. Maybe something as formal as godparents, or perhaps less structured but carefully maintained. Like the male friends Claudette LaMelle depends on for stereotypical male roughhouse she feels is important, to do "Kung-Fu, wrestly kind of stuff," with Evan and to "check that he's not in a dress."

Role-modeling is only a piece of the single-parenting puzzle. More critical: creating a support system. You hear the sigh of relief when single parents name the cherished few who pitch in to supply moral support. And kid-sitting. Jesse Williams, for example, knows he can't do it alone. That's why he has strung a safety net around his family. For him, a counselor he reaches out to as the need arises, at Spaulding for Children, specialists in placing African-American boys. For the boys, an involved godmother, plus Jesse's own extended family nearby, and neighbors who keep an eye. For a couple of the kids, connections with biological relations and nurturers from the past. Jesse also has a "friend" who's crazy about his gang, "but she's Buddhist," meaning not the Christian influence he'd prefer.

The biggest believers in bracing the family with hands-on helpers—strong shoulders available for an occasional good cry—are parents like

Jesse and Elmy. The ones whose badly banged-around kids prove, at times, to be loose canons. If you've got a child—how about several—reeling with rage, then resources, both from within your personal network and from professional services outside, can become lifesavers. We're talking, Elmy says, about kids like one of his: "angry with parents that abused him and abandoned him and died too early for him. All that anger goes onto the person who symbolizes them"—meaning the new parent. If dredging up and resolving buried torment is no party for two parents, it can be perdition for one.

Even if a child isn't dealing with outsize demons, a single parent needs a reliable cushion, where couples more likely rely on each other. Nearby family members, obvious candidates at first glance, sometimes do come through with flying colors. They certainly have for David Aiello. Indeed, his sprawling family has been his locus of support all along. His mother baby-sits a night a week, and other relatives give Dad the breaks he needs, whether to house-clean or to recharge.

The family portrait grouped around single adopter and child, however, is not always this pretty. Or, even if it glows, it's not always a potent factor in adoptive-family success. Curiously, the single adoptive parents' committee has discovered that extended family, whether they live in the same community or far away but visit often, doesn't much influence the prognosis. What does? Having a "core of positively responding intimates," whether kin or kindred spirits, or a mixture of both.

Close relatives don't always prove to be ideal members of the supporting cast. Some lone parents, such as those who poured out their tribulations in the book *In Praise of Single Parents*, complain that their own parents never accept that they've chosen single-parenthood. Others find their folks or siblings too steeped in stale notions about adoption, notions no parent wants whispered around the children. Yet others discover that offers of help come with too many strings attached. Some parents barge in, feeling it their right and their duty to fill in if their daughter hasn't "been passed off safely into the hands of a mate."[11] As biological children often do, adoptees may help repair family rifts, but not necessarily, and especially not if adopting solo rates as one more rebellion.

Even if family fits snugly into the support network, friends often prove to be the best hedge against the isolation that can descend on lone-parent households. If pals tried to nip the mad adopting scheme in the bud, as many do, they have first to get over initial objections. Some come around when the child does, offering critical help in the hectic early days. But these longtime intimates may drift away. David Aiello, for example—the more parenting consumes him, the less he finds in common with his old crowd, single guys without kids. While his buddies haven't abandoned ship, they're bored by the little comedies and tragedies that mesmerize new parents. "I don't want to become a singles-basher," David apologizes, "but I'm kind of getting to be that way."

Solo parents, especially adoptive ones, gravitate to like adults, who in turn become linchpins in the chain of comforters encircling the family. Even in Canada, where the American-style support-group syndrome is a mere sprout, single adopters flock to fledgling organizations. In the United States, it almost goes without saying that such parents can locate an organized self-help group. Cells get so specialized that Pam Soden in New York, for example, can join one dedicated to mature women who adopt older children.

People fashion all manner of props to ease the pressures of parenting on one's own. Phyllis Rogers, for instance, was sharing a big house with a bunch of housemates when she first adopted. Instead of moving out, she moved her child in. "I had full responsibility for my daughter, but I could ask them to watch her for a few minutes while I went out for a gallon of milk. It was a nice way to come into single-parenting."

No matter where adopters find their allies, they quickly realize they can't rear a child alone. Every single-parent family needs its angels.

SLIGHTLY BETTER FAMILIES

Given the emotional dynamite dragging them down, kids adopted late *do* tend to disrupt the peace in whatever families they join. However, research shows that single parents can expect somewhat *less* bothersome behavior than can couples. In other words, something about one-parent households slightly soothes the soreness that causes kids to act out.[12]

What might that something be? Here are the going theories. Number one: the simplicity factor. It's easier for traumatized children to develop a single rather than a couple of new intimate connections. Number two: parental focus. Turbulent kids may more readily calm down if an adult is able to put all primary-relationship eggs in one basket. Only singles can do that. Number three: special personality qualities among this population of adopters. In one study, researchers found single parents to be emotionally mature, with a high frustration tolerance and low susceptibility to the opinions of others—all of which, apparently, can work small miracles on maladapted youth.[13] The same investigators speculated that these parents need to give nurture more than they need to get it. They believe single adopters tend to have a self-sufficient nature, with solid emotional boundaries that create a safe space for a child who has known severance and failure in early attachments.[14] Put simply, these parents take the pressure off; fast intimacy is not necessary.

Whether or not having only one parent offers some kids a modest healing edge over having two, *one is definitely not a disadvantage over two*. Research to date has been very clear about this. In fact, in *Special-Needs Adoption*, the authors conclude that "single-parent families are a nurturing and viable resource for adopted children. Adoption outcomes are quite good and appear to compare favorably with those observed in two-parent families."[15] In some cases, single parents are even more pleased than couples. Fifty-three percent of lone parents, versus 34 of dual, whose kids were placed after age six reported "very positive" results.[16]

However well adoptive families that don't fall apart altogether function, maybe you'd expect, as I did setting out, that more single-parent arrangements would crash than the norm. Pat O'Brien's pessimism about chances for success if unmarried white professionals who've never had kids adopt notwithstanding, solo adoptions apparently don't crack up more often than standard adoptions.

You might also expect that singles would have a unique set of issues after they bring their children home. Yet, when researchers quiz them about child-rearing, they sound just like adoptive couples. Themes don't change with family configuration. Except for two items—the support system, already discussed, and the money crunch, discussion coming— single adoptive families are indistinguishable from the nuclear variety.

The crunch. With only one person bringing home the bacon, in most cases there's no financial fat. And when you combine one earner with the greater likelihood that singles support youngsters with extraordinary needs, shortfall can spell crisis. In the United States more so than in Canada, qualified families can get subsidies, tax credits, and adoption loans at preferred rates. But benefits don't make up for a second income.

In Canada, medicare, though currently in the chop shop, still comes in handy when families adopt children with psychiatric or medical conditions. Stipends, though available in some jurisdictions, are, however, scarcer and stingier than those south of the border. Adopters have to take it upon themselves to investigate what assistance they're entitled to. Facilitators may not know, or may have a lackadaisical attitude if they work in agencies catering mostly to upscale clients.

If you're on your own and contemplating adoption, you don't have money to burn, and you've read this far, you may be getting cold feet. The specter of family and confidantes who might accuse you of being a nutbar, the less-than-huggy reception that might greet you in some downtown office, the idea of waiting forever for a child or of wading through the complexities of overseas adoption could put your dreams on hold. More likely, if you don't already have in mind a child who'll test you till kingdom come, you might feel like backing down. But wait.

For all the troubles a child long out of diapers might tote into your life, if you're anything like the single adopters I met, the task will be more than worth it. Bear in mind that I met quite a range of adopters, raising quite a range of kids. Some, even if their little ones have already been through hell, like Wendy Miles has been, have, as parents, had it relatively easy so far. True, their children tend to be younger, not into the emotional blender of adolescence. But even parents like Jesse Williams and Elmy Martinez, who became dads when their boys were into or almost into the volatile teens, are in seventh heaven. They are no less in love with their children and with parenting than those who give birth or adopt babies at birth.

Noteworthy too: some kids hit with a sledgehammer in early life adjust with amazing alacrity. Think about Elmy's son Luis, for example, into the terrible teens when he arrived, after the system had raked him over the coals. Yet, as you learned in an earlier chapter from Luis's own words, his transition and progress have been unreasonably smooth, and he's a together guy, now in his twenties.

Remember: a bad start does not guarantee a walk on the wild side later, any more than a good start promises a stroll in the park.

Statistically, kids adopted beyond infancy do have more hurt in their hearts and more healing ahead. The process can be long, even nasty, but also immensely satisfying for adults who help them pull their shattered lives together. Even single parents grappling with scary behavior seem to share Elmy's attitude: lots of kids growing up in healthy-enough families anguish their way through adolescence and drive their parents to tear out their hair. What else is new?

Pam Soden sews up the consensus among the singles I interviewed, most of whose kids have psychological Satans to slay: It's hard, yes, but "it's the best thing I've ever done in my life."

Rainbow Kin

*Here [in the United States] I feel people see me with a black child and
think "Either she married a black man and that's wrong, or she adopted
a black child and that's wrong. There's no way she could possibly have
gotten that child 'the right way.'"*

—Tanis Doe, a Canadian living temporarily in California

Charlotte Meyer, skinny as a swizzle stick, shudders recalling the poster
she spotted in her Berkeley neighborhood. Staring back at her: a photo
of a little boy resembling Aaron, her African-American preschooler,
above the caption "Stop stealing our children and calling it adoption.
Take back our children!"

Before I waded into America's adoption arena, I didn't suspect that
race-matching would be *the* heavyweight contender for hottest controversy. That people might trade jabs about children of color joining
beige parents in one of the most racially riven countries on earth
wouldn't have surprised me. But adopting an African-American child
myself gave me a ringside seat to an ideological sparring match that
knocked me for a loop. Were the gloves on, I wondered, because white
families scoop up large numbers of nonwhite children? No. The numbers, I would learn, are minuscule. Only the fight is mammoth.

How deep the rage history has built.

Before the 1960s, Caucasian parents almost never adopted babies
who were anything but Caucasian. Why not? Society favored unifor-
mity in families and, in the era before easy birth control, there were
enough adoptable white infants to go around. But changes to the racial
status quo and in the status of women, stemming from the civil-rights
and counterculture crusades, put the issue of recoloring families on the
adoption map. Yet, even by the mid-1980s, two decades into transracial
adoptions, fewer than 20,000 African-American babies had gone to
white families, including 2,500 in 1971, the peak year. After 1972, when

the National Association of Black Social Workers (NABSW) issued a manifesto condemning the practice as "cultural genocide," traffic slowed to about 1,000 a year. It was still in that groove in 1994, when the NABSW reaffirmed its resolution: "It is the right of a child to be raised in a permanent, loving home which reflects the same ethnic or racial group."[1] At its height, black/white matches affected no more than 2 percent of all adoptions, and by now probably account for less than 1 percent. Nonetheless, the subject still exacts the lion's share of debate.

Not in Canada. Here it's such a nonstarter that it barely got a nod in *Adoption in Canada*, the 1993 study of hot spots in our system. It's not that kids with African ancestry don't enter families with European ancestry, or that no one objects, but rather, that it isn't dynamite. Native children inserted into non-Native homes, however, is. (More on this in the next chapter.)

Numbers partly explain the Canadian difference. If the disputed adoptions are numerically marginal in the United States, they're a footnote here. Difficult even to estimate, they disappear into other categories, particularly under the "hard-to-place" heading. This is not to polish Canada's favorite image of itself as a cosmopolitan Shangri-La. Let's not kid ourselves. Today, the powerful use official multiculturalism to stir the racial pot, keeping it on simmer or heating it to a boil as their interests dictate. And way back when—from 1629 to 1793, to be precise—Canada even dabbled in slavery. This wound, however, is not in the same league as America's defining atrocity. Hence, whereas transracial adoption rankles here—mostly reverberations from our neighbor—it carries ferocious symbolic weight in the United States despite inconsequential numbers.

Where did the rumble over these adoptions get its start? Back in the sorry history of American child welfare. As social work professor Ruth McRoy explains in "An Organizational Dilemma: The Case of Transracial Adoptions,"[2] before the mid-1930s, private nonprofit agencies barred nonwhites. Blacks instead relied on a sophisticated network of self-help organizations built up since the days when they were barely out of shackles. But, as public agencies began to supersede private ones, in the North the door squeaked open to black children. Not, though, to equal services. White kids were fast-tracked into adoptive families, while black kids were segregated into permanent foster care. There began the pattern of a system overburdened with children of color. It could have been worse; only the African-American tradition of informal adoption saved greater numbers of kids from a fosterage fate.

In the 1950s and 1960s, when masses of blacks migrated north with little money, schooling, or preparation for urban life, households began to splinter. Removed from life-saving extended kin, their need for family support services skyrocketed. What did they get? Primarily foster care in already-strained homes.

Meanwhile, chaos came to private adoptions. Since the 1920s, a lucrative fee-based business in placing newborns in white families had been ticking along. But the Pill, abortions, and single parenting, compliments of the 1960s, stemmed the baby supply. Although these changes affected all women, costly abortions, plus prohibitions on Medicaid coverage, increased the pool of African-American adoptees.

Simultaneously, the undersupply of white infants left adoption agencies reeling. And remember, this shake-up was happening in the Age of Aquarius, which warmed professionals' attitudes toward mixed placements. Families were also lining up. They hoped they were headed for life in Camelot. But, Leora Neal writes in *Transracial Adoptive Parenting: A Black/White Community Issue*, "many had blinders on as to the depth of racial prejudice that exists in America and the various subtle as well as overt forms that it takes."[3] Doubtless, motivation varied. For some, it was personal: infertility and the desire to parent. For others, political: a belief they could smash America's Berlin Wall of race by changing colors in the intimate family portrait.

To survive, adoption agencies seized on the era's dream of color-blind harmony and understanding. Borrowing on established practices of placing war orphans and Native children in families of a different batch, placers began approving transracial combinations. It's worth remembering here that, but for these two exceptions—foreigners and Indians—sameness in families had always been of utmost importance to adoption arrangers. Whether dealing with religious background or eye color, they were meticulous about matching children with carbon-copy parents. Why? Because an aura of shame surrounded adoption; hence, it was a duty to make adoption invisible. To this day, it galls opponents of mixed families that the rules went out the window when the system ran out of white infants.

How did agencies, till then true believers that Protestant, blue-eyed babies belonged with identical parents, rationalize the switch? McRoy explains: "Agencies emphasized the half-white heritage of children with black and white birth parents so that white families could, in some way, identify racially with the child they adopted." As a sweetener, they even relaxed eligibility criteria. Suddenly you didn't have to own a house or belong in a high tax bracket to adopt.

In this spirit, why didn't placers also reach out to black families who could sooner identify, since society sees ebony before ivory in children's faces? Because, beyond unconventional matching, it was easier and cheaper to do nothing else new. Besides, most workers were clueless about African-American culture. Recruiting minority personnel and families—such commonsense initiatives were too far out in left field from social work's comfortable pew. Instead, McRoy goes on, practitioners labeled black kids "hard to place" and families "hard to reach."

Economic self-interest and bureaucratic laziness, however, were the least of the bogeymen at work. Racism was the bigger culprit: the belief that well-off white families offered superior homes. And social workers, "servants of the existing moral order," as they've been called, were not about to rock the boat.

By the 1990s, however, you'd think that the boat would have capsized; that the "best families" nonsense would have drowned in its own backwater; that by now no one would have to make waves over the absence of cultural sensitivity; that the system would have perfected the art of outreach to all constituencies of potential adopters; and that the boatload of black children run aground in foster care would be nothing but a bad memory. Think again.

The traditional system, though better, still masters the art of exclusion when it comes to nonwhite adopters. And the predicament of kids stuck in system limbo is worse than ever. Contemporary social perils—AIDS, crack cocaine, welfare cutbacks, routine imprisonment of black males—have combined with the perils of antiquated adoption practice to precipitate a chronic state of emergency. It affects all kids, but hits minorities hardest.

By all accounts, the numbers are staggering. At any one time, there are 40,000 to 60,000 kids in care in Canada. In the United States, at least half a million. In the thirty-one American states with published data, black kids make up 57 percent of children in the system; in New York City alone, 80–90 percent. These figures become even more worrisome when you realize that African Americans younger than eighteen account for only 15 percent of the nation's children. Although most incomers languish for seventeen months, nearly a third of black youngsters get trapped for five years. Estimates of the numbers cleared for adoption and waiting in foster and group homes vary: 100,000 is the conservative figure. Most sources agree that roughly 50 percent of legally free youngsters—whose parents have volunteered or been forced to relinquish all claims to their kids—come from minority backgrounds. Infants and toddlers account for about half of this group.

THE "NO" SIDE
Even with so many kids choking the system, headed for nowhere but the trouble instability breeds, opposition to transracial adoption didn't die down. The seam was still raw in 1988, when Sydney Duncan delivered a conference keynote, "Healing Old Wounds," in St. Louis, site of the original 1972 manifesto. Duncan founded Homes for Black Children in 1969 in Detroit, a model that has inspired imitators. But here she was, sixteen years after the clash, still trying to explain why it had to erupt and why it has such a long shelf life.

The bitterness, she said, harks back to black consciousness that arose with the civil rights movement. On one hand, the 1960s' integrationist mood motivated whites to adopt black children. On the other, newfound self-love invigorated African Americans to build on their strengths. "For a people who have always taken pride in the care of our children, the transracial adoption movement was an attack on one of the few sources of pride in our history."[4] Duncan's themes—the value of children, the need to shake off white paternalism—echo through black writing. Azizi Powell, for example, adoptive mother and director of black adoption services for a Pittsburgh agency, writes:

It should be expected that African Americans would so strongly value blood ties. We are a people who were created by the tearing asunder of families beginning on African shores and continuing legally and church-approved, under American skies. It was a commonplace occurrence for United States slave holders to sell Black children away from mother and siblings, and fathers from them all. Black blood ties were of no significance. And because blood ties did not matter to whites, they mattered a lot to blacks.[5]

Again and again in the mountain of material—books, press clippings, speeches, newsletters, workshop tapes—African-American child-welfare professionals reconfirm their stance against transracial adoption. The W.K. Kellogg Foundation reports are typical. Its *Families for Kids of Color* initiative brought together key players in U.S. adoption. While the foundation isn't officially pro or con, "in every dialogue we heard passionate resistance to transracial placement of children."[6]

That passion gradually nudged influential organizations, such as the Child Welfare League of America and the North American Council on Adoptable Children, to change their tune. Now, in the voluntary sector, most policy-setters and child advocates support the "right" to matched families. While language differs, and some go farther than others, the black social workers have packed a wallop.

What's their position? They are not, they say, out to reverse racism and seek revenge, but rather to claim their children and control their destiny. They fear that black children cannot possibly thrive in other-than-black families. That pernicious racism dooms kids to developing so-called white psyches, to becoming what Audrey T. Russell called a "psychological mongrel" at the original NABSW proclamation meeting. They fear adoptees will feel like pariahs adrift from both consanguine and acquired communities.

From early on, it was also clear that black nationalism informs the struggle to keep the children within (not to say all opponents of transracial adoption endorse the call to nationhood). Russell's presentation, for example, made no bones about the fact that nation-building linked up inextricably to the cause of keeping the children away from outsiders.[7] Today, such adoptions remain an anathema among the new resegregationists, as well as among many blacks who reject those politics—which is no big mystery, considering the current state of American race relations, along with worsening disparities. Choose any socio-economic marker, from infant mortality to income, and the same old picture of stubborn inequality emerges.

From the beginning, the rhetoric has been red hot. Here's Russell again: "The power barons have decided against gas chambers anymore (that's much too nasty and obvious and folks get perturbed even 25-plus years later); they now choose more subtle and insidious means for just as lethal a purpose."[8] Some opinion-makers assumed transracial adopters would catch hell from other whites. Social worker Leon

Chestang, for example, wrote of the adoptive family: "In the eyes of the community, its members become traitors, nigger-lovers, do-gooders, rebels, oddballs, and, most significantly, ruiners of the community."[9] Other skeptics, convinced children of color couldn't get a grip on mental health in these maverick families, speculated kids might fare no worse in congregate care—orphanages, group homes, etc.—whose terrible consequences have long been known.

Yet other criticisms from way back still dog transracial adoption today. For example, because adopters generally prefer healthy newborns, whites would mostly adopt black infants. Hence, older and impaired children would still get stalled in foster care. Finally, opponents assumed Anglo families, unaccustomed to transcending racism's ravages, could not prepare black children to cope. Love would not be enough to implant in them the steel core they'd need.

Nicolle Tremitiere, an adult adoptee, agrees.

I love my mother very much, and I know how much she loves me. But there are certain things about being black in America that a white mother just can't teach a black child.... There are 12 adopted kids in my family, and we're a mixture of everything.... But the world is not like my family.... In the real world, a child must know who she is and where she belongs. If she is black, her path is easier if she has black parents to guide the way.[10]

In Toronto, Zoe, near thirty, also grew up in a large family: stepfather and his four adoptees, together with Zoe's adoptive mother, Elisabeth, who is Dutch, and her biological daughter. Zoe, the baby of the clan, was the only nonwhite. Elisabeth tells me that, as a child, Zoe was obsessed with race, so much so her family nickname was "Honky." Zoe is still obsessed. Being "a conscious black person" consumes her. Race references punctuate her every sentence.

Not only is she hell-bent against transracial adoption, she's dead opposed to blacks and whites "intermixing" romantically. Friends, yes. Lovers or life partners, no. Zoe's opposition goes so far she can't accept that her birthmother, with whom she was reunited just before the woman died, told the truth from her deathbed—that Zoe's biological father is white.

Why race matters so deeply to her daughter still mystifies Elisabeth.

She speaks of her own 1960s-style "colorblind" attitude, details the family's multicultural mix, describes Zoe's grade school—"white kids were a minority"—and mentions Zoe's one black girlfriend from childhood. An upbringing not so lily white, Elisabeth feels, as to have isolated her daughter.

Zoe, by contrast, rummaging through her memories, draws a blank on everything except her sense of isolation. She recalls spotting an occasional face like hers, but it surfaced from life in a white sea. She cites cottage country, with nary a minority person of any description, as a perfect example. Ironically, to illustrate Zoe's comfort, Elisabeth chooses the same example. "Zoe always loved the cottage."

Even in her mostly Caucasian high school, Zoe steered clear of the few other black students. (Bizarre though it is, two of those teenagers turned out to be her half-siblings. They happened to attend her school because, after Zoe's birthmother collected her children from her native Jamaica, they lived with her and their white stepfather in that school district.)

Elisabeth, perplexed by what went wrong, feels she did the best she could with what she knew and within the limits parenting six kids imposes. Interestingly, Zoe, whom I met separately, said just about the same thing.

Would Elisabeth adopt a black child today? Yes, "but with a difference. I'd expose her to more African culture."

THE "YES" SIDE

Boosters are less vocal than detractors because political correctness muzzles the meek. Elizabeth Bartholet, Harvard Law professor and adoptive mother to two Peruvian boys, is not among the timid. She trounces race-matching. In her controversial book *Family Bonds: The Politics of Adoption and Parenting*, she takes the view that in an anti-discrimination era when "in the rest of our communal life we have come to accept as one of our most basic principles that race should not matter," the adoption world stands out as a reprehensible anomaly.

During the 1980s, some whites, stonewalled when trying to adopt children of color, complained to civil rights authorities. As well, some foster parents, rebuffed for racial reasons when attempting to adopt their charges, waged legal challenges. The courts have been schizophrenic in interpreting laws and policies that favor in- over cross-race adoptions. The legal muddle, judges' own personal values, and misinformation about outcomes for children in mosaic families have contributed to a pattern of fluky verdicts.

The ethical status of race in U.S. adoption is still murky, though the legal status is clearer. The 1994 Multiethnic Placement Act (MEPA) prohibits federal-fund recipients from delaying or denying foster or adoptive placement due to race, color or national origin, though it does compel states to recruit families reflective of kids in care. MEPA has met with a mixed, though, it seems, mostly negative, reception in the adoption community, especially though not exclusively among blacks. Certainly the law has stirred fears that the financial plug will be pulled on some minority adoption programs, since they emphasize racial matching. Worse, critics say, MEPA will clear the way for those white adopters who "don't see color" and who are, consequently, ill-equipped to raise children different from themselves.

Equipped or not, white adopters and would-bes aren't the only ones who think they should be allowed to parent kids of color. Some onlookers agree. With *Losing Isaiah*, the Hollywood blockbuster about transracial adoption, as a news peg, the *Jamaican Weekly Gleaner*, North American edition, for example, ran a front-page editorial, "Adoption: Not a black/white solution," by Toronto writer Ashante Infantry.

> The most important issue is that children be placed in homes
> where they are wanted, loved and nurtured.... Whites who
> willingly adopt black children have gone beyond the color and
> cultural barriers and understand that a child is a child. Of
> course the climate we live in requires they ensure this black
> child is educated about the history and culture of their race.[11]

Some adopters I met are even more outspoken in their opposition to the ban. In Detroit, Jesse Williams, a single black man who adopted five boys, disagrees "vehemently" with race restrictions. "Children should be allowed to go with people who are going to provide them with love, period." Gil Cowan, also fortysomething and African American, lives near Pittsburgh with his white male partner, who adopted two black youngsters. Cowan, a bus driver, dismisses the black social workers' position as "ridiculous." Adopting families don't have a problem with race, he figures, so why create one?

Parents of all skin tones and cultural persuasions in my small sample, whether they adopted transracially or not, oppose any race-based embargoes in adoption. Only one woman, Linda Miles, started by saying children should always be placed with like families. Even if a child has to languish in-system till a similar family is found, while willing white adopters wait? No, Miles concluded. Speedy placement, even if it means a mismatch, matters more than racial sameness. However—and this is crucial—to say a very small random cluster of families objects to race-matching is not to say they advocate transracial adoption. Rather, most rank priorities this way: first choice: in-race placement; second choice: cross-race; last choice: putting a child's security on ice while holding out for adopters who racially replicate the child.

When I arrived at the 1995 conference of the North American Council on Adoptable Children, I was edgy. NACAC meetings draw more than a thousand parents, adoptees, and professionals, including big names and big opponents of families like mine. This was my first foray, toddler in tow, into a setting where some might regard me as a reviled species—white adoptive mother to a black child. Coming from Canada, where parents like me are not public enemies, plus living in a Toronto district where diversity is unremarkable, my family hadn't drawn much notice, let alone fire.

But in the United States, and in an adoption crowd which is on record rejecting my kind of family on principle—frankly, I didn't know what to expect. Dirty looks? A drubbing? I needn't have worried. In workshops and in private conversations with African Americans, a spirit of cooperation prevailed, something like "Right or wrong, you're raising one of ours. Let's come together to give him the best environment in which to grow up proud." Workshop presenters took advantage of the assemblage to help parents who haven't been on the receiving end of racism throughout their lives to see the world through their children's eyes, and to prepare for it. They showered attenders in coping strategies and resources. Even those speakers whose golden rule reads "Thou shalt not adopt across race" put the already-adopted kids and their needs first. In subsequent conferences, I've seen that same clarity of purpose shine through.

White adopters of black children I met in the United States, though not in Canada, expressed uneasiness similar to the emotional butterflies

I brought to the conference. Because of the bad rap their family has received, after adopting they initially felt guarded. In the privacy of their homes, they worried they'd have to tiptoe around in a combat zone. In the outside world, however, in the real-life aisles of supermarkets and malls, things have not gone badly. Gale Allen, for one, often gets asked about his connection to the kids. He describes a typical *tête-à-tête*.

"Are you a foster parent or a social worker?" asked a black stranger.

"I'm his father. He's adopted," Gale answered. "I thought, 'Oh no, here it comes.'"

"That's great," the woman said.

Similar feelings of paranoia unnerved Melanie McClure one day in a department store. A Sacramento lawyer and coparent in a lesbian couple raising two African-American siblings, Melanie was pushing Charlie in his stroller when she noticed a black couple noticing them. As the woman approached, Melanie thought, "Oh, oh ..."

"Whose baby is that?" the woman wanted to know.

"'He's mine,' I said. She just looked at him and said, 'Well, honey,' and gave him a big hug right there. A perfect stranger ..."

Karen McGregor, who lives near San Francisco with her three adopted black children, says, "African Americans have been very supportive to us as a family." When she goes shopping, they frequently strike up conversations about the kids. However, Karen has had some grief from security staff who've shadowed her in stores. They act obnoxiously because, presumably, they've been instructed to tail kids of color, the little shoplifters. Occasionally, Karen says, sales clerks, white or black, also get rude to show their disapproval of families like hers.

Other adopters interviewed reported no significant problems. Everyone had a disturbing, but isolated incident or two, some with blacks, more often with whites. (Take into account they likely have more contact with whites, which predicts a skewed outcome. It doesn't prove Chestang's theory that adopters are bound to take heat from other whites.) Most telling, trouble wasn't pervasive, and race-related run-ins were rare. Often, events perceived as having racial overtones might not have.

Like something that happened to the Meyer/Glotzer family in Berkeley. Son Aaron got into a playground ruckus. A few white parents on the scene "way overreacted." Did they go ballistic because Aaron is black? Or would they have been equally exercised were he white?

Hard to say. Though it's reasonable, given such circumstances in an acutely race-conscious society, to suspect racial undertones when sparks fly, mind-reading is not a foolproof business. Just ask Pulitzer prize-winning journalist, David K. Shipler, whose latest book, *A Country of Strangers*, maps the psychological terrain where blacks and whites meet. It's a place, particularly for African Americans, that demands constant decoding of words and events, and where assumptions are never safe. Karen McGregor has certainly learned that lesson. She recalls a woman who kept gawking. Karen assumed the lady was protesting transracial adoption. Turns out the woman grew up in foster homes and never had a family. Seeing an obviously adoptive one piqued her own pain. She was eyeing them with envy, not with scorn.

On the other hand, David Glotzer, a dead ringer for Richard Dreyfuss, didn't need a fortune-teller to decipher the meaning of a black colleague's reaction. She let him know in no uncertain terms that he'd "obviously taken [Aaron] by some nefarious means and that [he] didn't belong with me."

I could go on for pages with anecdotes both positive and negative. The vignettes only prove that opinion inside the adoption world is neither uniform nor color-predictive. The same holds true in the outside world. The few scraps of research from both the United States and Britain suggest splits. For what it's worth, in 1991 *CBS This Morning* asked 975 adults, "Should race be a factor in adoption?" An almost identical cohort of blacks and whites, 71 and 70 percent, said "No." The poll mirrored what Gallup reported twenty years earlier, just a year prior to the NABSW edict.[12] ("For what it's worth" because I'm skeptical about public-opinion polling. I can't help wondering whether the media use polls to probe popular attitudes or to shape them.)

Two near-identical studies done overseas in 1979 and 1989 among mid-income blacks in the same South London area found considerable support for transracial adoption. In the first go, 71 percent were "completely accepting." A decade later, half were "rather accepting." By then, such adoptions had slowed to a trickle in Britain, and a third of respondents were "strongly opposed," up significantly from the initial study.[13]

The numbers—which, everything considered, may amount to a 50/50 split—are least interesting. More intriguing are reasons respondents give. While some favor transracial adoption as an integration vehicle, many offer a lesser-of-evils argument: better loving white families than loveless alternatives. Most worry that adoptions erode cultural identity and risk alienating children from the black community. They also believe black families are better equipped to instill survival skills and cultural pride. In short, *concerns even among many who go along with mixed matches mirror those expressed by steadfast opponents.* Yet more noteworthy: research consistently uncovers keen interest in adopting, if survey families knew how, if racial prejudice wouldn't disqualify them, and if financial help were available.

The truth of the matter is that birthparents of color usually have few choices. Chances are that no specialized adoptive programs for minority families exist in their community. Even if one does, they may not know about it since restricted mandates and budgets limit how far the word or the work can spread. It's easily the case that the only agencies they do know about will trot out the old lie: black families don't adopt. The agency then drops a pile of "Dear Birthmother" letters from eager nonblacks into the pregnant woman's lap. Even if there are one or two profiles in the stack that are racially congruent with the birthfamily, nothing else that matters to the birthmom may match up. Perhaps, for instance, she's intent on open adoption, but the would-be parents are set on closed adoption. Perhaps she's down on religion, but they're up on church-going. There's little doubt that race matters to mom, but other things may matter more, things she can't get from families of her racial mix that are on offer.

In this tricky choosing business—tricky because so much in adoption hinges on birthfamilies hamstrung by few choices and adoptive ones comparatively blessed with many—one point bears emphasizing. As a rule, neither biological nor adoptive families seek racial difference. The exceptions: white adopters parenting a child of color may prefer second children from a similar background. Likewise, a birthmother who places more than one child may prefer to keep siblings under one roof.

Normally, however, people set out to solve their problem, whether infertility or untimely pregnancy. The Meyer/Glotzer family is typical. They sought a healthy newborn, period. They would fast learn, however, that Caucasian infants are as scarce as minority babies are plentiful. In addition, their liabilities as adopters—past forty, childless,

Catholic–Jewish combo—bumped them to the back of the queue for white newborns. The transracial option appealed to Charlotte because her child would have African-American relatives through her sister's marriage. For David, the decision wasn't as automatic. He worried about family acceptance, and about layering Jewishness onto a child already burdened with the specter of racism atop standard adoption issues. David canvassed his family and found an attitude of welcome. He worked through his worries, and came out eager. He and Charlotte went on to adopt two black children.

What about the birthparents who picked them? It's a story of immediate availability and matched values over race. Hannah, their second child, was born to a middle-class African-American couple in Maryland. Neither the mother, a college student, nor her common-law husband was ready for kids. They chose Charlotte and David for their child-rearing attitudes. But, had the birthfamily had speedy access to philosophically similar black adopters, it's a safe bet they'd have chosen them.

When a birthmother picked Lori and Bob Clemmons near San Jose to adopt her biracial son, Jesse, she told them tradition and religion governed her choice. While she would have preferred a dual-heritage couple, nothing mattered more than a married pair who follow old-fashioned family values and Christian fundamentalism, both dear to the Clemmonses.

HOW DO KIDS FARE?

Does Jesse's first mother have reason to hope her son will flourish? Like it or not, the answer is "probably." The only twenty-year longitudinal study of transracial adoptees in the United States wrapped up in 1991, reporting positive results in *The Case for Transracial Adoption*. By all standard measures, the kids fared more than fine, and on par with in-race adoptees. Results reinforce what investigators have been saying all along: nonblack homes don't necessarily handicap black children.

This is not to say there's no reason to be up in arms about transracial adoption. Obviously, many people object passionately, which is fair enough. But, if the research can be trusted—there are those who say it can't—there's little reason to balk out of concern that these families routinely harm children.

While the pattern of positive findings may hearten proponents, it's cold comfort to adoptees like Zoe who grow up conflicted about who they are. And indeed, studies do confirm that transracial adoption can lay a snare for racial identity.

Estela Andujo, for example, compared teenagers of Mexican background placed in Anglo and Hispanic adoptive families. Those in Anglo families thought of themselves as American, while the others self-identified as Mexican American.[14] It needs mention here that findings like Andujo's uplift those who believe race doesn't, or at least shouldn't, matter. Elizabeth Bartholet, for one, finds "positively heartwarming" those studies in which adoptees describe themselves as American, human, or biracial rather than black. McRoy found a tick similar to the one Andujo noted. "From my research, black or biracial children who were in families living in predominantly white areas, attending predominantly white schools, had more difficulty developing a positive and unambiguous identity. Unfortunately the majority of transracial families do live in mostly white areas."[15]

Surprising as it may seem—and it even catches researchers off guard when they stumble onto it—racial identity and self-esteem are not always flip sides of the same coin. In other words, adoptees can possess strong self-regard even with a weak sense of connection to their origins. Feeling remote from one's roots doesn't automatically equate, or so researchers claim, with psychological hangups.

Zoe as a youngster, by way of illustration, was so estranged from her beginnings that she vaguely feared other blacks. Yet, she is Ms. Self-Confidence today, and always was, according to her mother. Indeed, she's so assertive and self-possessed that I hadn't realized how petite she is until her mother happened to mention Zoe's height.

Research is one thing, individual stories another. The former gives us the big picture, the latter the nitty-gritty of each atomized life. When it comes to transracial adoption, the twain don't always meet. I've read the research. Over the past few years, I've also attended at least a dozen workshops on race and culture issues in adoption. Panel and audience participants invariably include young adult adoptees from the families under scrutiny.

The kids suffer; there is no doubt about it. Some suffer more, some less, some sooner, some later. This is hardly surprising, given that race and culture are such big-ticket items. When added onto the other major ticket item, adoption, they potentially make the going pretty rough. The latest panelist I heard—a Korean adoptee in her twenties—is just beginning to question her insistence, to date, that she's Caucasian and comfortable with the delusion. Now she has two children and wonders how she can raise them with pride in their heritage if she can't face her own honestly.

Though coming to terms with racial and cultural identity can prove a singularly rugged and lonely path for adopted kids who aren't like their parents, not all the kids would say they'd have it otherwise. Consider, on the one hand, Zoe, who can think of few fates worse than a rainbow family. On the other, Liza Steinberg in Oakland, California, who says these adoptions "can work and work beautifully ... and I'm the living proof." She's careful to add she's "pro family," not "pro transracial adoption."[16]

Saying it can work doesn't mean it's all smooth sailing. "Before I was adopted," Liza once wrote, "I was separated from two families, my birth mother's and my birth father's.... I was also separated from my culture and my race ... the hardest and most painful things I have dealt with in my life. And they are HUGE."[17]

By definition, all adoptees have troubled waters to navigate. Racial difference means one more river to cross. In Liza's case, though raised in Zoe's times, when parents flew by the seat of their pants, she and her family were able to bridge their differences. One of four kids from varied backgrounds adopted by a Jewish couple, Liza grew up in an otherwise whitewashed world. "I knew that who I was was okay at home. ... But I knew that when I went outside ... it wasn't okay for people," she says, echoing a theme, take note, that comes both from adoptees who wish they'd had same-race parents and from those who wouldn't trade their adoptive family for anything.

Liza, again typical of all kids, but especially of adoptees, yearned to fit in. That's why, when she first happened upon a black community filled with people resembling her, she finally felt comfortable and "didn't want to go home." Zoe breathed the same sigh of relief on her first visit to Jamaica.

Liza, however, did go home, and over time, despite "the many ways in which you feel disconnected from your race" especially as a "black Jewish girl in a white Catholic high school," she says with a belly laugh, worked out her own way of belonging. Having parents sensitive to her issues, as a result of their firsthand experience with anti-Semitism, helped.

Liza's background, she feels, yields up benefits and drawbacks. On the plus side, "you get this 'comfort thing' where you can go into different environments." On the minus, a boyfriend who abandons ship to avoid having white, Jewish grandparents in the family fold. With understanding, peppered in humor and scorn, she alludes to being "too black" for some people and "not black enough" for others.

Liza's watchwords: be prepared. An adoption coordinator at Pact, a San Francisco adoption alliance for children of color, Liza helps families prepare to adopt. If parents share traits with the coming child, all the easier for everyone. But, she says, if they don't, they'd better take stock. Two inventory hot spots: housing and hair. Liza has little patience for candidates who cringe when she questions their reluctance to move from mono- to multiracial neighborhoods. She gets exasperated with parents who don't get the hang of their kid's hair, yet won't go to a black salon. If they can't handle a minority moment, themselves at center stage, trouble is brewing, she says.

For Zoe, trouble came in many forms, including a short bob. Her hair was a "complete mystery" to her family. Instead of untangling the puzzle, they snipped with the scissors. Today, Zoe flaunts her dreadlocks. They symbolize rebirth, just as the memory of her near buzz-cut in childhood, not stylish then, represents the hopelessness of transracial families.

WHAT'S STOPPING MINORITY ADOPTERS?

Among mantras peppering the adoption literature: though child-placers try to find minority families, few are willing to adopt. It surprised me how frequently I ran across this nonsense, blithely tossed off as common knowledge, yet often followed by a segue into custom adoption—as if it doesn't count.

Indeed it does count, since children get warm-hearted human beings instead of a cold-hearted system to raise them. In adoption by custom, untouched by the courts, the surrogate family might be headed by relatives, friends, or neighbors. Such informal child-minding is not some rural curio. Even in the desperate zones of today's inner cities, some kids still find succor with parent substitutes. Granted, with families scattering to the winds, as they do these days, stand-in parenting isn't what it used to be. And what with the mesmerizing cult of the individual dumbing the continent, little wonder African Americans have veered from their rich communal traditions. Yet, "child keeping" still goes on.

In Brooklyn, adoption social worker Chester Jackson, a big teddy bear, only recently found out, by accident, that the woman he called "Mom" was actually best friend to his mother, known to him as an aunt. Single, raising six other kids on welfare, his African-American mother, who died when Chester was thirteen, needed her network to raise her children. Her girlfriend accepted the job as a rightful role. The truth, though, was hidden from the boy, perhaps to protect the family from welfare snoops.

Factor arrangements like Chester's into the adoption definition, and what kind of picture emerges? One strikingly different from the myth. Suddenly, supposed nonadopters come through as the biggest child-absorbers of all, providing refuge for an estimated 900,000 kids even today. In addition, these "other mothers," typically single grandmothers, tend to take in more kids—at least three—than do legal adopters.[18]

In fact, even when it comes to formal public-agency adoptions, one government study found that African Americans adopt 4.5 times more per capita than others.[19] In 1982, for instance, the adoption rate was 18 children per 10,000 families for blacks, compared with 4 for whites.[20] Remember, however, that public agencies usually place older, needier kids, often in sibling groups, not healthy new babies one by one. The higher incidence of adoption by blacks, far from suggesting any relief from race prejudice down agency lane, probably hints at something else: black families' superior willingness to take in more than one child at a time, even if the kids bring hefty challenges.

In 1980, sociologist Robert Hill discovered that more than 3 million black families would have been willing to embrace the 100,000 kids with African ancestry in foster care at that time. While not all the enthusiasts were necessarily suitable adopters, even by scrupulous selection standards surely 3.3 percent were. That's all it would have taken to move the children into homes. Yet, as the black community was well aware, the chances their members would, if they offered to adopt, make the grade were abysmal, as the National Urban League would soon demonstrate. In 1984, two League studies revealed that, of

800 black adoptive applicant families, only 2—that's 1/4 of 1 percent!—were approved, against a national average of 10 percent.

Let's cut to the chase here: given the abundance of eager families, plus the rate of custom and formal adoptions, it's a bald lie to say minorities don't adopt, or that their children are significantly less adoptable.

Another factor reveals the fib. Agencies dedicated to finding matched families for children of color have eye-popping success. Even three decades back, when Homes for Black Children opened, it placed more youngsters than the combined total for the twelve other Detroit agencies. Or, take the stunning accomplishments of One Church/One Child, which now boasts thirty-five satellites across the United States. Founded in 1980 by Father George Clements, a black priest who got Papal dispensation to adopt four teenage boys, the program urges every African-American congregation to find families, and they do. Another dozen or so specialized operations, including the Institute for Black Parenting, show what the right approach to placing minority kids can accomplish.

Or consider recent revelations from the North American Council on Adoptable Children (NACAC). Seventeen specialty agencies placed 94 percent of their black and 66 percent of their Hispanic children, compared with 51 and 30 percent at standard agencies.[21] Why do adoption main-streeters flunk? With predominantly white professionals running the joint, "just about all guidelines impacting standard agency adoption [are] developed from white middle-class perspectives," NACAC found. Adopting is a storm in red tape. Affluent applicants, though they may wince at the waste and stupidity of the paper chase, nonetheless fill out the forms, gather up the documents, and get the whole mess notarized. They have money, fax machines, Internet access, insider contacts, even perhaps gofers, to get the job done in triplicate, on time. But other applicants, suspicious that the hoop-jumping—especially the needlessly invasive homestudy—is designed to discourage them, opt out before they're screened out.

Cost is the biggest barrier blocking blacks who might otherwise adopt. Fees can pose a problem even for the wealthy since the symbolism of buying babies may offend people whose ancestors were bought and sold. Besides, paying to parent doesn't add up in a culture where adults traditionally rear others' children. The NACAC investigation into obstacles to matching minority kids with like families tells the tale.

> Transracial placers also distinguish themselves in their almost consensual treatment of adoption as a business that, like most other economic endeavors, revolves around fundamental forces of supply and demand. As a worker at one of these agencies plainly stated "Adoption is like any other business." ... In strict accordance with the "economic" mentality, the eight typically spoke of children in their agencies as commodities, acquirable by any family willing to pay a fair market price for them. They assume that prices for children—like those of other salable goods—vary according to characteristics possessed by the good in question. For one transracial placer, this principle helped explain "why we *only* got $6,000 for a couple of our children last year." The word "only" is appropriate considering the average fee charged by the eight was $9,562 and that one agency received $20,000 for each of the placements it completed. Another admits ... "most families of color who approach us can't come anywhere close to meeting our fees."[22]

Should adopting be auction-block and highest-bidder commerce? Should it commodify kids, rank them on a salability continuum: healthy white newborns fetch the highest price, while darker-hued, older children fetch the lowest? Even practitioners who'd say "Of course not" and mean it don't have unlimited maneuvering room. Because fees mean survival and some adopters are lined up, no recruiting necessary, checkbooks at the ready, the cost-effective impulse kicks in. Agencies frequently place on the basis of economic self-interest and "to concede to the demands of the most powerful interest groups they must deal with: white prospective adoptive parents."[23]

DEMOCRATIZING ACCESS
Only a seismic shift in attitudes and actions can bulldoze barriers. There's no mystery in what the quantum leap will take. Specialty agencies have already tested the blueprint.[24] For starters: make cultural sensitivity a priority. Hire professionals whose backgrounds mirror target adopters'. Locate services in prospect neighborhoods, near public trans-

port. Work night and weekend shifts. Learn to recruit and retain an untried clientele. For instance, discover and use communication channels familiar to new candidates. Get out of the office; mount aggressive but sensitive outreach. Respond quickly and openly to all comers.

Create user-friendly homestudies: kitchen chats, not office probes. Make them informal and informative, not investigative, or, for kin adoptions, beyond a safety check, dump them almost altogether (as Alberta recently did. New York and Illinois also offer less-stringent alternative licensing for caretaker relatives). Kill excessive paperwork. Talk up subsidies. Pare down fees. For non-negotiable payments, detail the services they cover. Stop the fictive family ideal. Screen in, not out. Ferret out strengths, not weaknesses. Cherish whatever gifts families offer. In short, keep what's best for kids, not for bureaucracies, at the eye of the quest.

HELPING KIDS THRIVE

No matter what anyone thinks, some of the coming generation are being raised by parents different from them. "These children can't wait for the debate to be resolved," Pact's directors remind us. "We must respect families as they exist."[25] As Sydney Duncan noted in her wounds-healing speech, "Any time adults argue about children it has to threaten their security, and if someone is arguing about the rightness of your home, that is the ultimate threat."

Too many youngsters already suffer the Catch-22 of family and race as an either/or proposition. They're the ones who latch onto their foster families. Then, when they come up for adoption, their caretakers apply. The system says, "Forget it, wrong color" and only then starts shaking the bushes for an acceptable household. By the time the child moves into an appropriate setting, s/he may have spent years with the only real family s/he's had. This is matching gone mad.

The madness starts when an agency, which in the current climate has a case of nerves about releasing a child of color to white adopters, nonetheless assigns the child to such fosterers. Why to them? Because traditionally few agencies did the requisite outreach to build a multicultural storehouse of foster and adoptive homes. Instead, they took the easy way out by relying on long-favored Anglo foster families. Today, if it turns out a child can't go home, too few culturally kindred adopters are on hand. Agencies weren't geared up for the onrush of the changing ideological tide. Now, they're trying to play catch-up. Meanwhile, kids get caught in the cross hairs of a system that espouses race-matching in adoption but, in ability to deliver, lags far behind its rhetoric. For public agencies, where the heart of the problem lies, the new Multiethnic Placement Act will both let them off the hook from giving race such prominence *and* put them on the spot to recruit a more representative cross-section of foster and adoptive families.

While researching in Washington, DC, I caught a TV interview that captures the current contradictions. A white couple who'd fostered a black child for several years tried to adopt him. "Don't even think about it," their worker advised. The boy, and his brother, whom the family also wanted, were eventually placed with African Americans.

The child was miserable; he wanted to "go home." The adoption fell apart, and the brothers were brought back into the system. Later, the foster mother spotted the boys' pictures in an ad seeking black adopters. She badgered authorities for parenting permission, to no avail. Eventually she went to court, where her adoption bid succeeded. Footage of the family at home, including an interview with the child in question, confirmed the mother's version. The kid just wanted to stay with this family, but no one asked him.

This absurdity, reversed only by luck, mocks the notion supposedly ruling child welfare: the pursuit of a child's best interests. Children are served when their nurturing links—however repugnant to whomever—receive a cushion of support. Even well-known campaigners for in-race adoption, such as Leora Neal and Al Stumph, make the case for intercommunity cooperation for the sake of children when the system, by their reckoning, fouls up by producing hybrid homes.[26]

But coming together for the kids in American cities blighted by significant apartheid is easier said than done. Indeed, the original NABSW fiat uses the fact of separate worlds to warn against transracial adoption. It highlights how far off their beaten tracks many white adopters would have to veer in order to have contact with the black community. Cognizant of this sad truth, placers urge parents to go as far afield as necessary because kids need same-race confidants and role models for their self-esteem and for their armor against racism.

The best salve for a sense of belonging, everyone agrees, is for

adoptive families to live in neighborhoods where difference is ordinary, where kids can rub shoulders with peers from a background like
their own. Good advice. Some presumably follow it, or already live in
such locales before adopting. But only two families in my small sample
live in a conspicuously multicultural milieu. Otherwise, I met black
families living in black areas, and white and mixed families in mostly
white precincts. If they described their environs as global villages, the
village didn't include many blacks. Asked about nearby blocks, embarrassed parents scrambled to come up with one African American.

This even held true for a few families who, after adopting, relocated
for job changes or for added space. They moved a considerable distance, within or to a new city, without shifting racial ground. Despite
ready justifications—housing prices, good schools, etc.—the parents
clearly have access to middle-class neighborhoods with a good mix of
people, but stay put in familiar enclaves. No wonder some black
American social workers from big cities, where there's a mélange of
neighborhoods, complain that white adopters taking cultural-sensitiv-
ity courses from them nonetheless continue to live in white suburbs.

It's a shame when adoptees miss out on an environment where they
can blend in. But even those marooned in largely segregated neighborhoods have a decent chance today of living with parents who account
for their difference. Among newer families I interviewed, only one
seemed to have missed the point entirely, and even these parents were
correcting their early mistake. No matter where they live, all the others
I met take to heart a view of their households as heterogeneous. We
adopted a minority child, so now we're a minority family, they stress.

Though none of these families set out to find kids racially different
from themselves, happenstance brought the gift of love where they
least expected it. The treasure of diversity together with the travesty of
racism—at root responsible for the overabundance of adoptable children of color—changed and enriched lives in ways people never predicted. It created conditions for trespass into worlds they might
otherwise never have known.

Sacramento lawyer Margery Evans-Knapp, for one, had very little
contact with African-American co-workers. "After the children came
along, suddenly everyone knew my name ... and I thought, 'Oh, it's
because of the kids.' But actually, when I finally said something about
the children to one woman who'd been so friendly to me, she said, 'Do

you have kids?' ... I realized it must have been a difference in me, that having these children must have made me reach out more."

Now she counts on those contacts for parenting advice. Other adopters, especially in the United States, get tips on culturally savvy parenting from stellar adoption agencies. The luckiest families enjoy follow-up services, continuing education, even troubleshooting. Whether they have top-notch or bottom-drawer professional help, they make it a project to connect with others who share their children's roots and mirror their family's composition. For example, the McGregors in Fremont, California, with a small black population, compensate by gathering an assorted circle around them through I-Pride, an organization of multicultural families.

Unfortunately, some blinkered oddities who view race and culture as nonissues still manage to adopt nonwhite kids. And, sad to say, the Multiethnic Placement Act may further pander to this mentality in the United States. On the side of progress, however, nowadays a growing percentage of people adopting a child who doesn't look cloned from them—whether the difference involves race, nationality, abilities, whatever—try, as far as possible, to make their child's world their own. In the transracial case, for example, for those adopters who previously might have seen the struggle against racism as someone else's fight, it brings them into the fray. Many parents can probably relate to Jana Wolff, who confesses in her book, *Secret Thoughts of an Adoptive Mother*, to starting out unenlightened about the realities of race and ending up transformed "in ways that scare some of my friends."

Clearly, multiracial adoptive families in these times are more likely than those from Zoe's day to have *meaningful contact* with their children's communities of birth. They are less likely cultural tourists, dropping in on the occasional festival.

Marian Wright Edelman, president of the Children's Defense Fund, writes: "It is utterly exhausting being Black in America—physically, mentally, and emotionally. While many minority groups and women feel similar stress, there is no respite or escape from your badge of color ... [and] the daily stress of nonstop racial mindfulness."[27] What Edelman calls "this extra Black burden" writer Marita Golden calls a "black tax" on daily existence. As her son "careened into adolescence," Golden felt "flushed with trepidation."

Soon Michael would inhabit that narrow, corrupt crawl space in the minds of whites and some black people too, a space reserved for criminals, outcasts, misfits, and black men. Soon he would become a permanent suspect.... Women would think twice about entering elevators alone with him, cops would ... watch him a little more closely.... By the time my son was twelve, every day I wondered when he left me in the morning what would be the manner of his return to me at night.[28]

Most parents in these pages have more than inklings of what these writers are talking about. For instance, people have told Terry McGregor how blessed his kids are to have him as their dad, meaning lucky for them to be in a white family. As if that erases the "black tax." Parents like Terry know better. They know white families are no bonus for black kids. Boys' mothers especially prepare for the day their sons become "permanent suspects."

Parents of young children concentrate on more benign forms of harassment because more lethal ones are too disturbing. Yet, it's hard to keep flashes of life-threatening risks from your mind's eye. How can anyone not quake, when, under dubious circumstances, police shoot black males? And when investigators then typically clear the shooters of wrongdoing? (If these incidents always made me rabid, since adopting they also make me apoplectic with fear for my son.) While adoptive parents cannot live inside their children's skin, neither can they live in LaLa-Land.

Before this book, had you asked for my take on these controversial adoptions, I'd have said, "I'm for them, provided parents don't toss off difference with the standard trivializers, such as 'We're all the same under the skin.'" I don't agree with Zoe about much, but I do share her view that race-blindness is its own kind of bigotry. Today I'd say I've gotten over my naivety. I've come to understand that adoption saddles every adoptee with psychic weight that pushes the limit. Adding extra baggage like ethnoracial difference between child and parents can blow the scale. The research may say kids manage the surplus surprisingly well, but the anecdotal evidence suggests that the lighter they travel, the easier the journey.

So, am I for or against transracial adoption? Call it a cop-out, but I don't think there is a simple answer. Nonetheless, some aspects of the issue couldn't be simpler. First, it's easy to condemn those who verbally crucify individual transracial adoptive families; they bring nothing to the debate but grief for children. Second, it's easy to take a stand against any child languishing in system limbo on any pretext, no matter how high-sounding. It's easy to stand for families, the most suitable—considering all the factors—and *quickly available* refuge open to a child in the context of a deeply flawed adoption system uninclined to rapid metamorphosis. There's no abracadabra to instantly defeat defects that have taken the best part of a century to construct.

The bottom line: kids need homes, and they need them fast—faster than the system will self-correct. Faster than specialty agencies can do for waiting children what the system too often leaves to chance.

Yet, even now there's no excuse for letting transracial adopters go their way without scrutinizing their credentials. Do they know what they're getting into? Those qualified to judge must feel confident that a given family has an aptitude for diversity and for zooming in on the specific heritage of the child they want. Assessment tools for culturally competent adoptive parenting, though not state-of-the-art, do exist, and do get used to some extent in the United States. But training is still a matter of chance or self-selection—if indeed parents can find programs or courses—not a prerequisite for the job.

Ultimately, I agree with human-rights activist and altogether-formidable human being Tanis Doe. A single lesbian in her thirties, deaf, and physically disabled, she adopted, while working in Jamaica during her twenties, one of her deaf students, now a teenager, in an open arrangement with the girl's birthfamily. Tanis believes it's "favorable to find likeness of some kind" to cut the risk that children will feel like "foreigners in their own home." She mentions a differently abled lesbian friend who adopted a diff-abled Japanese girl. "If you told me the Japanese part had to match with the adoptive family, I'd say 'No, *you have to look at the whole kid.'* ... *No child is one thing. There's incredible diversity in each child*" (my emphasis). Tanis reckons the girl will be better off with her "family of likeness"—even though mom isn't Asian—than in a Japanese two-parent standard-abilities household. In the list of alikeness variables, Tanis includes birthparents' values and preferences.

All of this, of course, argues for an incredibly diverse collection of waiting adopters. Indeed, if the system ever commits to wrapping every child in a constant, copacetic family, a pool of prepared families congruent with the kids consigned to care will be the first hint real change is in the hopper. Livable subsidies and lifelong support services will be in there with them. Without these boosts, there's little reason to hope impressive numbers of youngsters will be spared the gross indecencies of a government upbringing.

SEVEN

Native Adoptees:
A Special Case

There is no formal adoption ceremony among Native Americans, no word for "orphan," no such thing as a child without parents, because the Native American extended family is so important.

—Jim Cadwell, Native American Child and Family Resource Center

What makes the Native case different from that of other culture and race transplants? For starters, North American Indians belong to a family of nations whose rights were trampled on by European settlers from the moment they arrived. Our forebears and governments perpetrated the standard violations all too familiar to First Peoples, from stealing land to stealing children. Though the younger generation was never voluntarily relinquished by their parents or their nations, authorities corralled them into what is, in effect, international adoption.

What else makes the Native case unique? Whereas other types of cross-matches, whether in domestic or in foreign adoption, tend to work, these tend to falter. Some families, of course, beat the odds. For one, think back to the Halketts in Calgary. You'll remember that, in this single-header household, divides are wide—north meets south, the daughter, Jenn, is Inuit, while her adoptive mother, Cathy, is white—but this family is a going concern. Exceptions aside, what jinxes the prospects for healthy adjustment? Many factors, all of them complex but all with roots traceable to the subjugation of Indian nations. It produced the plagues of poverty and demoralization many aboriginal communities and individuals battle today.

How did the campaign that would produce generations of cultural orphans work? Through a two-stage attack on the integrity of Native families, communities, and cultures. Working in cahoots with churches—Catholic and several Protestant denominations—the federal government hatched the plan and partially financed it. Residential schools, which go back to the late 1800s, was the first fork on the road to planned ruin. Church and state ganged up "to civilize the barbarians."

But lurking behind this ostensible motive was another rarely mentioned imperative. The Crown didn't want Indians, whose lands had been treated or stolen away from them and ways of living imperiled, getting uppity and trying to reclaim what they'd lost. Assimilation was a way to blunt resistance. Assimilation meant expunging the culture of birth by inculcating Christianity, the Queen's English, and a Eurocentric worldview. To this end, tens of thousands of kids across North America were systematically abducted from their parents and plunked down in church-run, live-in schools far from their familiar environments and influences.

Just how civil were these schools? Here's a typical assessment:

> I personally attended Indian Residential Schools for eleven
> years and on leaving it took me another eleven years to
> mentally undo the devastation.... One school principal in
> Brandon used to call us God's children three times on Sundays
> at the three services and the rest of the week call us dirty little
> Indians. No one ever hugged us or told us they loved us. We
> were mere numbers, strappings, beatings, hair cut to baldness,
> being tethered to the flag pole, half day school with
> unqualified tutors, and slave labour the other half were
> commonplace.[1] (Abhorrent though this snapshot, it doesn't
> refer to sexual violations perpetrated by caretakers, mostly
> clergy, against so many of these children.)

Pupils weren't happy, but in fact this stab at using "education" for cultural genocide was a stunning success. By the time most residential schools shut down in the 1970s—the last one in Canada closed in 1988 after a wave of child-abuse scandals—they'd done maximum damage in curtailing transmission of essential aboriginal values. A recent study by the Nishnawbe-Aski Nation of teenage suicides in Northern Ontario concluded that the "residential school annihilated a generation of parents."[2] It's a finding that echoes throughout a growing body of investigations into what's wrong with Indian families.

This annihilation set the stage for the second line of attack, known among Natives as the "sixties' scoop." The schooling experiment, which among other hobblers robbed children of the experience of family life, rendered them unprepared to raise the next generation. Just as their parents and communities had been devastated by the loss of a generation, so, too, they had been groomed to produce another lost tribe. Babies were born to broken human beings, many of whom did what broken people often do: abuse themselves, each other, and their kids. Referring to a young Ojibwa boy-in-care's suicide, Native playwright Drew Hayden Taylor contextualized the tragedy: "a culture forced by oppression to prey on itself."[3] To make matters worse, the reserve system, racism, and the curtailment of hereditary rights—hunting, fishing, etc.—had reduced many communities and individual families to lives of grinding poverty.

Under the sweeping powers of the "child in need of protection" clause in Canada's Child Welfare Act, social-welfare authorities, came, as they saw it, to the rescue. Here and in the United States, where a similar "rescue" was under way, some private welfare agencies helped with the dirty work of uprooting children and planting them far from home. For public consumption, the mission hinged on vaguely humanitarian-sounding motives. First: save children from "unfit" parents. That white, upper-middle-class urban social workers got to be arbiters of fit First Nations' parenting on reserves was overlooked. Other unnoticed fine points: the interlopers knew little about Indian cultures. And wedded to an ethos of individual pathology, they didn't bother their heads about why whole reserves were reduced to squalor. Just remove the kids—which they did in astounding numbers. As an example, in 1955, less than 1 percent of kids in care in British Columbia were Indian. By 1980, the percentage had risen to 36.7.[4]

Across the country, during the "scoop-up," aboriginal children were severed from their families at five times the national removal pace.[5] In Manitoba alone, for instance, from the mid-1960s to the early 1980s, about 3,000 children were plucked from their parents.[6] In Canada today, Indian youngsters account for about 40 percent of permanent wards, and as much as 70 percent in regions with the highest concentrations of Native Peoples.

From the beginning, the child-protection system liked to hand out one-way tickets to Indian kids. Instead of going home again, they were routinely farmed out to white fosterers forever, or to adopters across the continent, and in some cases even around the globe. Receiving families, depicted as "good, God-fearing" folks, were typically untrained, unprepared, naive, and well-meaning. They had no notion they might be doing anything dubious. On the contrary, they'd been led to believe by church and state that they were deliverance incarnate.

The same legalized kidnapping and five-star cultural insensitivity at placement was going on in the United States too. U.S. surveys between 1969 and 1974 revealed that over 80 percent of Indian children put up for adoption—aboriginal kids were being adopted at 20 times the national tempo[7]—were placed in white homes[8] at a rate of about 1,400 annually.[9]

Shirlene Parisian, who runs a repatriation program for Manitoba First Nations, laments that in her province "there's not one Indian person who has not been touched by the loss of these adoptees."[10] Indeed, it's safe to say there's not one North American Indian who hasn't been hurt.

When Tove Kilburn adopted three Native infants through Vancouver Children's Aid over twenty years ago, she thought love would be enough. A statuesque blonde, Tove grew up in Denmark, where it was "almost fashionable" to adopt internationally. She always planned to, and to work on behalf of "more unfortunate" youngsters. Besides her three children mentioned, Tove adopted two girls from Bangladesh, and gave birth to her sixth child. To this day, she continues her long-time practice of an annual hands-on stint in Bangladesh orphanages run by Families for Children, an organization based in Canada.

Recently divorced from her husband, a pilot, Tove, now fifty-five, has returned to her early career as a flight attendant. She lives in a luxurious South Vancouver home, a swimming pool outside, the inside crammed with elegant furnishings and collectibles. Ironically, her posh digs are barely a ditch away from Indian land with ramshackle bungalows and strewn yards. Why ironic? On the one hand, her kids were raised planets of privilege away from so many Native kids. On the other hand, the children's encounters with racism have barely removed them a stone's throw from the nearby reserve.

Tove braves a sunny face and waxes positive about parenthood. But her veil is too sheer to hide the pain. The pain of so many now-dashed hopes "that, with education and love, I could prepare them to go out there," feeling good about themselves.

After growing up with a books-and-museums grasp of their heritage, the three, now in their mid to late twenties, are troubled. One son,

Sioux–Cree and Anglo, "looks white" and "would like to forget his Indian half." The other son, Mark, whom Tove describes as "the love of my life [whose] spirit is so great," has proven particularly unprepared for the troubles. As a child, the boy was beset with behavior and learning problems. No one knew why. Tove ran from one specialist to the next, who put Mark through one test after another, getting nowhere. After years of research, Tove found the answer: fetal alcohol syndrome (FAS).

In the 1970s, FAS was not a recognized condition. By the time it was, Mark's life was menaced with alcohol and drugs, and the problems they bring, including the law. In a note she sends after we meet, Tove tells me Mark was recently beaten up in a racial incident on their doorstep, after which he fled to the United States, where he was later arrested. Nothing new for a young man who has survived many racial run-ins, including stabbings and broken bones. Panic still grips Tove whenever an ambulance whizzes by at night.

The note also mentions that her daughter's Haida birthfamily ran a search ad in a local newspaper. "I'm very excited for her," Tove writes, though the twenty-four-year-old is not ready for reunion. When she is, going home again may not be all it's cracked up to be. Five West Coast communities that tracked seventy-five adoptees who tried found none was able to hack it.[11] Mark has dabbled in reserve living and in various healing rituals, to no great effect. But Tove still hopes they hold the key to his redoing.

Despite heartbreak at seeing "my dreams for my children crumble ... there's so much these kids have to face. I just wasn't prepared," and despite mounting taboos against aboriginal adoptees going to non-Native families, Tove is still a believer. With today's knowledge of FAS, plus support services available to adoptive families, nonexistent when she needed them, she feels households like hers can work. Several times during our meeting, she points out that the available alternatives—foster homes or orphanages—are worse. Love may not be enough, she concedes, but "I made a big difference in all my kids' lives."

The tales Tove tells of identity crises and crazed behavior run through anecdotal accounts of North American Indian children grafted onto dominant-culture families. Parents' cultural sensitivity usually makes a big difference for adoptees' adjustment and esteem in racially mixed families. But among those adults who adopted Native kids, in the past certainly, only the very exceptional brought the requisite sensibilities, such as being knowledgeable about, or in any real way attuned to, aboriginal perspectives. The whole idea of patching Indian kids into families that were anything but Indian, after all, was to assimilate them. Placers were not exactly on the lookout for white families who had any kind of in with Native clans.

Because there's so little experience to go by, it's hard to judge if adoptive families more savvy to their children's heritage would make a major difference. Until recently, open adoption joining Native birth and non-Native adopting families was unheard of. To the minor extent that such connections exist today, it's too soon to assess the impact. In one small Canadian study, though, even Indian kids whose Anglo parents reached out to their children's bands didn't fare better than totally disconnected peers. Perhaps that's because as the researcher himself, Christopher Bagley, has speculated, links were too superficial to matter.

Some commentators believe that, in the Native case, culture clash is not the crux of the crisis. That is not to say they dismiss the crossover factor. They don't underestimate how easily the minds of Native adoptees can get disfigured. How can kids not have low self-esteem and feeble cultural pride when their peoples continue to suffer grave indignities? How can adoptees feel good amid the demeaning messages, especially living, as these youths do, inside the culture that turns out the bad images? While some commentators take all of that into account, they point to what they consider even more potent cripplers bringing down the success rate: FAS, FAE (fetal alcohol effect), and other traumas in early life.

Christopher Bagley, a social work professor, studied thirty-seven transculturally adopted Native teenagers against control groups of international adoptees and of Indian kids raised in original families from which a sibling had been removed. Bear in mind that authorities supposedly remove only those children who are from hopelessly dysfunctional families, so the stay-at-homes should prove a mess.

Bagley found among Native adoptees "much poorer levels of adjustment, more problems of depression, low self-esteem, and suicidal ideas as well as much higher levels of acting out behavior," including a three-times-greater incidence of self-harm. The Native in a non-Native family was "significantly more likely than any other parenting situation" to fracture. By age fifteen, one-fifth of the thirty-seven had split from their adoptive parents. Meanwhile, the adoptees' brothers and sisters who stayed with the birthfamily weren't so maladapted.[12]

You could make a case that what Bagley observed may not have *as much* to do with the Indian factor as a first glance suggests. After all, it's not that bizarre for any adoptee, or biological child for that matter, who has a checkered past to leave home sooner than we normally expect. No matter who adopts older children—even babies after a rough ride in the womb—they may end up with runaways. This risk applies irrespective of the adopter's roots or the child's, and even if both are the same. But when Native adoptees hit the road early, we're quick to cry "adoption breakdown." We forget that they and their families may continue to be emotionally intertwined, perhaps even in touch, or just temporarily disconnected.

Besides, we all know adolescence can be crazy even for the sanest-seeming kids. Ten years down the pike—maybe sooner, or even much later—most straighten out, and the family establishes the next stage in its version of normal. When it comes to Indian/non-Indian adoptive units, however, society doesn't extend the same breathing space to sort themselves out that it automatically bestows on other families. Granted, the record has been dismal, but that's no excuse for forgetting that some families, given time, make it. Also, "success" means different things for different individuals and different families. And getting to that place may be no more rocky for the families under discussion than for any family, adoptive or not, whose kids have hell to pay for an unfair start in life.

Here's the age-old "cure" the system prescribes when it removes children from Native parents. Make a slipshod effort to keep the kids in extended-family or community foster care. Fail to find takers, or, if you do find them, don't monitor arrangements. More likely, place the kids in non-Native fosterage. Offer few services to the biological household; just wait for the miracle that will reverse family fortunes. Provide puny supports to the foster children and family. Do little or nothing to make sure kids stay in touch with relatives. Follow the dump-and-wait principle until mom comes pounding on your door, demanding her kids back. Send them home for a while, until the next crisis erupts. Then remove the youngsters again and place them with a different white family. Keep this not-very-merry-go-round spinning till kids "age out" of the system. Eventually you won't have to intervene because they'll run away from easy reach, or they'll graduate from child protection to juvenile justice.

Sound outrageous? It is, but it is also common. Gail and Don Barth, who live in a small community near Vancouver, know just how callous the system can be. When I met them, they were on the verge of adopting a twelfth child to join their international crew of nine adopted and two, now-adult birthchildren. The adoption in progress: a newborn sibling to their two Native kids, whose birthmother suffers from FAS. Birthmother and Barths share in a workable open adoption.

In cobbling together their large and unusual family, the Barths have seen system-bungling *par excellence*. To illustrate just how insane things get, they tell me about two other Indian kids they fostered. By the time the brothers arrived on their doorstep, age four and five, child protection had bounced them around to a variety of caregivers. Temporary had defined their lives. They'd endured severe malnutrition—even rickets—and "extensive abuse" at their stepmother's hands. After a year and a half with the Barths, who would gladly have adopted them but for British Columbia's embargo against non-Natives adopting Natives, the social worker called to say they'd be reuniting with their family.

Gail, a dynamo, flew into action, organized a letter-writing campaign begging authorities to ease the boys back into reserve life slowly. Prepare them. Let them maintain their ties here. For the first time in their lives, they have stability. Right or wrong, you put them in a non-Native family. Now do what's best for them. But no. Authorities didn't care what was best for the boys. They cared about what was expedient for the system, and about burnishing their own image as politically correct. Social workers showed up unannounced and took the kids away, just like that. Months later, the children were apprehended again, after their stepmother battered them again.

Sooner or later, Native people had to sort out the crisis. They had to reach out to their scatterlings, and had to stop government stealing at its source. Emboldened by African-American salvos against transracial adoption, aboriginal activists in the United States compelled Congress to pass the Indian Child Welfare Act (ICWA) in 1978. It formalized tribal authority over placing children.

Federally, Canada didn't follow suit. Instead, the provinces enacted a patchwork of policies and laws to slow the old habit, and to involve band councils in adoption planning. Though provisions vary, they require that public agencies either nix non-Native adopters and go the extra mile to find Indian families, or consult with the birthmother's band when drafting an adoption plan.

Have laws and practices stemmed the traffic? Haphazard statistics make a numerically accurate answer anyone's guess, but existing data indicate "Yes." Yes, though more so in the United States, where the legislation has a few teeth. But even the U.S. law has proven a bittersweet victory, according to Native American child-welfare experts convened for *Families for Kids of Color*, a project of the W.K. Kellogg Foundation. Their assessment? A half-decent statute further reduced by stingy implementation money, mushy accountability structures, and misty critical terms. Loopholes create openings for bitter custody battles between white adopters or candidates and Native families or authorities. Cases can get pretty complicated.

> The true cause for prolonged custody battles ... is a general lack
> of compliance with various ICWA provisions, the lack of a clear,
> formalized tribal notice provision for voluntary adoptions
> within the ICWA, and efforts by financially motivated attorneys
> and other placement workers to deliberately circumvent ICWA
> rules. A fourth problem involves Eurocentrism ... [evident in]
> the so-called "existing Indian Family Doctrine" ... [which]
> suggests that native families who live outside of a reservation
> and do not actively participate in stereotypical Indian rituals or
> events are not "truly" Indian; by extension, the reasoning goes,
> ICWA rules do not apply to children who are being removed
> from such families since those children are not being deprived
> of their culture or tribal connections.[13]

A flawed law. No agency to enforce it. Little financing behind it. Child welfare low on some tribal agendas. Overlapping players in the child-placement riddle: the Bureau of Indian Affairs, private adoption agencies, tribal social services. This hodgepodge affects fewer than 2 million people, some with reservation and others with urban mindsets, belonging to more than 500 tribes scattered hither and yon and speaking about 250 indigenous languages (more than 50 in Canada). When you add that these people are fighting roadblocks in every avenue of a comeback from the war against their very existence, you hardly have a formula for overnight success.

If the ICWA isn't equal to the task of keeping children in the Native fold, Canada's array of laws and policies is even more impotent. Just look at findings in the *National Adoption Study*: though overall placement numbers are down, in 1990 most adoptable Indian children still went to unrelated non-Natives. Totals dropped, by the way, for various reasons, including a growing reluctance on the agency side to put Indians in other-than-identical families, and a growing reluctance on the adopter side to welcome the kids. Based on the record, people fear these families won't work. On both sides, there's also a growing desire to do what's right and, at the moment, the winds are blowing in favor of Native kids in Native settings.

Yet, some professionals, Native and not, along with would-be adopters and Indian birthmothers, still believe there's nothing wrong in forging such families. They cite positive-outcome examples as proof that these kids and these parents are meant for each other.

In such a climate, where an apparent majority of stakeholders oppose creating the families in question, against a minority resisting the tide, it's not surprising that both Canada and the United States have seen imbroglios between white adopters, or hopefuls, and Native birthfamilies or Indian bands. In a much-publicized British Columbia case, Teena Sawan, a young, single Cree mother, not a penny of cultural capital to her name, agreed to a private adoption. Compared to Sawan, the adopters, Faye and Jim Tearoe, were loaded: white, married, older, home-owning, devout. When Sawan revoked her consent within the proscribed ten-day provincial limit, all hell broke loose. The powers-that-be sided with the adopters, while their lawyers dragged out the legal process long enough to make it unlikely the courts would order the boy returned (a standard ploy in custody cases).

The Tearoes kept the child, and the Supreme Court of Canada refused to hear Sawan's appeal. End of story. The mess, detailed in *The God-Sent Child: The Bitter Adoption of Baby David*, by journalist Kim Westad who followed the case, hinged in part on the "Indian Family Doctrine."

David was depicted as not really Indian because his mother had lost touch with her tribe, because his birthfather is "Canadian" (read: Caucasian), and because David has light skin.

In this particular travesty of justice, promises to protect the integrity of Indian families were a lot of hot air.

Sawan, it seems, did not set out to deliberately avoid an Indian home. Apparently, she just did what came naturally after a life in ten white foster families—including some where she'd been beaten and molested—cut off from her culture: turn to the society she lived in. Unlike Sawan, some birthmothers do look for non-Natives on purpose. Most provincial adoption laws mandate child-welfare authorities to notify the band or tribal council when a Native birthmother selects outsiders. Some provinces give Indian authorities a proscribed period to find more suitable adopters. In certain cases bands do find an alternative. In others, they veto the proposed placement without providing a Native substitute, leaving the child indefinitely in foster care, often, ironically, with white families.

To avoid tribal involvement, some women who can't, for whatever reasons, keep their babies turn to private agencies. In these circumstances in Canada, there's not a lot Indian leaders can do. In the United States, by contrast, a tribal council has some leeway. Take the case of a Navajo woman who tried to place her baby with whites. Her tribal court, under ICWA, intervened. It ruled the child could move in with the couple but had to link with her lineage through a supervised schedule of visits.[14] That the mother was able to shimmy past the law in the first place, ICWA critics say, reveals its flaws.

But, challenging what women themselves choose for their offspring makes some people fume. Marilyn Shinyei, for example. She runs Adoption Options in Edmonton, a private agency specializing in open arrangements. Indian birthmothers come to her looking for "anything but a Native family. They want their kids off the reserve" or out of urban slums. But the problem, as Shinyei sees it, is that even though 25 percent of prospective adopters she meets say they'd welcome a racially different child, most mean "anything but Native. People are scared of the politics.

"No other community or cultural group has that power over where children are placed. Think how whites or blacks would react if told that the equivalent of the band council would determine the fate of their kids." Shinyei also contends that adoption of meaningful numbers of kids by aboriginals is unrealistic. "Native people have so much healing to do, they can't present us with many healthy families. Besides, most healthy ones are already parenting extra kids."

Shinyei's discomfort with collective over individual rights is a cultural anomaly, one quite different from what Indians traditionally prize. For Natives, there is no such thing as a motherless child. Children belong to everyone, not solely to biological parents and their kin—which is all very nice in theory. However, factor in the abysmal state of many aboriginal communities today, and the identity mishmash many Indians suffer, and it's no mystery why some mothers imagine their kids will be better off in a white world. They hope that living on the other side of town will have its compensations.

Authors of the 1993 *National Adoption Study*, University of Guelph professors Kerry Daly and Michael Sobol—in a spirit opposed to the U.S. legislation—propose helping mothers who prefer non-Indian adoptive placements. "Native birth mothers should be given the right, conferred in exceptional circumstance [the meaning of 'exceptional' isn't spelled out] by judicial review, not to inform the Band Council of the intention to place their children in non-Native homes."[15]

There's a North American Indian proverb that goes something like this: there are no cures for plagues from the gods of plague. The cure for the pain of lost children will come only from Natives themselves. Indeed, on the long road back to dignity, they have been chipping away at the child-protection colossus, just as they have at every obstacle visited upon them.

In Canada, however, they are recovering in a country deeply muddled about the notion of nationhood. Here, it is not taken as axiomatic that all nations, big or small, even if they exist within a larger country, have indestructible rights. Instead, many Canadians look at national rights subjectively, reducing them to a question of personal preference. (The dominant Anglo psychology on Quebec makes a good case in point.) It's true that North American Indians enjoy wide public sympathy in their quest to reestablish their circle of nations. Yet, the tendency to deny or dilute national entitlements, like determining your own child-welfare policy, is rampant. Canadians don't have a problem grasping that Peru, for example, has every right to set its own adoption laws, binding on all Peruvians and prospective foreign adopters. But we do, it seems, have trouble transferring that principle to Native nations. Eventually, as Indians succeed at self-government, presumably the muddle will sort itself out. In the meantime, laws and agency practices being what they are, both birth and would-be adoptive parents have to take guidance from their own conscience.

In the United States, in the monumental task of improving the welfare of Indian children, certain ideas have wide currency. Some cropped up at the Kellogg forum: codify, as part of Indian customary law, tribal concepts of permanent placement. Push early tribal enrollment to establish children's heritage beyond a doubt. Strengthen tribal–state links, especially to heighten recognition for Indian leaders. Provide adequate money and technical assistance to implement ICWA. Include questions about the law on bar exams, then update and retest lawyers. Make sure social workers serving Native clients pass cultural-competency courses. Increase adoption subsidies to families. Finally, push the courts to expedite child-custody cases quickly.

Other needed reforms already appear in bills that may become law: amend ICWA to oblige anyone planning a voluntary adoption to notify the child's tribe and certain family members. Limit the time period during which these parties can intervene or men not married to the baby's mother can claim paternity. Require judges presiding over hearings for adoption or for terminating parents' rights to ensure the adults know their ICWA rights. Another provision would protect continuing contact between adoptees and their tribes.

Canada lags so far behind that we still dither when it comes to ensuring the growth of Native-run adoption agencies, even though it's long been known they find Indian adoptive families sooner than do mainstream agencies. (This is not to overestimate the state of aboriginal social services, beleaguered by underfunding, understaffing, and inadequate training.) In the Northwest Territories at least, we no longer dicker about the legitimacy of custom adoption. There, informal child-keeping has always been the norm. At the age of majority, the kids involved never had to plead with some hostile authority for hints about their family of origin because birthfamilies have always belonged in the kinship circle. Kids grow up knowing who's who. The 1995 Custom Adoption Recognition Act, the establishment of adoption commissioners, and the 1996 Supreme Court certifications of such adoptions under the new system mark an advance in acknowledging and supporting cultural practices.

But this is a baby step. Clearly, some of the American proposals are much needed here, beginning with livable subsidies. Beefing up benefits while paring down cultural dissonance between workers and clients would do a lot for kids the system too often treats like dross. So would preventing social workers, lawyers, judges, and others from using the "Indian Family Doctrine" to help non-Natives in custody fights over First Nations' kids.

These same initiatives, given a boost in the United States, could go a long way in improving the status of children in Indian country. But, as Ray Moisa writes in *News from Native California,*

> the true roots of the problem of cultural genocide, however, as represented by the routine adopting out of Indian children, lie in the dire economic, medical, and social conditions that abound on the reservations. Until those problems are remedied, the long-term welfare of all Indian children and families remains in jeopardy.[16]

EIGHT

World Households

International adoption is the only option other than death for some kids.

—Gail Barth, British Columbia mother of twelve, nine adopted

Given the magnitude of the problems facing relinquishing countries, intercountry adoption, even properly conducted, is meaningless. It presents an idealized life for small numbers of children, as an alternative to a global policy. This is a duty for international cooperation....

—Damien Ngabonziza, Secretary General,
International Social Service in Geneva

Focusing on the particular—a single child's life—can sharpen our vision of the whole.... Seen in its broader context, international adoption may increase our sense of urgency about the millions of lives still at risk.

—Cheri Register, adoptive mother to two Korean girls, and author of Are Those Kids Yours?

January 3, 1995. "She's here in the room with me! Can you believe it? She's so beautiful," my friend Ruby's* voice staccatos over the crackling phone link between Asunción, Paraguay, and Toronto. Giddy on euphoria fueled by exhaustion, she relays every detail about her infant. Before we say good-bye, I ask if she'll be okay until her husband, biting his nails back home in Chicago*, arrives closer to their court date. She's shaky, Ruby admits, but managing, thanks to lots of company and support. Her *pension* is full of foreigners, there, like her, collecting the children they've arranged to adopt.

I put down the receiver and weep. Joy that Ruby finally has a baby. The incomparable magic of motherhood ahead. Behind her, year after year of failed infertility fixes, month after month of dreading the blood that always flowed.

Bittersweet tears as memories, not long distant, wash over me. My own dilemma comes back. What if, in North America, my partner and I couldn't in short order find a relatively healthy newborn or toddler? Would we go to some poor country, where, with doggedness and a fistful of dollars, even unconventional antiques like us—then-unmarried, past forty—can usually find a youngish child more quickly than at home?

The fear I could never shake—the specter of a stolen or bought baby—again sends a shiver up my spine. Though foul play reputedly doesn't factor into adoptions from some suppliers, particularly in Korea and China, our foray began when Korea was making it tougher and before China made adopting easy. Besides, if I didn't speak the language or have a handle on the culture of my prospective child's homeland, how could I grasp what was going on during the adoption process? Even if I met the birthmother, how could I know she was for real, not a paid actor, or a "breeder" producing babies for the foreign market? Given limp adoption controls and active outlaws on the adoption highway, I couldn't get beyond the sense of risk involved, however small. And unlike those relieved that they won't have to mess with birthfamilies if they adopt far away, I feared the distance. The more I learned about open adoption, the more I wanted at least to know the who and the whereabouts of my child's first family.

February 15. Ruby, now six weeks in Paraguay, sobs on the phone. Turns out her local lawyer is a sleaze. Ruby doesn't have a clue what's up. The court date, previously fixed, is now a mystery since the judge handling her case, who favors international adoption, has been replaced with one who opposes it. Will the adoption go through? It has to; there's no going home without her daughter—though, horrors, it happened to an Italian couple down the hall. Since then a few other parents laid down bribes in a bid to get out faster.

Why the sudden urgency? Some scandal about abducted children. As we speak, local headlines decry the loathsome foreigner, especially the Ugly American. Police are tromping room to room in the main hotel housing adopters, looking for the babies in question. No one has knocked on her door. Not yet ...

Eleven heart-pounding weeks later, Lady Luck will pull Ruby from her nightmare when she and her baby board a jet for home.

Overseas adoptions began after the Second World War and intensified after the Korean War. Back then, though some infertile couples adopted, families were as apt to have "kids of their own" and to welcome foreign orphans for humanitarian reasons. Wars and civil strife—Vietnam, Cambodia, Romania, etc.—commingled with poverty would continue to supply waves of needy waifs. Meanwhile, the demand side of adoption—principally North America, Western and Northern Europe, Israel, South Africa, Australia, and New Zealand—would radically change. Access to birth control and abortion would climb. Single-motherhood would shed its shame. Infertility would disappoint many baby-boomers trying to conceive later than usual. And some who'd written off parenthood as beyond reach—singles and gays, the most obvious examples—would begin to challenge social conventions. These factors would turn a rescue mission driven by the needs of children into a business driven by the parenting desires of affluent adults.

As the number of adoptable babies in industrial countries plummeted in the 1960s, the developing world emerged as the new cradle. Now it supplies an estimated 15,000 to 20,000 intercountry adoptees each year. So critical are poor countries to family-building in rich ones that cross-border deals now outnumber domestic ones in some destinations. In 1991, Canadians brought home at least 2,448 children from distant lands, outstripping local adoptions by an estimated 750.[1] In the United States, the numbers of foreign adoptions fluctuate but regularly make up one-fifth to one-sixth, or 7,000 to 9,000, of the yearly tally. From 1971 to 1991, an estimated 140,000 adoptees entered the United States. In 1987, the high point, 10,100 children came from eighty-three different nations.[2] The source countries vary. From the 1950s to the mid-1970s, Asia, with Korea in the lead, provided 90 percent of the children.[3] From the end of the Korean War until 1991, Seoul sent about 120,000 children overseas.[4] By 1980, however, the focus started shifting to Latin America, with its legacy of bloodshed and misery.

Other countries, such as India, open and close. The on–off cycle follows the vagaries of international political gamesmanship and the ebb and flow of public outcry against exporting children. Although foreign adoption brings a bonanza to a small coterie of intermediaries—lawyers, facilitators, translators, hotel operators, bribe-taking bureaucrats, assorted hustlers—it's not big business; it's merely a cottage industry.

And because adoption isn't in the serious-money league, it only occasionally adds up to chump change in rivalries between the United States and its challengers for a slice of world domination. Among sending countries at the moment, only the Russian Federation and the People's Republic of China (PRC) toy with the American grip on power. The Chinese case shows how adoption can sneak onto the political agenda.

In the parrying between the United States and the PRC, America has assumed the mantle of human-rights guardian (which, given its service record, especially as a fabulously rich country, to at-risk kids in its own backyard, is cheeky to say the least). Hence, it seizes on any story that makes China look like a heinous violator. So, for example, the 1996 Human Rights Watch/Asia report describing Chinese orphanages as virtual death camps for baby girls and disabled children made worldwide headlines.

Don't misunderstand. This is not to rhapsodize about Chinese orphanages. Bear in mind, though, that North American adopters who've toured more than just showcase facilities say that, as orphanages in poor countries go, China has better ones and bad ones. Skeleton staff and funds, conditions ranging from half-decent to deplorable, where survival of the fittest dictates the mode of care—these are not unique to the PRC. But China is special in a crucial way: it's high on America's hit list. Hence, the world witnesses heartbreaking images from China sooner than from dungeons that doubtless exist in some other poor but "friendly" countries.

The Dying Room and *Return to the Dying Rooms*, 1995 British shockers secretly filmed in about a dozen orphanages across China, put klieg lights on the deplorable examples. The documentaries don't make a convincing case for the existence of alleged torture chambers, where the weakest are deliberately starved to death. But the films do provide a grim hour of TV, with footage reminiscent of Romania's well-documented houses of children's horrors. Sitting through the official Chinese response provides lighter entertainment as they attempt to throw the baby out with the bathwater. They deny everything by assertion. All is well in Orphanage-Land.

Where is this sad story leading? To the observation that international adoption can become a football in the big-power game. Right now, in its contention with China, it suits U.S. and allied interests to have their citizens seen as saviors of little Chinese girls, abandoned because of the still-powerful preference for boys. Supposed good-guy countries rescuing urchins from the alleged bad guys plays well in the West. Obviously, international adoption also suits the Chinese, since they've streamlined the normally cumbersome process. Indeed, China now holds the title for having the fastest, most efficient system on the planet.

How do searchers learn that China, or some other source, is the country of hope at any given time? Easily. Once they hook into the international adoption network anywhere on the loop—through an agency or a newsletter or the Internet—they can stay abreast of best bets. Even before the World Wide Web, the adopters' grapevine hummed with hints and rumors. In the adoption world, a good personal experience is gold. And because globe-combers who manage to find a baby empathize with the empty-handed, they eagerly beat the tom-toms with news of where dreams can come true.

After the fall of Ceausescu, for example, Romania became the destination *de jour*. Within eighteen months, foreigners scooped up about 10,000 children before humiliated authorities turned off the spigot.[5] In a related example, the collapse of the Soviet Union brought the kind of chaos that temporarily favors the outflow of children. In 1993, Americans adopted 1,110 kids from that part of the world.[6]

Would-be parents go to the ends of the earth for various reasons. Likely they want a newborn, but, with reason, despair of finding one at home anytime soon. Or they want an infant who, at first glance, resembles them (most searchers are white), and figure—again, with reason—they'll have better luck in a bigger arena.

They may go abroad because they're intent on a healthy baby, though this train of thought baffles. The typical sending country, after all, can hardly be touted as a paragon of pre- or antenatal care. Package tours descended on Romanian orphanages, nonetheless, where early deprivation was an art form. Yet, adopters who dream of babies "out there" getting a better start than they do here can be right. Take the case of China's newborns, who tend to be healthy at birth and still shipshape if quickly whisked away from institutional life. Babies from eastern Europe, by contrast, suffer from an estimated ten times higher incidence of fetal alcohol syndrome than kids born in the United States.[7]

And little ones who've done time anywhere in the warehouses of the world come with disabilities inflicted by orphanage culture. Adjusting and attaching rarely come easily to children who've survived by fending for themselves and fearing adults.

Adopters' decision to travel is linked to various race- and culture-conscious motives. Perhaps they support prohibitions in their own countries against adopting children with Native or African ancestry. While they hope these children can be placed with matched families, they doubt that foreign babies in countries that don't practice adoption outside of kinship can find homes. For these adopters, incorporating a child of color into the family in their home country is not okay, but it is all right to adopt one from abroad.

Others, even if they agree with domestic transracial adoptions, nevertheless feel ill at ease with the politics. Yet others simply want to escape the notice and hassles that can hound mixed families, especially black and white ones in the United States. Given acute color-consciousness, which burdens race with such exaggerated importance, some would-be parents ask themselves, "Who needs it?" and answer, "Thanks anyway, not us." Undeniably, some adopters do subscribe to a racial pecking order, with blacks at the bottom. Whatever the reasons, there's no denying that preference for newborns, particularly lighter-skinned ones, plus prospects for cutting the waiting time, lead the list of globe-hoppers' whys.

But there's another reason: fear. Some people are scared to adopt in North America. Scared of open adoption. Scared the birthmother will change her mind while she still can, but not soon enough to spare them from broken hearts. Scared there's a birthfather in the wings who'll learn his baby has been placed and will drag their family through a long reign of terror in the courts. Maybe win custody—when the child is three or four! Baby Jessicas may be few and far between, but her image lingers in the adoptive brain.

Connie Spanton-Jex, who, with her husband, Rod, adopted two young brothers from Colombia, feels "much more secure" than she would have adopting in nearby Washington, DC, or indeed anywhere in the United States. "I'll never have to give these kids back. There's no one out there looking for them ... [no] father coming back and saying 'I didn't know she gave the kid up for adoption.'"

Connie also bemoans the interminable wait they would probably have faced at home. Because Rod is deaf, and Connie, who hears, is an interpreter, they felt their setup was ideal for a deaf child, a chore to locate domestically. Historically these children have disappeared in the system, their hearing deficits un- or misdiagnosed. Even though it's easier to find them now via the Deaf Adoption News Service (DANS) on the Net, the majority wait in faraway orphanages.

Some would-be parents flee to avoid roadblocks they expect at home. About twenty years ago, Joan MacDonald, a divorced mom and Toronto schoolteacher facing forty, figured foreign adoption was her only hope. Children's Aid made it abundantly clear she wouldn't be getting a child through them. By comparison, the international pathway was a breeze, enabling Joan to adopt two girls, one from Korea and one from India.

Attitudes Joan bumped up against two decades ago still stymie many singles today. David Aiello, for instance, wasn't looking for new and perfect, but he wasn't ready for a street kid either. He checked out his chances of adopting a youngish and not exceptionally messed-up child here. The consensus among the circle he consulted, lawyers mostly: single males are out of the running. Adoption authorities in Guatemala, however, either didn't notice or didn't flinch at his gender or his marital status.

Ironically, many globe-trotters now end up with high-needs kids coming out of institutions, not with newborns. In other words, they frequently adopt clones of those the system should be plugging here. However, assuming the prospective parents are nontraditional—say, single and male, like David—if they try to adopt on their own turf, and especially if they're trying for a baby, they can easily get the cold shoulder from public agencies, and even private ones. Their contact mightn't even mention the pitiful situation of waiting kids. It seems incredible, but, for devalued candidates, adopting exactly the youngster who urgently needs them can often be done easier and quicker far from home.

Finally, families look elsewhere because special-needs adoption is promoted harder and smarter than it is domestically. The lucrative global family-making business gets the full commercial treatment, from irresistible ads to inflated promises—the usual business rap, which works. Hence, many newcomers are easily lured into fleeing their own jurisdictions.

RESCUERS OR ROBBERS?

David Aiello, a very bright guy, looked at me as if I were speaking Swahili when I asked where he stood on the ethics of international adoption. He didn't know what I meant. After a synopsis, he answered this way:

> There's me and then there's a child and the question is: are those two good together? ... I don't even think about any sociological or political commentary about whether that's right for any reason other than what has to do with me and him.... I know there's a Guatemalan minister of something or other who says that "our children are our heritage and they should stay here in our country." Well, that doesn't address the issue of what's good for [the child].... The child deserves the dignity of his own individuality and is not anyone's resource—no politician's, no country's, no nothing.

Among ways of viewing crossnational adoption, three lenses eclipse the rest. There's David's one-on-one approach, in which something fundamentally good gets complicated by needless bureaucracy. At the other end of the spectrum, the global view, in which something basically bad gets further convoluted by its connections with child-trafficking.

Between these two: so-called ethical international adoption, which demands hypervigilance. Accordingly, families follow the beaten path, scrupulously observe the law, hire "reliable" intermediaries, and focus on orphans in institutions. They insist on proof the youngster they're about to take out of the country has no willing kin, and is domestically unadoptable, given local laws and cultural norms, and that they are the child's last shot at a family. Plus, adopters donate money, and maybe become activists in the cause of improving family security in their children's native lands.

David Aiello has good company in his conviction that adoption is, above all, an interpersonal matter. He can count on the likes of Harvard law professor Elizabeth Bartholet, who adopted two boys from Peru, and who authored a provocative book, *Family Bonds: Adoption and the Politics of Parenting*.

You need only step through the door of this world and look around to realize that there are vast numbers of children in desperate need of homes and vast numbers of adults anxious to become parents. It seems overwhelmingly clear that efforts to put these groups of children and adults together would create a lot of human happiness. But the legal systems in this and other countries have erected a series of barriers that prevent people who want to parent from connecting with children who need homes.[8]

Uncompromising opponents of intercountry adoption are first to admit the magnitude of misery. Damien Ngabonziza, for one, secretary general of International Social Service (ISS), based in Geneva, which tracks a caseload of about 12,000 cross-border adoptions annually. More about his position later. The point here is only that no one on either side of this issue denies the need; swords cross over how it should be met.

Members of the me-and-the-child school are not prone to paralyzing moral quandaries. Rather, like Bartholet, they see a perfect symmetry of needy tots and desirous would-be parents. They see toddlers forced to live by their wits, scavenging dumps at the bottom of the food chain. They realize that families, too stretched to feed another mouth, are forced to hand over offspring, in some cases to creepy institutions where scabrous tots, starved for affection, barely subsist. They hear about women whose unmarried pregnancies confer shame and ostracism, and whose progeny are fated to become nobody's children. They see themselves as a way out for the domestic servant, likely raped by someone in her master's house, who will, if she tries to keep her baby, lose the measly wages that probably feed her entire family. They see themselves as a godsend for children who haven't the foggiest hope of being adopted in their own countries.

From that perch, we are all part of a human family sharing a planetary community. Adoption shrinks the global village. National borders are bothersome intruders on what should be trouble-free family-making. Those who can should care for the children of those who can't. You may not be able to fix the cruel world, but you can make a difference in the lives of small, precious children, one by one.

Besides, they say, it's not for us to judge if some mother, ground down by a hard life, wants better for her baby, which to her means a well-off family in a faraway land. Relinquishing parents are simply doing there what they do here—the best they can for their child within existing choices.

Distance adoption, they stress, elevates youngsters from conditions where they have virtually no chance of a decent life. Indeed, they might not even survive. Adoption transplants them into a setting where they have an above-average crack at a charmed life. And that within the context of bringing children into families who crave them but usually can't have them. That's a lot of joy all round. What could be wrong?

Everything, according to opponents. By their reckoning, neither personal goodwill among would-be parents nor abject poverty among relinquishing families and nations justifies international adoption. The practice, critics point out, has nothing in common with mutual aid among equal partners. Rather, they say, dramatic imbalances divide receiving and sending countries. Not incidentally, they chide, adopters come from wealthy nations and big powers, especially the United States, that plunder natural resources from weak nations, devastate indigenous economies and ways of life, buy cheap and sell dear.

They add: many relinquishing countries, such as those in Latin America, have been brought to their knees by foreign debt. Financing it has forced them to cut, not cultivate, services that weld families together. Some senders, Guatemala, for example, have seen scores of civilians maimed, murdered, or "disappeared" under a U.S.-backed regime. Others—South Korea, exhibit A—live in a state of virtual American military occupation. These examples only begin to hint at the inequities between adopting and supplying republics.

Opponents complain that imperialism's bad attitude of entitlement—the world is my market—gets altogether too grabby in thinking the world is also its womb. Those opposed assail the arrogance of what one international adopter described this way: "[the] blithe assumption at the heart of much of the foreign-adoption literature ... the best thing that could possibly happen to a poor, brown-skinned child from an impoverished country would be a new life in a white family in the marvelous land of Burger King and Barbie dolls."[9]

Critics cringe at the Western vanities involved. For one: the presumptuousness of people who lay eyes on a baby born in a foreign land and say things like "The second I saw her, I knew she was meant to be mine." They quiver at the sight of the jet set, with their viewcorders, featherweight strollers, and portable layettes, coming from countries living high partly by keeping countries like theirs down.

What gives people from the usual set of suspect nations any moral right, opponents ask, to maraud around the globe, treating small human beings as just another resource to rob, whether they do it legally or with dirty tricks? Why can privileged citizens from exploiting countries go where they please and help themselves to the children of underprivileged women in downtrodden nations? A feminist critique bolts in here as well: Where is the sisterhood in this? some ask.

Who, you might wonder, regards global family-making in these terms? The chorus of condemnation sounds harshest from relinquishing nations, though echoes murmur from all corners. Not surprisingly, the most enthusiastic supporters live in receiving countries. That is not to say people in sending countries unanimously condemn the adoptions. In fact, public opinion runs both ways.

The protesters' lineup includes some prominent child-welfare advocates in source countries, and some, like Ngabonziza, working in Western-based international organizations. A minority of stakeholders scattered throughout destination spots agree with the clamor. State University of New York social work profs Kenneth J. Herrmann Jr. and Barbara Kasper, for example, think distance adoption lets the world community off the hook in terms of family planning and battling poverty. "Ironically, although adoption may contribute to the well-being of tens of thousands of children, it may contribute to the continued oppression of tens of millions."[10]

No matter where they come from, the disenchanted sing this same tune. It has other lyrics: most foreigners prefer newish-borns, the blonder the better. However, true orphans—confined to institutions, freed for adoption, *and* completely disconnected from kin—don't fit this profile in adequate numbers. As a result, the demand creates irresistible pressure to jack up the supply. It leads to what Maria Josefina Becker of the federal Brazilian child-protection agency calls the "production of abandonment."

To the extent that they actively undertake the search for children to be adopted, couples and agencies involved in international adoption, their generous and humane motives notwithstanding, increase the pressures favoring a rupture between the poor child and his or her family rather than strengthening the ties between them.[11]

Second, detractors say, searchers subscribe to a Western concept of adoption, which grates on local customs. "In some cultures," Ngabonziza explains, "it is inconceivable that blood relationships can be extinguished or that someone totally strange can parent your child, let alone someone from a different clan or country."[12] Besides, if this kind of family-building makes sense where you come from, why not do it there? Heaven knows there are enough kids back home who need you.

Margot Wilson-Moore, in Victoria, BC, knows firsthand what Ngabonziza means about conflicting mores. Her adoption of Anjoli from a Bangladesh orphanage dumbfounded some locals. Margot, by the way, speaks Bengali and was at that time living in a village, Chuchuli, with her family while working on her anthropology doctorate.

Why, the perplexed wondered, would she adopt a stranger when she already has birthchildren and could, presumably, have more? Why would she take in someone with whom she has no ties, let alone blood ties? It's not like she's a relative or family friend. And why on earth would she choose a girl, especially one of lowly and likely illegitimate birth, whose mother might have been a domestic? And a dark-skinned foundling to boot—why would she want such a child?

Cultural discord also comes up around notions of abandonment. Maria Josefina Becker points out that poor parents normally place children in institutions, not intending to cast them off permanently, but rather to ensure their survival for a spell when family fortunes bottom out. That's why Margot can imagine, as she does, that Anjoli's birthmother might one day show up at the place where she left her baby. In case that happens, Margot periodically sends photos and updates to the orphanage.

Third, cultural loss always factors into the critique: loss for originating countries, for family left behind, and for children who leave. Kids may be in rags, reasoning goes, but they have a place in the scheme of things in their tattered homelands. Every mind and pair of hands matters in the project of securing justice for all children. Besides, disparagers say, unbreachable ties to their people and place, if broken, bring other damages down on children, such as those of living as a displaced person.

This line of thinking infuriates advocates. Elizabeth Bartholet writes:

> The critics of international adoption engage in a tremendous amount of false romanticization.... The children we are talking about ... live in states of near-total deprivation. Those who survive to grow up are apt to face virulent forms of racial and ethnic discrimination in their own countries, based on their racial or ethnic status or simply on the fact that they are illegitimate or orphaned.[13]

Tove Kilburn in Vancouver, who does volunteer work in Bangladeshi orphanages, and who years ago adopted two girls there, fumes. "When you're born in a gutter, I don't think you have a culture. These kids come from a stinking sewer. I don't think we're taking them away from anything at all."

What's more, proponents say, many modern adopters work darn hard to help their children access their heritage. Language lessons, culture camps, peer support groups, community picnics, festivals, a house full of books and paintings and crafts, homeland visits—these may not be the same as living a culture day to day, but it sure beats what adoptees would have known of their worlds had they gotten stuck in them. And so what if many adolescents whose adoptive parents pave their way into their past and whose families celebrate their children's traditions go through a period of rejecting contact? It's like piano lessons: at least the foundation is there to learn more later on.

Fourth, fault-finders say, flimsy and disarrayed social services in some sending countries attract the dregs of the entrepreneurial class to adoption. Remember, adopters come from countries that enjoy comparatively organized and controlled adoptions. Back home, most parent hopefuls wouldn't dream of trying to buy a baby. But, when they arrive in chaotic countries, if baby-sellers hit on them, the temptation to park scruples at the airport can overcome better judgment.

HUSTLERS AND HORROR STORIES

The idea for this book came to me as lessons from our sojourn to parenthood started sinking in. Among the books that got me going: Bartholet's *Family Bonds*. My marginal notes ran the gamut, from full agreement (Yes! Down with the obsession for blood-linked families) to strong disagreement. Wherever she described misdeeds in adoption between nations—"enormously exaggerated" and not "significant in the larger picture"—my scribbles became a string of question marks. I believed then, as I still do, that licensed operators handle most of the business and work within the law, at least within its yielding margins. Yet, I wondered if disreputable dealings were no more than a trivial sideline. I soon started keeping a file. It bulked into one of the fattest accumulations for any theme in any chapter herein. There is so much underhanded stuff to summarize in a few pages, I barely know where to begin.

Fees might be a good place. Adopters working through private, foreign intermediaries, called "facilitators," expect to be hit, on top of the usual expenses, with hefty costs. Besides travel, there are translators, special documents, distance communications, and a raft of unanticipated charges that can nickel-and-dime them into debt. In the United States, but not in Canada, private domestic adoptions can cost a fortune, too, if prospective parents cover a birthmother's allowable expenses. Hence, for U.S. adopters, a private deal abroad, barring big snags and long delays, can end up costing less than a similar adoption at home.

Joan D. Ramos, an adoptive parent and worker who investigated the state of ethics in remote adoptions, claims that "frequently parents bring many thousands of dollars *in cash* to pay the foreign intermediary who arranged the adoption."[14] Yet, legitimate types don't demand cash. Bribe-takers, birthfamilies selling babies, and the scoundrels who arrange the sales do demand it. If travelers have aboveboard intentions, why would they cart so much hard currency?

They carry it not only to pay those facilitators who are not exactly law-abiding, but also in readiness for local "customs." They may include tacitly required hurry-up or thank-you "gifts" to lawyers, judges, or any professionals along the path with power to prevent or proffer the pot of gold for which adopters have come. One family I met admitted, off the record, that they went, pockets bulging, to a meeting with the judge who'd been stalling their finalization for no apparent reason. Their lawyer hinted His Honor was waiting for an incentive. As it turned out, the judge signed without one. But, had it been necessary to grease a palm, they'd have done it. They'd been through so much, worked so hard, come so far, and, above all, already had their babe in arms. Giving the infant back was unthinkable. By comparison, it's easy to understand that a judge's payoff was peanuts.

Stories of graft along the adoption assembly line are common. In *Double Take*, Kathryn Cole tells a rollicking good story about her socialite broker in Manila who bought her way through the adoption of Cole's daughter. So much money, always beribboned to boxes of sweets, changed hands that Cole joked there must be a shop that "specialized in bribe biscuits with tins sized to fit the favor being sought."

Adoption skullduggery runs the gamut. There are credentialed men and women in suits mining the gray area in adoption law that muddies the international field. There are flimflam men pursuing foreign dollars in newly destabilized countries. There are Mafia types running black-market baby rings in some established sending countries. Then there are the adopters, many of whom would sooner go home to an empty nursery than with a child acquired through crooks. However, opponents charge, and even proponents admit, that temporary ethical blindness is an occupational hazard, especially after parents have a baby in sight. Yet other adopters smell a rat and couldn't care less, so long as their urgent journey leads them to a child.

In some places, Romania being the best recent example, petty criminals with connections and cultural smarts seize on a cash cow. They ferry foreigners to families in dire straits who are dreaming of deliverance for their children. Deliverance, promises the salesman, is waiting on your doorstep. What's a child worth? He offers a little cash and a few trinkets, treasures otherwise unattainable by the birthfamily. The seduction starts to work. Perhaps the best gift they could give at least one of their children would be nirvana, on offer at their door ...

While penny-ante cons may try to work solo, normally they stooge for higher-ups, often those responsible for expediting adoptions. Here's a small but typical sampling of scams reported since the 1980s by international child-advocacy bodies and/or major news services.

- **Paraguay.** That country, open since 1989 and the leading South American supplier of adoptees to the United States in 1995, suspended new applications for a year following a state-run investigation. It found many cases where women had been blackmailed into giving up their newborns, and where mothers or poseurs sold children for a few hundred dollars and a radio. Those implicated included lawyers, doctors, nursery operators, psychologists, notaries, and fake birthmothers.

- **El Salvador.** It halted overseas adoptions in 1994 after a band of lawyers was charged with fraud and corruption. The closure came after years of reports that scouts, working for lawyers, routinely combed the countryside for hungry mothers to coax into handing over their babies for enough money to buy a few sacks of beans.

- **Ecuador.** In 1988, following press reports of adoption improprieties, the local office of Defense for Children International investigated. DCI found a klatch of lawyers monopolizing the business. In some cases, they and adoption authorities hired poor women to kidnap children, often from public markets while their mothers worked. In other cases, poverty-stricken parents were bribed or guilted into giving up their babies to guarantee them a good life. If money and moral suasion didn't work, threats were used. The same tactics were employed to force yet other vulnerable women to masquerade as birthmothers, or to sign relinquishment documents for the abductees.

- **Argentina.** A 1988 series of raids discovered cartels of career criminals and adoption professionals procuring babies in suspicious ways. The infants were held in hideaways waiting to be sold for $20,000 each to foreigners, or, failing that, for $1,000 to $2,000 to local elites. Leandro Isla, a law professor who represented Defense of the Child in Buenos Aires at the time, estimated that four out of every five adoptions in his country were illegal, about half involving brown-bag payments to birthparents and middlemen. He cited cases of women selling a baby a year, including some who come and go from Paraguay and Bolivia.

- **Guatemala and Honduras.** In 1987 "fattening-up farms" were uncovered in both countries. Their aim? To improve the health, and hence the price point, of young children in their care, rounded up in irregular ways. The estimated yearly value of Guatemalan adoptions, by the way, is $5 million, going mostly to a handful of lawyers.

- **Brazil.** In 1986, police arrested seven suspects after recovering twenty children under three years old from clandestine nurseries where they were being readied for travel. Police claimed that about sixty people, including doctors, caregivers, court officials, and drivers, were in cahoots with the ringleader, an adoption lawyer.

- **Sri Lanka.** In the late 1980s authorities busted a German–Sri Lankan couple running a seaside "hotel" hosting local mothers and their newborns—twenty-two when police arrived. Foreigners came there to browse and to pick, for $1,000 to $5,000, the child of their choice. The dirt-poor mothers got about $50 per sale.

Scandals like these, out of Asia, Latin America, and now eastern Europe, remain sidebars to the story of international adoption. While no one knows how much of the trade is tainted, the 1993 Hague Conference on International Law found evidence of "extensive" child-trafficking. Though illegal and quasi-legal adoptions are part and parcel of this underworld, not all roads lead unlawfully procured children to families. Modern slavers smuggle minors across borders to become fresh recruits for brothels, porno flicks, and criminal gangs in sundry nations.

For adoptive purposes, most children funnel from poor to rich countries. Occasional reports also suggest folly within and among developing nations. *Time*, for instance, reported that approximately 4,000 Thai boys are sold annually to middle-class Malaysians needing heirs. As for stolen and bought babies within national borders, no case gained more notoriety than Argentina under the generals.

A notable newer feature of international adoptions involving murky arrangements—a growing militancy among birthfamilies who feel they were duped. A small number now reach across the seas in hopes of learning about, contacting, or even recouping lost children. In the most celebrated Brazilian case, a toddler, kidnapped as a baby and adopted by an Israeli couple, was repatriated in 1988 after her birthfamily won a prolonged court battle in Israel.

The subject of abuse in the commercial-adoption web wouldn't be complete without mention of the most extreme charge—that some foreigners mine babies for their body parts. Rumors that adoption and organ transplants are linked persist despite no proof. While the gossip may garner almost no believers in receiving countries, it apparently enjoys significant credibility among ordinary citizens of sending countries. In 1994, after a baby-snatching story erupted in Guatemala, a mob assaulted two American women, believing their adoptees might be slated for the scalpel. This was not the first time crowds have blown their fuse.

Dr. Janice Raymond, medical ethics and women's studies professor at the University of Massachusetts, believes the blowup is warranted. In *Women as Wombs*, she makes a carefully documented case that nefarious activities probably exist and that we are too quick to dismiss them wholesale. On many bases, including the oft-ridiculed risk of a hookup between adoption and organ-trafficking, Raymond pleads against international adoption, which she sees as a cheap, morally repugnant form of surrogacy.

You won't hear adopters quoting Raymond. They're aghast that anyone would impugn such evil motives to even one of their fellow travelers. But those who slam the adoptions, no matter how they rate the rumors, say searchers simply refuse to get it. They refuse to understand how the child chase engenders a growth medium for bizarre beliefs. If you live in a military dictatorship where people go missing permanently, it's no stretch to believe an adopted baby may become the source of a kidney for another child. Or, if you live in a society where adoption as we know it is unthinkable, some suspicions will inevitably push the envelope. Ultimately, divides between adopting and surrendering families and nations cut so deep that they give reasonable doubts and unfounded fears more than enough room to breathe.

THE THIRD WAY

Gail Barth, forty-five, who looks ten years younger and bounces with the energy of a twenty-five-year-old, is about to become a grandmother. Although her three children by birth have grown and left home, she won't have time to crochet booties. She still has nine adopted kids, age three to thirteen, to raise. Gail, her more subdued husband, Don, a flooring layer, and their brood live in Cloverdale, a lush farming community near Vancouver.

Their household is unusual not only for its size, but also for its makeup, which includes Koreans, Haitians, and Native Indians. Though Gail never intended to adopt outside Canada, the provincial social-services ministry bushwhacked her bids to adopt at home once too often. Tired of the obstacles, she looked abroad and found a smoother road.

Once on it, it was full steam ahead, with occasional detours back into domestic adoption.

In 1988, Gail and Don added to their family two brothers, preschoolers, from Haiti. With an interpreter, the Barths met the birth-family, living in hungry poverty, to kick off an open international adoption, with one visit so far. The boys' mother sought a family abroad after one of her thirteen children—the twin to one of the adoptees—died from a treatable disease, probably dysentery. On a subsequent trip to Haiti, the Barths visited the birthfamily again, only to find the mother deathly ill with TB. They arranged travel from her village to Port-au-Prince, and paid the $250 (Canadian) cost for her lifesaving treatment. She recovered and returned home, but not before asking Gail to adopt another of her babies. Although Gail initially agreed, once the mother was cured and able to cope, the Barths backed off.

"We believe in keeping families together if at all possible," Gail stresses. They also believe in what's known as "socially responsible" international adoption. Gail, crushed by her apparent infertility even after she'd had three children, underestimates neither the gut power of the parenting urge nor the gutter ethics of the baby merchants. Accordingly, no matter how life-and-death your feelings about finding a child, and whether or not it leads to heartbreak, you turn on your heel if anything *en route* to bliss looks bad.

But, if you make reasonable efforts to stick to a squeaky-clean route and to ensure that leaving the country is the child's only chance for a family, then, and only then, would your adoption win Gail's blessing. If you do import a child, then you should go on to export foreign aid—a rule of thumb in Gail's school of adoption thinking. That's why, in 1992 she founded the Canadian Foundation for the Children of Haiti, an outpost of a Haitian charity. Among other things, it has helped build a hospital by raising funds, gathering building and medical supplies in Canada, and by sending a volunteer work crew. Gail and Don both wielded hammers on that job.

This is only one of many health and social-welfare projects that international adopters support. Some parents send money of their own volition, while a few countries, China, for instance, now demand a "donation" along with more usual fees. As a result of adoptive experiences that politicized them, some parents join solidarity circles in their own communities committed to family-support efforts in their children's countries of origin. Hence, proponents argue that adopting abroad creates over here a new constituency agitating for change, while, over there, it helps on the ground.

They also claim adoption embarrasses governments into doing more for homeless kids. That's probably wishful thinking. In Latin America, for example, the emotional voltage against exporting children runs high and blows fuses at various points. Hence, intercountry adoption does provide a handy platform for speechifying against American imperialism. But does "Yankee go home" translate into cleaning up conditions that break up families, or even into clearing out corrupt adoption officials, let alone outright crooks? Doubtful. Critics say that, far from tightening the noose, sending "problem" children out of the country siphons pressure *off* do-nothing governments. Meanwhile, adoption rakes in badly needed foreign currency, estimated, for instance, at $15–20 million annually in Korea in its heyday.[15]

Finally, the ethical train of thought upholds the intercountry solution as a way station along the track to a reordered cosmos. Signal lights on adoption will flash red, accordingly, as countries industrialize and stabilize. Foreign adoptions will fall by the wayside as domestic solutions rise, thanks to better social services and more enlightened attitudes toward unmarried mothers and fatherless children.

Just look at South Korea. It has all but closed what was a wide-open door. As that country recovered from the war and became richer, it even ran a promotional campaign for local adoption. However, South Korea, the only example, is unconvincing. Given an entrenched bias for blood-related boys, along with other persistent taboos, domestic adoptions actually dwindled after the public education campaign. By 1991, 23,000 children were living in orphanages. About 4,000 more join them each year.[16] To date, the global report card shows that the fluidity of adoption borders follows passing geopolitical fancies. Nonetheless, advocates of socially responsible adoption contend that the practice helps poor countries and their kids in the transition between bad and better times.

HAPPY TRANSPLANTS?
I met Mi Ryung MacDonald, twenty-five, at a public meeting on adoption. At age five, she was adopted from Korea by an Anglo single mother. Although Mi Ryung was one of the presenters on stage and I

was in the audience, I barely noticed her. She sat at the far end of the panel, almost into the wings, coiled inside her slumped body. When she finally spoke, she came across as meek and mixed up, racked by cultural displacement.

That's why it was such a shock when we met a couple of months later, along with her mother, Joan, and sister, Molly, at their modest home in an alphabet-soup Toronto neighborhood. That night, I realized that retiring Mi Ryung has personality to spare. And, far from nondescript, she's drop-dead gorgeous. Decked out in black—a backwards baseball cap crowning her high forehead, her silky hair tied back in a ponytail, jet-black bike shorts and tunic, fire-engine red lipstick against her flawless skin—she looked like a magazine cover.

My first impressions, however, weren't all wrong. She is bursting with confusion. But Mi Ryung is a work in progress. Hammering bit by bit out of her identity haze, she's struggling toward a comfort zone. Having grown up not sure whether "I was white or Korean or anything," and wanting "to be more Canadian," she's now "slowly accepting who I am, and I'm proud that I am Korean." Pride started to set in three years ago after a journey of self-discovery to the land of her birth and the orphanage of her memory.

Before that, she preferred her Western name, Nancy, and eschewed contact with Asians. Now, she still "feels awkward" in "big groups of Oriental people" but doesn't mind "one on one." She's "scared," though, "to go into the culture and try to find my roots.... It's kind of like a pull between wanting to be accepted and ... a fear of them not accepting me." She adds, "But I don't know how much I want to be accepted because they have a very different lifestyle [from mine]."

Obviously, Mi Ryung still has a way to go. Her befuddlement, in light of the research findings, makes sense: ethnoracial coherence is *the* trick area for transnational adoptees. Knitting the unusual threads of their origins and fate into a coat that fits can become a lifetime's project.

International adoption critics have always claimed the kids would feel rootless. Indeed, many adoptees don't easily incorporate a firm sense of group affiliation, neither with their country of origin nor where they land. When they look in the mirror, some don't like what they see. There are even those who pretend they see something else. Mi Ryung's mother, Joan, believes it's no accident her daughter, as far as she knows, never dates Asian or white guys. "I don't think she feels like she belongs in either group," Joan comments.

Research on friendship patterns among transplants is revealing. Apparently, it's unusual for kids to count peers of like origins among their best friends. A large, recent U.S. look at adopted teens, including transracial and -national subjects, mostly Korean, found 20 percent wished they were a different race.[17] In the same vein, a major report on intercountry adoptees in Canada found about 10 percent, originally from Korea, Bangladesh, and Haiti, thought of themselves as white. More than 4 percent of parents in the sample also saw their kids as white! More than 25 percent believed their children of color perceived themselves as Caucasian.[18]

Some important caveats: *Most adoptees in most studies, far from torn apart by identity conflicts, express adequate ease with their heritage and self-concept.* In fact, they're sometimes more comfortable with themselves than are white domestic adoptees and birthkids in lookalike families. Remember, the normal teenage preoccupation with finding oneself isn't necessarily smooth sailing in families where few obvious differences mark its members.

Also, the fact that some kids wrestle harder than others with connectedness doesn't make them psychological cripples. Like the cross-racial research, cross-country outcomes point to more than passable self-esteem *even with* faltering ethnoracial awareness. Mi Ryung's sister, Molly, who is twenty-four, comes to mind. These two young women are like day and night. Molly, a diminutive force, all dimples and dark eyes, was adopted at age eight from an orphanage in India. Yet, she seems perfectly at home in her own skin and in her eye-catching family—"I was proud.... It was like 'That's okay. We're different, but we're unique'"—and at ease with the asymmetries of her interior world. Self-assured, assertive, and seemingly mature for her age, beyond a passing curiosity, she doesn't feel connected to her ancestry. But, for her, to date it's not been a problem.

What about racism? Has it been a problem? Joan and her daughters say "No." Now and then people stared, maybe inquisitively, maybe disapprovingly. Racial slurs were very rare. This should surprise opponents of intercountry adoption since they claim life in a mismatched family brings out meanness in onlookers. But does it? The only easy part of the answer, if the research is right, is that most transplants do brush up against some prejudice. However, "some" can mean encountering one or two ignoramuses, as the MacDonalds have, or it can mean necessary, constant alert. Advocates say that, whatever dangers discrimination poses, they are trifling compared with the prejudice adoptees born outside marriage—and fatherless girls, in particular— would face in the lands of their birth.

On variables not directly related to race or culture, study after study paints a rosy picture of how adoptees fare, whether adopted at home or abroad. They integrate into their new families, get on well with parents and sibs, like themselves, make friends, get good grades—the list goes on. Compared with nonadopted sisters and brothers, and same-age kids next door, what's their most outstanding characteristic? They're indistinguishable in their demographic group.

Here's the "but." Children adopted beyond infancy are less likely to conform to the positive portrait. Everything can be tougher for them: familial, emotional, social, and educational adjustment. In general, older means harder on everyone, including at-home and in-race adoptions. But adding cultural difference and faraway roots ups the ante for a troubled transition. Throw in exceptional trauma, like surviving in a war zone, on top of more familiar heartaches, like losing one's family and living in institutions, and kids can feel forever on the edge. Their new families can, too.

Just look at what's happening among Romanian adoptees, most of whose parents predicted health problems they hoped doctors could cure, but little else they believed love couldn't cure. Two new Canadian studies have found the children, five years later, lagging behind, with IQs ten points below average. Besides cognitive delays, the more time served in orphanages, the greater their communication and behavior problems.[19] It remains to be seen what these early forebodings will mean later on.

Though age, early agonies, and cultural dislocation taken together do spell jeopardy, they are not, as Molly attests, surefire forecasters. The MacDonald sisters got the package deal in risk factors, yet their journeys have differed radically. Mi Ryung has been plowing through angst from day one. And why wouldn't she? Besides hurts accumulated through five orphanage years (she was abandoned at three months), she came with language that was gibberish and with habits that seemed queer to her new family. She had food preferences no one could name, let alone cook. She was delivered, in an airport, to strange-looking people in an unfamiliar place. (Twenty years ago, adopters got little advice about preparing to greet a foreign child. They were led to believe all you need is love.)

How did Mi Ryung react? With shock. She refused food, except Popsicles, four days running. Joan recalls, "I tried cooking rice.... I figured rice was rice.... How naive I was." Through the Yellow Pages, Joan found a Korean grocer, whose family stuffed Mi Ryung with homestyle noodles. A rough start. But Molly, with similar markers against a smooth ride, has, by comparison, sailed through.

Mi Ryung, who'd say Molly's in denial, may be right. At the very least, it's safe to say that racial- and cultural-identity issues take a long time to resolve, and that what's comfortable at age twenty may become less so at thirty. The same questions don't strike all adoptees at the same time or with the same ferocity, but they do tend to lie in wait.

ADOPT INTERNATIONALLY: YES OR NO?

About sixty countries, approximately a third of them sending nations, decided it was high time to control these adoptions. They intend to do it through the Hague Convention on International Adoption, introduced in 1995. The multilateral treaty, with its minimum standards of practice, aims to ensure only legally available children, cleared for border-crossing as a last resort, leave any country. Signatories—about a dozen so far—must ratify the convention, enact enabling legislation, and establish a "central authority" to oversee adoptions. "Central," by the way, can mean a single federal overseer, such as the United States will eventually open, or it can mean a region-by-region model, Canada's choice. Five provinces—British Columbia, Manitoba, Saskatchewan, New Brunswick, and Prince Edward Island—already have Hague legislation.

Supporters of international adoption seem confident that the new protocols will enhance the integrity of the practice. Because only accredited, licensed agencies will be allowed to operate in Hague countries, the convention will undoubtedly put an end to the most flagrant abuses. Some interested parties following the treaty's progress point out, however, that the plan, which was designed to expunge legal headaches, ridiculous delays, and outrageous fees, will add bureaucracy, thereby likely upping time and costs. (Could a hidden benefit emerge from this irony? Will more people figure they might as well adopt at home?) Those who are skeptical about the Hague Convention say it will pile another high-sounding document atop the moral-minded dust-collectors, like the U.N. Convention on the Rights of the Child, that too often mean little in children's lives.

Recently, Barbara, an old friend I'd not seen for a decade, called. Then, out of the blue, we bumped into each other at the hairdresser's. My adoption story riveted her, reviving her unresolved urge to have kids, something she and her husband haven't been able to do. Barbara is forty-seven.

Since our reunion, they'd decided to try adopting. They'd prefer a baby. What were their chances? she wanted to know. Crummy, I told her, though slightly better if they'd shift to an older child, maybe from this continent, possibly from another. "You're telling me to consider Colombia or some such, but the other day you said that you ruled it out. Why?"

Because, I explained, the rules are spongy; you need a firm conscience. Until and if all adoptions, worldwide, come under strict controls, would-be parents have to sketch their own family-making map. In my own case, I was skittish about adopting from the third world, and, besides, I wanted a semi-open adoption at the very least.

But, I stressed to Barbara, it's a personal decision in which you trade off one set of risks for another. Unless you adopt an older child who looks a little like you and do it here—which today I'd heartily recommend if you can pry one loose from the bureaucracy before you're a pensioner—someone will try to make you feel like a bad guy (if they don't think you should be beatified, that is). You have to decide what kind of aberration you can live with being: one who adopts from the wrong race or from the wrong place. "It all boils down to what one of my adopter friends calls 'choosing the *least-uncomfortable* option.' The adoption free-for-all being what it is, there are no other guideposts."

As If Kids Mattered

It is time to move beyond the lip service paid to children ... by supporting families so that abuse will not occur in the first place, and by absolutely guaranteeing the future safety and developmental integrity of children who have been abused and neglected.

—Richard J. Gelles, The Book of David:
How Preserving Families Can Cost Children's Lives

Ultimately, this book is one story of how a society, rich in knowledge about what children need, and in resources to offer them the earth, continues to shaft so many of them. Harm comes in countless ways. At issue here: denying ever-increasing numbers of this generation the basic toolbox of life: a loving family for keeps.

So far the 1990s, the decade of the smart machine, hasn't been clever at making amends for this chronic injustice—familyless kids—perpetrated in the name of child welfare. Indeed, it hasn't been a congenial period in which to raise a voice for anyone who barely gets a glance in the best of times. Exhibit A: kids who risk entering and those already knocking around in the child-welfare system. Climbing onto the political agenda usually eludes these cast-offs. In the United States, though, they got a break when President Clinton sponsored an executive order which aims to double adoptive placements of waiting children by 2002, speed up the transfer of kids from temporary to permanent addresses, and make the public more aware of adoption.

In these chilling days of winner-take-all, losers don't often get such notice. Not when governments worship "fiscal responsibility" and wash their hands of social responsibility. Not when they toss the social safety net into the shredder. Not when they pare down "frills" they say we can no longer afford, doodads like daycare and welfare, universal health care, and quality public education. Instead, we're told, it's payback time for profligate spending. The piper doesn't mention that the deficit-building binge brought fewest benefits to those who had the least to begin with, the same people now sacrificing the most to pay the bill.

Many families, already fragile or in trouble before "structural adjustments" hit, felt the full weight of downsizing when it downloaded onto them. They have become casualties of the globalizers' greed.

Simultaneously, in the name of restraint—which is proving a record payday for the banks and the usual few—the powers-that-be are checking out on communal responsibility to protect people in the line of fire. Among the results, the underclass is surging, more families are going to seed, and more children are landing in care. Yet, the system lumbers along on dated laws, policies, and practices. With these, it cannot possibly rescue kids on a ruinous trajectory because they have no moorings.

True, we don't have perfect knowledge about what it would take to morph the child-welfare system into a panacea for problem-ridden families and kids. But we know enough to make a qualitative leap. To that end, here's a grab-bag of ideas, braided together by three threads: putting children first, speeding-up services to families and kids, and creating a user-friendly system. The laundry list, by the way, is a cut-and-paste job that borrows from here and there. But one wellspring of inspiration deserves special mention: the W.K. Kellogg Foundation's *Families for Kids of Color*.

- Opinion-makers in the field would join forces to hammer our adoption-hostile culture into its opposite: adoption-positive. Down the line, staff from every kind of child-service setting would outdo one another in promoting a motto something like this: "Children have as a birthright a safe, nurturing, forever family. For every child at least one loving, committed adult." Turning this credo into a household refrain wouldn't be haphazard. Rather, the effort would flow from orchestrated campaigns under child-welfare auspices.

- It's not enough to talk the talk. Everyone, top to bottom—from the executive director to the janitor—working in adoption agencies, would, as Pat O'Brien at You Gotta Believe boldly suggests, behave like a recruiter. This mentality matters because, as the record shows, one-to-one contact between believers and the uninitiated brings families forward into adoption.

- In tagging little ones tumbling toward a cruel childhood and in taking fast, preemptive action, the buck would stop someplace on the helping axis. Professionals would be held accountable for following strict protocols on suspected abuse. From the first known slap or hint of danger, interactive databases would track suspect families and link professionals serving them.

- The system would swear off this bad habit: being lackadaisical about social sicknesses in families. Indeed, families at risk, not those a millimeter from ruin, would grab the spotlight. Disaster prevention would supersede emergency triage. Yet, faltering adults, no matter how far gone, would get the intervention equivalent of mouth-to-mouth resuscitation to help them onto their feet, and to hold them on *terra firma* so their families could stay together.

- If biological parents couldn't cut it after best efforts, by them and by rescuers, within a year, then an alternative route to permanency would already be cleared for their kids. Planning would not start when families failed, but would be finalized long beforehand.

- For kids who had to be removed, speedy disposition would be so routine that drifting would send the system into high alert.

- Bouncing kids around would be absolutely *verboten*. As a rule, they'd experience only one make-believe family and spend no more than a year in care. A coordinated multidisciplinary squad, working under a case manager and through a single streamlined process, would assess the child's situation and draft a permanency plan. One professional from the unit would serve as the primary caseworker and as the child's buddy, at least through to placement.

- Those who remove kids and those who place them—private and independent practitioners included—would be joined at the hip. Yoked together both within the public stream and across the adoption-services spectrum, they could better collaborate to break the bottleneck relegating children to system Siberia.

- Protection and placement services, including the courts, would focus to a fault on the least-harm premise, and on "the best parenting system for the child and not the adult. In our society, we are still blaming the parent that cannot successfully parent and forgetting that the child has a right to be parented."[1]

- Children would be consulted, given as much control in shaping their destiny as they're capable of handling. Laws would enshrine their right to be heard. Adults responsible for restringing the web of children's core relationships would respect the kids' wishes, unless totally outrageous.

- Preserving vital ties to significant people from pre-placement days, and to cultural origins, would become almost sacred in protection and adoption. The importance of continuing the lines, of strengthening a child's tether to his or her roots, of integrating the past into the progression of his or her life, would become one of the basic building blocks of adoption. Guaranteeing continuity for kids, in much the same way parties to a civilized divorce do, would become the norm. By extension, confidential adoptions and closed records would go the way of the dodo bird.

- Birthmothers would be swaddled in supports that allow for real choice in raising or relinquishing their newborns. Girls know the score: keep your baby, and welcome to poverty, social isolation, McJobs. Morally, the community may not condemn you, but normally it will not, beyond subsistence, offer a hand. As a result, many who opt for adoption do it under the rubric of choice and the reality of no such thing. Ideally, young moms could choose freely, knowing that, if they decide to bring up their baby, the help they need will be there. This is not to argue for teenage parenthood, which is fraught with personal and social fallout, but against forced relinquishment masquerading as free choice—a blight on the entire history of adoptions. At the same time, young parents, like everyone else, would be savvy about the adoption option. They'd be much more favorably disposed than most are now, thanks to a shining example of public education. The upshot: more, not fewer, adoptable babies.

- Kincare would catch fire, reigniting not only in groups with a tradition, but across the society. Extended family, very broadly conceived and without bearing on blood, would become the first line of hope. In fact, many children, as Pat O'Brien likes to say, already have a potential guardian angel: an aunt, the school janitor, the neighborhood grocer. Those in charge of the kids would sleuth out these "relatives" and lavish incentives on them—stipends, courses, respite care, or whatever it takes—to become the child's permanent anchor.

- Where kin or kinlike folks weren't in evidence, the system would beat the bushes for every family that might embrace the child. By this, I don't mean to tarnish "stranger" adoptions. Indeed, I've tried to make the case for the equality and legitimacy of the entire palette of family types. Still, it behooves us to remember: the more links a child maintains with his or her earlier world, the easier adoption will likely go.

- Faded ideas about "good" families, based on such flimsy criteria as structure and income, would never enter the conversation. Instead, concern would center on how much a given candidate wants a particular child, and the applicant's capacity to respond to the breadth of that child's needs with or without financial or other assistance. Far from fretting about household form, child-placers would relish today's smorgasbord, thereby putting an end to the old game of playing favorites.

- Another tradition would bite the dust: singing the praises of "comfortable" white couples as choice adopters. In fact, the chorus has been gradually updated to include families of color and those of lesser means. Yet, among standard agencies, the tendency to privilege the old elite by failing to reach out enough to others continues to make the lyrics ring a tad hollow. Excuses for not creating a diverse waiting list of adopters have outlived their staledate.

- Instead of examining would-be adopters for parental worthiness, which is a lot of subjective hooey in any case, the homestudy focus would shift. It would prepare people to become worthy parents of adopted kids, who have unique issues atop the regular stuff of growing up. While some agencies already use the study as much to train as to assess applicants, in many private adoptions, candidates (read: mostly professionals chasing babies) don't have to learn a thing. They just have to impress their studier that they're not hazardous to children.

- Before birthfamilies select adoptive parents, intermediaries would give them a mini-course on the whole tableau of modern adopters. Why? Because in the same way as those prospective parents fixated on a newborn need their horizons nudged, those birthfamilies bent on Bill and Suzy ought to learn, for example, that Jim alone or Jill alone, or maybe Jill and Jasmine together, can make fine parents too. In the final cut, facilitators would honor the birthparents' choice, but only after broadening their vista.

- The profit motive would be excavated from adoption; ostentatious fees would be no more. Government regulation of private and independent adoptions would force the art of family-making to dissociate from artless commerce. There'd be strict controls on allowable charges and rates, plus a subsidized, sliding-fee scale for consumers. These, in concert with more generous subsidies—based on family income, not only on adoptees' extraordinary needs—would level the playing field. Financial aid, by the way, needn't necessarily mean new nickels; in some locations, more than pennies could be purged from foster care. Without costs holding them back, a true cross-section of the population could step forward.

- Standard agencies would stop relying mostly on families that try, on their own steam, to adopt. Here's a novel idea: child-welfare/adoption authorities would go all out to sell the public on adoption as a normal way to build a family. They'd hire hotshot advertising types to design the pitch. They'd make average citizens acutely aware of waiting kids. What's more, when families braved entering the bureaucracy, they'd be treated with kid gloves and to a speedy turnaround in completing their adoption.

- The adoption system would be diverse and collaborative, but also competitive. Public agencies in particular would race to incorporate specialty-agency innovations in finding, matching, and sustaining adoptive families. In the United States, smaller private and voluntary service-providers usually outdistance the rest at placing racial minority, older, and special-needs children. Generally speaking, this nervy little troop of upstart agencies is neither uptight about nontraditional adopters nor hamstrung by the either/or rigidity—either a birthfamily or an unrelated adoptive family—needlessly trapping so many kids in in-care gridlock.

If I had my druthers, adoption would be a public responsibility, not a private or semiprivate business, a charity, or a voluntary venture. Though people closer to the community and at arm's length from child welfare have the passion to reimagine adoption, volunteers, in my view, need be vigilant against government desires to have its work done for free. Having said this, the sad fact remains: the state as parent notoriously lacks sensitivity and imagination in dealing with its children. Besides, bureaucracies are allergic to speed. Hence, at the moment, I'd opt for outside agencies *under government contract* as the way forward. In the United States, there's some precedent for such a move. Various jurisdictions already purchase foster and adoptive services from small, community-based agencies. In some cases, the purchasers award higher payments if contractors fast-track kids from foster into adoptive homes. In other words, better outcomes bring financial bonuses.[2] This is a far cry from the status quo, which, in effect, rewards agencies for keeping kids in no man's land.

- Money would be divvied up to discourage long-term fostering and to kick-start growth in the use of every permanency package so far divined. Job one would have two prongs: (a) inoculating precarious birthfamilies against breakdown, and (b) finding temporary caregivers prepared to sign on for life if necessary—assuming things click between them and the child—and eager to keep the first family in the child's orbit.

- Authorities would routinely relate to families—birth, foster, adoptive—as partners in making the best-possible plan for children with whom they're involved. As things stand, more often than not care-connected families feel the system flubs it when it comes to valuing their contributions.

- The public system would smarten up, find ways to get over its tendency to diminish the people it touches. The harsh slap of disempowerment, stinging birthfamilies worst, goes to the heart of why they avoid the public route like the plague unless their babies are apprehended and they have no choice. Were they in the driver's seat during the adoption process, as they can be in the nongovernmental sphere, more birthfamilies with newborns might go public. The benefit? Blurring the baby/bigger kids and affluent/average adopter schisms between private and public adoptions.

- Protection and placement would be enlaced in accountability mechanisms, answerable to constituencies other than professional bodies and government overseers, which themselves can be part of the problem. One direction in which accountability needs more than a facelift: inclusion of local communities. Indeed, locals would be in on planning and executing reforms to make services more effective and responsive. And performance standards, instead of being airy-fairy, would be measured by "an exacting bottom line: every waiting child must be placed swiftly and appropriately in a family setting that affords stability and lifelong ties."[3]

- All agencies would start behaving, like some do now, as if adoption goes beyond the piece of paper that assigns parental rights. Adoption is a pivotal, lifelong process for all affected parties. Therefore, supports, on an as-needed basis, would accompany them along the journey. Services would not cluster, as they tend to, around the starting blocks.

- Provinces and territories in Canada, like individual states in the United States, have responsibility for adoption, which accounts for the otherwise incomprehensible disparities from one place to the next. Trying to adopt across lines on the national map can be as slow and frustrating, if doable at all, as adopting from some banana republic. Though the case for standardizing laws is old and compelling—for one thing, it would make it easier for kids to find families—the subject has no bounce in Canada. In the United States, the National Conference of Commissioners on Uniform State Laws has been working for many years on the Uniform Adoption Act, but it's a ways from satisfying all interested parties and being ready for the books. Yet, to broaden prospects for placing children within their own country, the practice of tying them up with red tape into territorial patches will have to be pitched out.

- Perhaps the most convincing evidence of a robust system would emerge from radically reformed judicial proceedings. For starters, the courts would stop playing footsies with child-welfare dawdlers. Between them, these two slowpokes consign kids to limbo for years on end. Finally, the legislative end of custody would be guided by children's, not by adults', best interests, and an unfaltering dedication to safety.

These proposals by no means cover all reforms whose time has come. They merely begin to map routes for getting out of some of the old ruts. But even these ideas, if widely applied, could confer on many more children a chance to enjoy the halcyon days of youth. Doubtless, even a small number of the proposals, if taken seriously and applied universally, could have a big impact on the practice of adoption.

I think about how they might have affected David and me when we ventured into the adoption world of the 1990s. From that first call to Children's Aid, we would have been treated like royalty. The intake worker would have rolled out the red carpet to ensure that we'd make it into the office and that one more child would be spared a life of avoidable misery.

How would it go from there? The worker would be glad to see us and certain that, if we meet some basic requirements, we could be a family of three within months. Though we went in with our hearts set on an almost-flawless toddler at oldest—and s/he would listen to our dream—s/he'd move the conversation toward the reality: babies are few and far between. Besides, given our age, we can't afford a long wait. There are, however, as s/he'd remind us, lots of tots stalled in the system. These words wouldn't come as a big surprise since the plight of these youngsters would have a public profile. S/he'd urge us to consider pushing our limits, to at least meeting some families who've stretched theirs. S/he'd give us literature, maybe a video, invite us to an orientation session, encourage us to call with questions, then send us home to read and think. Before we go, s/he'd tell us about courses we'd get to prepare for adoptive parenting, about pre- and post-adoption services, about support groups and available subsidies. We'd go away feeling that, if we chose a child from care, we'd be cushioned to meet the challenges.

If we came back, the first item of business? Introduce us to several families parenting one or two kids adopted past babyhood. We'd visit over-the-hill urban professionals, temporal types like us, not householders doing God's work raising twenty-five kids with extraordinary needs from around the globe. We might be in awe, but they'd spook us. In other words, the system wouldn't try to prettify older-child adoptions, or make us feel we'd need old-time religion to take on the task. Nor would it persuade us in the abstract, but it would show us in the flesh what might be ahead were we to raise kids who've had a rocky start.

If we proceeded to the homestudy, it would ready us for the kind of family we're about to form, which doesn't have familiar cultural references. We'd explore, for example, adoption from the child's perspective, the meaning of openness, our preparedness, or lack thereof, to help a child prize his or her heritage if different from ours. Indeed, the home-study would help us define the kind of child who might feel most at home with us and with whom we'd be most comfortable: age, gender, background, special needs, etc. But, more important, it would jump-start the lifelong process of constructing sensitivities and skills to help us excel in our job as parents. This, instead of wasting a lot of time recalling—fancifully reconstructing, is more like it—the early relationship we had with our parents, or our fantasies about ourselves as parents-to-be.

For the sake of argument, though, let's say the Children's Aid Society wasn't our first stop, but some private agency. There, too, the facilitator would fill us in on the kids who don't find families in a flash. At the same time, s/he wouldn't rule out the possibility that a newborn's birth-parents might choose us. There's no point trying to foist an unwelcome child on any adopters, but every point in checking whether they have malleable minds. In our case, as it happens, David and I were putty, but no one tried to reshape us. Had anyone on our route been on the job for kids who don't find families in the blink of an eye, we might have ended up with one system child, or even with two youngish siblings. As I said in the preface, we couldn't be happier with the son we were blessed to find. But that we had to work so hard and go so far afield to find him, rather than the system at home working so hard to find us for kids who aren't grabbed up in an instant—herein lies the nub of what's so dreadfully wrong. And until the system stops would-be adopters long before they head to the border, it will continue to deserve the harshest rebukes.

This teaser of how the journey might have begun for us, if the system had its priorities right, hints at how different things might be for children if even a small part of the wish list above, however inadequate, was in working order. In fact, elements of this far-from-perfect compass for a new course have already been massaged into practice. Farsighted laws, pacesetting private and specialty services, even the odd renegade public agency and family court—thanks to tireless child advocates, and rebellious social and court workers—have been turning the tables. In these transitional days, bits and pieces of the system do yield under the weight of progressive impulses. Indeed, pioneering agencies lead the way. Read almost any issue of an adoption newsletter and your heart will warm to the ingenious pilot projects that spring up. Though truer in the United States than in Canada, the ingenuity for taking a giant step already exists. The wheel doesn't need to be invented; it only needs to be turned.

What's good, however, is still hit and miss; what's wrong, widespread. The net result: the child-protection/-placement juggernaut remains manacled to a set of family values, bureaucratic reflexes, turf considerations, and bottom-line thinking that bring needless calamity on an appalling number of kids.

As standards, even the sketchy inventory above will be filed away as madcap musings unless stakeholders and the bigger body politic kick up a fuss. Unless we prevent policymakers and purse-string holders from continuing to imperil young lives—admittedly an audacious ambition at this historic moment. Governments have sunk to new lows in averting their glance from the most vulnerable among us. Complicating matters, the kids involved could not have less political coin. Most don't come from just any family; they are the children of the damned, which in the final analysis explains why they suffer such rough justice.

Demanding a pro-social agenda with protections for children— here in the form of a timely permanent family—is particularly brazen. It is brash, given the long-disgraced affinity for letting kids amble endlessly and pass through the hands of dozens of helpers. Brash, given the newer affection for shifting collective responsibilities onto private shoulders. However, the fact that those who should listen often appear to have closed their ears to all but a select few shouldn't stop us from raising our voices. Instead, we need to pump up the volume.

Moseying unprepared into the peculiar ether of adoption at the start of this decade, it felt more like I'd entered the twilight zone than enlightened human services on the lip of the millennium. Yet, looking around later, I saw harbingers of change. Signs show up among those child advocates, adoption promoters, and child-placers who insist it is possible with all due haste to tuck children into the decent families they deserve—and to heck with whether that means birth or adoptive. Signs emerge from would-be adopters who refuse to go away when rejected because they don't fit some hackneyed old formula for family.

The system, one can only hope, might yet distill lessons from trendsetters who are polishing up the adoptive-family image and finding parents for children. It might yet abandon its line—families can't be found—in favor of this standpoint: there are umpteen homes, and the right permanency plan, for every child, including those whose needs far exceed the ordinary. In this mindset, all that's required is a little imagination to locate and groom the best prospects.

To conclude what is essentially a sad story on a positive note: I met a lot of people who agree it's high time to bring adoption out of the closet, and high time to swing open the doors to any competent adult or configuration of adults who define themselves as family. Most of all, they say, it's time to stop making excuses for keeping kids in family Neverland.

Afterword

When Marlene Webber first contacted me, she was thinking of writing a book about "this awful system." Initially I thought she was just another adoptive parent justifiably upset about the way she had been treated. As I listened, though, I heard someone who was genuinely concerned about the negative treatment of helpless children. I suggested some initial contacts, then forgot about it. Now that I have read her book, I am grateful that she completed her task, and that we can all share her findings.

As If Kids Mattered spares no jurisdiction in its indictment of current practices in the adoption business. That thousands of children in North America spin around for years in the revolving door of child welfare, when there are loving families desperately trying to adopt them, is an abdication of government responsibility and a failure of society at large.

It can be painful reading for those of us who have worked in child welfare and adoption. But it also presents a fair picture of the trailblazers—the social workers, parents, agencies and adoption advocates who defy archaic rules based on family values of yesteryear to bring together waiting children and parents.

Much of what Webber has to say will come as no surprise to those of us who have adopted. But rarely has such a wealth of information, so solidly researched, been packaged with such passion and humor.

She tackles the most contentious issues, stepping into the political minefield of gay and lesbian adoption, and dealing sensitively and realistically with the complex cultural and political issues around interracial and aboriginal adoption. She introduces us to adoptive parents who are wealthy, poor, culturally and racially diverse, older, single, gay—most of whom would not get past the traditional intake desk. We also meet their adopted children, who would not be considered prime material for adoption in many agency or government departments because of their age, severe disabilities, race and culture.

These are not perfect parents, or perfect children. Their relationships with each other are not trouble-free. What is so heartwarming, however, is the strength of commitment that these parents all display—"the 'C' word," as an adoption advocate friend of mine calls it. It is the commitment that seems to make the difference.

Despite the odds, this strange assortment of parents and children have fashioned warm and loving families. We begin to see what is wrong with the system through their words. And if we don't quite get it, Webber hammers the message home. Some readers may be offended by the strength or provocative tone of her language, but what she says is important.

Her strongest and most important message? All children should have the right to a permanent, loving family, no matter how the family is configured, and it is the responsibility of government and every one of us to see that this happens. Her wish list for a changed system should become part of the curriculum at all schools of social work, and read by all social workers and bureaucrats responsible for child welfare planning, as well as by politicians who ultimately have the responsibility for legislation and policy.

Webber is very much aware that there are no simple solutions to the issues in adoption, and she challenges us all to confront those issues. Only then will we begin to make a difference, and find loving families quickly for all those children who now wait.

My only reservation about this book—I wish I had written it.

—Sandra Scarth
Founder and Former Executive Director,
Child Welfare League of Canada

Notes

CHAPTER 1

1. Carole A. McKelvey and Dr. JoEllen Stevens, *Adoption Crisis: The Truth behind Adoption and Foster Care* (Golden, CO: Fulcrum Publishing, 1994), p. 19

2. Elizabeth Bartholet, *Family Bonds: Adoption and the Politics of Parenting* (Boston: Houghton Mifflin, 1993), p. 36

3. Patricia Irwin Johnston, "Speaking Positively: An Introduction to Positive Adoption Language" (Indianapolis: Perspectives Press, n.d.), photocopy

4. Bartholet, *Family Bonds*, p. 167

5. Karen March, *The Stranger Who Bore Me: Adoptee–Birth Mother Relationships* (Toronto: University of Toronto Press, 1995), p. 128

6. Ibid., p. xi

7. Jana Wolff, *Secret Thoughts of an Adoptive Mother* (Kansas City: Andrews and McMeel, 1997), p. 130

8. McKelvey and Stevens, *Adoption Crisis*, p. 18

9. Rita Simon, Howard Alstein, and Marygold Melli, *The Case for Transracial Adoption* (Washington, DC: American University Press, 1994), p. 11

10. Bartholet, *Family Bonds*, p. 72

11. Robert L. Woodson, *Wall Street Journal*, September 23, 1992, p. A14

CHAPTER 2

1. The primary sources for unattributed data in this chapter are: Edna McConnell Clark Foundation, North American Council on Adoptable Children, National Centre on Youth Law, American Public Welfare Association, American Civil Liberties Union, Adoption Council of Canada, and Child Welfare League of America and of Canada.

2. "Unadoptable Children," *Adoptive Families*, November/December 1995, p. 16

3. Margaret Wente, "To Save Children at Risk," *Globe and Mail*, September 21, 1996, p. D7

4. Kevin Donovan and Moira Walsh, "Missed Clues—Lost Lives," *Sunday Star*, April 20, 1997, p. A1

5. Louise Armstrong, *Solomon Says: A Speakout on Foster Care* (New York: Pocket Books, 1989), p. 27

6. David Bender and Bruno Leone, *Adoption: Opposing Viewpoints* (San Diego: Greenhaven Press, 1995), p. 87

7. Nadine Jacobson and Bill Holton, "Loving Elizabeth: A Blind Couple's Struggle to Adopt a Baby," *Family Circle* 108/14 (October 10, 1995), p. 94

8. Barbara Tremitiere, "Coping, Conscience, and the Difficult Child," in Hope Marindin, ed., *The Handbook for Single Adoptive Parents* (Chevy Chase: Committee for Single Adoptive Parents, 1992), p. 46

9. Bender and Leone, *Adoption*, 285

10. Joe Kroll, "The Impact of Welfare Reform in Child Welfare," *Adoptalk*, Fall 1996, p. 3

11. Carole A. McKelvey and Dr. JoEllen Stevens, *Adoption Crisis: The Truth behind Adoption and Foster Care* (Golden, CO: Fulcrum Publishing, 1994), p. 52

12. According to the North American Council on Adoptable Children (NACAC), subsidized adoptions run at $8 to $13 a day

13. If you have any lingering doubts about the orphanage solution, read *There Is a Better Way: Family-Based Alternatives to Institutional Care* (St. Paul, MN: NACAC, April 1995).

CHAPTER 3

1. See, for example, Sue Wells, *Within Me, Without Me. Adoption: An Open and Shut Case?* (London: Scarlet Press, 1994)

2. Judith S. Modell, *Kinship with Strangers: Adoption and Interpretations of Kinship in American Culture* (Los Angeles: University of California Press, 1994), p. 237

3. Ibid., p. 231

4. Marilyn Shinyei and Linda Edney, "Open Adoption in Canada," *Transition*, September 1992, p. 8

5. Letters to the Editor, *Maclean's*, June 27, 1994, p. 6

6. Marsha Riben, *Shedding Light on the Dark Side of Adoption* (Detroit: Harlow, 1988), p. 75

7. Carol Anderson, "Open Adoption or Open Exploitation," *CUB Communicator*, April 1992, p. 10

8. Jan Waldron, *Giving Away Simone: A Memoir* (New York: Times Books, 1995), p. 114

9. Ibid., p. 175

10. Karen March, *The Stranger Who Bore Me: Adoptee–Birth Mother Relationships* (Toronto: University of Toronto Press, 1995), p. 98

11. Susan Wadia-Ells, ed., *The Adoption Reader: Birth Mothers, Adoptive Mothers and Adopted Daughters Tell Their Stories* (Seattle: Seal Press, 1995), p. 8

12. Riben, *Shedding Light on the Dark Side of Adoption*, p. 102

13. Lois Ruskai Melina and Sharon Kaplan Roszia, *The Open Adoption Experience* (New York: Harper Perennial, 1993), p. xviii

14. Ruth McRoy, Harold Grotevant, and Susan Ayers-Lopez, *Changing Practices in Adoption* (Austin: University of Texas Press, 1994)

15. See, for example, Lois Ruskai Melina and Sharon Kaplan Roszia, *The Open Adoption Experience*; Kathleen Silber and Martinez Dorner, *Children of Open Adoption* (San Antonio: Corona Publishing, 1990); Kathleen Silber and Phylis Speedlin, *Dear Birth Mother* (San Antonio: Corona Publishing, 1991)

16. Silber and Dorner, *Children of Open Adoption*, p. 188

17. Silber and Speedlin, *Dear Birth Mother*, p. 69

18. McRoy, Grotevant, and Ayers-Lopez, *Changing Practices in Adoption*, p. 14

19. Judith S. Modell, *Kinship with Strangers: Adoption and Interpretations of Kinship in American Culture* (Los Angeles: University of California Press, 1994), p. 231

20. Ibid., p. 235

21. Waldron, *Giving Away Simone*, p. 214

22. Irving G. Leon, "The Crusade for Children's Rights," *Ours*, May/June 1994

23. Charlotte Vick, "Solomon-Like Settlement Avoids Baby Jessica Result," *Adoptalk*, Fall 1993, p. 7

24. Modell, *Kinship with Strangers*, p. 237

CHAPTER 4

1. David K. Flaks, "Research Issues," in Ann Sullivan, ed., *Issues in Gay and Lesbian Adoption: Proceedings of the Fourth Annual Peirce-Warwick Adoption Symposium* (Washington, DC: Child Welfare League of America, 1995), p. 21

2. David Frum, "Gay Rights?" *Saturday Night*, December 1995, pp. 66, 69

3. Kerry Daly and Michael Sobol, *Adoption in Canada: Final Report* (Guelph: Health and Welfare Canada, May 1993), p. 55

4. Helen Nestor, *Family Portraits in Changing Times* (Portland: NewSage Press, 1992), p. 60

5. Joseph Berger, "Adoption by Same-Sex Couples Not in Children's Best Interests," *Toronto Star*, June 3, 1995, p. A25

6. Carol Austin, "Latent Tendencies and Covert Acts," in Susan Wadia-Ells, ed., *The Adoption Reader* (Seattle: Seal Press, 1995), pp. 107, 111

7. Celeste McGovern, "The Feds Move to Horn In on Adoption," *Alberta Report*, June 14 1993, p. 29

8. Laura Benkov, *Reinventing the Family* (New York: Crown Publishers, 1994), p. 173

9. Ibid., p. 198

10. David Bender and Bruno Leone, *Adoption: Opposing Viewpoints* (San Diego: Greenhaven Press, 1995)

11. Stephan Lynch, *The Progressive*, January 1996, p. 15

CHAPTER 5

1. Kathryn Cole, *Double Take* (Toronto: Stoddart, 1995), p. 24

2. Hope Marindin, ed., *The Handbook for Single Adoptive Parents* (Chevy Chase: Committee for Single Adoptive Parents, 1992), p. 32.

3. See, for example, Shere Hite, *The Hite Report on Men and Male Sexuality* (London: Bloomsbury, 1981)

4. Shoshana Alexander, *In Praise of Single Parents* (Boston: Houghton Mifflin, 1994), p. 22.

5. "Single Parenting and a Changing Society" *Adoption Resource Exchange for Single Parents Inc. Newsletter*, Springfield, VA, Fall, 1995

6. Kerry Daly and Michael Sobol, *Adoption in Canada: Final Report* (Guelph: Health and Welfare Canada, May 1993), p. 7

7. Cheri Register, *"Are Those Kids Yours?"* (New York: The Free Press 1991), p. 7

8. "Single Parent Adoption: What You Need to Know," National Adoption Information Clearinghouse Information Sheet, Rockville, MD

9. James Rosenthal and Victor K. Groze, *Special Needs Adoption: A Study of Intact Families* (New York: Praeger, 1992), p. 115

10. Barbara Tremitiere, *The Large Adoptive Family: A Special Kind of Normal* (York, PA: One Another Publications, 1994), pp. 110, 111

11. Alexander, *In Praise of Single Parents*, p. 329

12. Rosenthal and Groze, *Special Needs Adoption*, p. 116

13. Ibid., ch. 7

14. Victor Groze and James Rosenthal, "Single Parents and Their Adopted Children: A Psychosocial Analysis," *Families in Society: The Journal of Contemporary Human Services*, February 1991, p. 74

15. Rosenthal and Groze, *Special Needs Adoption*, p. 114

16. Ibid., p. 121

CHAPTER 6

1. David Bender and Bruno Leone, *Adoption: Opposing Viewpoints* (San Diego: Greenhaven Press, 1995)

2. Ruth McRoy, "An Organizational Dilemma: The Case of Transracial Adoptions," *The Journal of Applied Behavioural Science*, 25/2 (1989), p. 145-160.

3. Leora Neal and Al Stumph, *Transracial Adoptive Parenting: A Black/White Community Issue* (New York: Haskett-Neal Publications, 1993), p. 9

4. "Healing Old Wounds," *Adoptalk*, Fall 1988, p. 4

5. Azizi Powell, "African American Perceptions of Adoption," *Transracial Adoption Manual* (San Francisco: Pact Press,), p. 49

6. W.K. Kellogg Foundation, *Families for Kids of Color: A Special Report on Challenges and Opportunities* (Battle Creek, MI: W.K. Kellogg Foundation), p. 15

7. Bender and Leone, *Adoption, Opposing Viewpoints*, p. 188

8. Ibid., p. 189

9. Rita Simon, Howard Alstein, and Marygold Melli, *The Case for Transracial Adoption* (Washington, DC: American University Press, 1994), p. 42

10. Nicolle Tremitiere, "I Should Have Had Black Parents," *Utne Reader*, November/December 1991, p. 60 (excerpt from *Essence*, April 1991)

11. Ashante Infantry, "Adoption: Not a Black/White Solution," *Jamaican Weekly Gleaner* (North American edition, April 7–13, 1995)

12. Simon, Alstein, and Melli, *The Case for Transracial Adoption*, p. 61

13. Christopher Bagley, "Adoption of Native Children in Canada: A Policy Analysis and a Research Report," in Howard Alstein and Rita Simon, eds., *Intercountry Adoption: A Multinational Perspective* (New York: Praeger, 1991), pp. 55–79

14. Estela Andujo, "Ethnic Identity of Transethnically Adopted Hispanic Adolescents," *Social Work*, November/December 1988, pp. 531-34

15. Ruth McRoy quoted in Dorothy Elizabeth Brooks, "Black/White Transracial Adoption: An Update," *Ours*, July/August 1991, p. 20

16. Comments made in a workshop on transracial adoption at the 1995 NACAC annual meeting

17. Liza Steinberg, "Straight Talk," *Pact Press*, Summer 1996, p. 38

18. Bender and Leone, *Adoption*, p. 158

19. Neal and Stumph, *Transracial Adoptive Parenting*, p. 9

20. Simon, Alstein, and Melli, *The Case for Transracial Adoption*, p. 5

21. Tom Gilles and Joe Kroll, *Barriers to Same Race Placement*, Research Brief no. 2 (St. Paul, MI: North American Council on Adoptable Children, April 1991), p. 8

22. Ibid., p. 18

23. Ruth McRoy, "The Case of Transracial Adoptions," *The Journal of Applied Behavioural Science*, 25/2 (1989), p. 157

24. See W.K. Kellogg Foundation, *Families for Kids of Color*

25. G. Steinberg and B. Hall, "Supporting Transracial Families. Start from Where They Are." *Transracial Adoption Manual*, Winter, 1994, p. 99

26. See Neal and Stumph, *Transracial Adoptive Parenting*

27. Shoshana Alexander, *In Praise of Single Parents* (Boston: Houghton Mifflin, 1994), p. 23

28. Marita Golden, *Saving Our Sons: Raising Black Children in a Turbulent World* (New York: Doubleday, 1995), p. 68

CHAPTER 7

1. Brief to Review Committee, William Clarence Thorns, Superintendent for the Peguis School Board, November 5, 1982, in Edwin C. Kimelman, *No Quiet Place*, Review Committee on Indian and Metis Adoptions and Placements Final Report to the Honourable Muriel Smith, Minister of Community Services, Winnipeg: Manitoba Community Services (1985), p. 210

2. Peter Moon, "School Wants Truth out and Victims to Heal," *Globe and Mail*, October 19, 1996, p. A6

3. Drew Hayden Taylor, "The Death of a Scoop-Up Child," *Globe and Mail*, April 12, 1997, p. D10

4. Pauline Comeau and Aldo Santin, *The First Canadians: A Profile of Canada's Native People Today*, 2nd ed. (Toronto: James Lorimer, 1995), p. 143

5. "Native Issues in Adoption," *Adoption Roundup*, Summer 1992, p. 4

6. Ibid.

7. Rita Simon, Howard Alstein, and Marygold Melli, *The Case for Transracial Adoptions* (Washington, DC: American University Press, 1994), p. 8

8. Ibid.

9. Ray Moisa, "Indians Resist Non-Indian Adoption," *Utne Reader*, November/December 1991, p. 58

10. Lila Sarick, "Adoptees Unearth Their Native Roots," *Globe and Mail*, April 7, 1994, p. A4

11. Ibid.

12. Christopher Bagley, "Adoption of Native Children in Canada: A Policy Analysis and a Research Report," in Howard Alstein and Rita Simon, eds., *Intercountry Adoption: A Multinational Perspective* (New York: Praeger, 1992)

13. Diane Riggs, "The Indian Child Welfare Act: Issues and Developments," *Adoptalk*, Summer 1995, p. 6

14. Ray Moisa, "Indians Resist Non-Indian Adoption," *Utne Reader*, November/December 1991, p. 58

15. Sobol and Daly, *Adoption in Canada*, p. 105

16. Moisa, "Indians Resist Non-Indian Adoption," p. 58

CHAPTER 8

1. Marilyn Shinyei and Linda Edney, "Open Adoption in Canada," *Transition*, September 1992, p. 37

2. James Rosenthal and Victor K. Groze, *Special Needs Adoption: A Study of Intact Families* (New York: Praeger, 1992), p. 106

3. Mary Ellen Fieweger, "Stolen Children and International Adoptions," *Child Welfare*, 70/2 (March/April 1988), p. 290

4. Michael S. Serrill, "The Gray Market in Third World Children," *Time* (Canadian edition) 138/18 (November 4, 1991), p. 60

5. Michael Serrill, "Wrapping the Earth in Family Ties," *Time*, November 4, 1991, p. 54

6. "Intercountry Adoption Statistics for 1993," *OURS*, March/April 1994, p. 9

7. "Global Trends in Adoption," *Adoptive Families*, March/April 1996, p. 11

8. Elizabeth Bartholet, *Family Bonds: Adoption and the Politics of Parenting* (Boston: Houghton Mifflin, 1993), p. xv

9. Judy Ashdenaz, "Indians," in Susan Wadia-Ells, ed., *The Adoption Reader* (Seattle: Seal Press, 1995), p. 143

10. Kenneth J. Herrmann Jr. and Barbara Kasper, "International Adoption: The Exploitation of Women and Children," *Affilia* 7/1, Spring 1992, p. 50

11. Janice G. Raymond, *Women as Wombs: Reproductive Technologies and the Battle Over Women's Freedom* (San Francisco: Harper San Francisco, 1993), p. 151

12. Damien Ngabonziza, "Moral and Political Issues Facing Relinquishing Countries," *Adoption and Fostering* 15/4 (1991), p. 78

13. Bartholet, *Family Bonds*, p. 157

14. Joan Ramos, "The Tough Ethical Issues of International Adoption," *Ours*, January/February 1994, p. 14.

15. Herrmann and Kasper, p. 50

16. Serrill, "Wrapping the Earth in Family Ties," p. 57

17. Peter L. Benson and Anu Sharma, "The Truth About Adopted Teenagers," *Adoptive Families*, July/August 1994, p. 20

18. Anne Westhues and Joyce Cohen, *Intercountry Adoption in Canada, Final Report* (Ottawa: National Welfare Grants, Human Resources Development Canada, January 1994), pp. 141, 171

19. Jane Gadd, "Adopted Romanians Lagging," *Globe and Mail*, May 24, 1996, p. A6

CHAPTER 9

1. O. Virginia Phillips, "Who Are the Real Parents?," *Pact Press* 3/2 (Spring 1994), p. 17

2. Diane Riggs and Kate Welty, "Privatization: The Future Is Now," *Adoptalk*, Winter 1997, p. 4

3. W.K. Kellogg Foundation, *Families for Kids of Color*, p. 3

Acknowledgments

Writing a book is a lot like the African proverb about raising a child: it takes a village. Mine was peopled with too many to include here, especially those who, through a quick chat, led me to interviews. While I can't, I regret, list everyone who tried to give me productive leads, at least I can mention some who made calls for me which resulted in key interviews: Helen Mark at the Adoptive Parents' Association of British Columbia; Pat O'Brien at You Gotta Believe! The Older Child Adoption and Permanency Movement, based in Coney Island; Debbie Thomas and Debbie Kelly at Project Star, in Pittsburgh; Virginia Butler at the Council on Adoptable Children, in New York City; Brenee Moore at the Judson Center and Mary Lee Pearson at Spaulding for Children, both in Michigan; Marilyn Shinyei at Adoption Options, in Edmonton. Thank you.

A few of these same folks, plus others, helped fill my files with useful material, or my head with ideas that became pivotal. Elspeth Ross at the Adoption Council of Canada and Pat Fenton at the Ontario Adoption Council are gold mines. So, too, is Pat O'Brien. I owe him special thanks for fixing me up with families, for ferrying me around, and for having such a big mouth when it comes to the plight of older children lost in the system. Were everyone in the field to believe, as Pat does, that there's a plan for permanency, and a family out there, to fit each youngster, were everyone convinced we can invent enough, innovative schemes to make that dream come true, books like this one wouldn't be needed.

Since Pat's is not the majority view, I turned to adoptive families, in particular, newer types, to figure out what's wrong with them or with adoption itself. Something had to be off, I reckoned, to make the child-welfare/adoption system frequently freeze at the thought of potential parents like me—forty-plus, then living common law—and other nontraditional comers. Something had to be fishy about today's families, and probably about the very idea of adoption, if the system could favor broken-down birthfamilies and ring-around foster families over permanent adoptive homes.

At the outset, my agenda—to examine *nouveau* adoptive households from the inside out—was a bit fuzzy. But as I listened to adopters, the focus sharpened. I heard a convincing case for adoption as just another regular way to build a family. I heard how the system, despite fine words, in practice often rejects that notion. In the process, it denies children loving care from at least one adult to call their very own. I saw evidence that adopting kids long out of diapers can work. I ended up with every reason to promote, along agency row, more affection for modern households that break the 1950s mold.

You'll be the judge of whether the families and I win the arguments. To the thirty-seven families I interviewed, my heartfelt gratitude for your willingness to expose your private lives to public scrutiny. I hope you'll feel I've done you justice. Apologies to those whose stories ended up on the cutting-room floor. The fault is mine: my failure to draw from you insights that differed from those I'd already gathered.

Thanks go as well to my agent, Jan Whitford at Westwood Creative Artists (née the Lucinda Vardey Agency). Being what's gently referred to as a "mid-list" writer—and what's worse, in Canada, a small market for almost any book, let alone special-interest themes in nonfiction—doesn't pay the mortgage. But there are other perks. On the list: working with Jan, who sees social value in the subjects that attract me and who does her best to help.

Compared with my previous books, this one went through more than the usual growing pains. Though I didn't always feel like thanking her during the process, in the end I appreciated my editor, Barbara Berson, for her substantial mark on the final product. I'm also indebted to Beverley Beetham Endersby for her light-handed copyediting.

At points in this long project I was, I confess, a pain in the posterior. My family and friends, bless them, were nice enough to pretend not to notice. The masochists among them, and my parents above all, even continued throughout to ask me how it was going, knowing I'd tell them more than they wanted to hear. Chetan Rajani, Sarah Spinks, and Jo Lampert, initially by e-mail to Australia and then here in town, really got an earful. Other friends, particularly Neil Docherty, Ana Jovicic, and Valerie MacIntosh, also listened more politely than they should have. Thanks, guys. Alison Griffiths and David Cruise put me onto two particularly illuminating interviews. Tessa Stein took care of me in Detroit. Hugs all round.

No one gets a bigger hug than my mate, David Carter. For a bunch of reasons I won't bore you with, writing this book was, at times, a bigger struggle than I bargained for—just as living with me was for David. Yet, he took my guff with good grace, even after the advance from the publisher was a distant memory. David also tried to give me good advice, most of which I foolishly ignored, and he kept smiling. Without his loving support, I doubt I would have finished what I started. Everyone should be lucky enough to have a partner like mine.

Index